William Shakespeare

KING LEAR

Edited with a Commentary by George Hunter
Introduced by Kiernan Ryan

PENGUIN BOOKS

PENGUIN BOOKS

Published by the Penguin Group
Penguin Books Ltd, 80 Strand, London WC2R ORL, England
Penguin Group (USA) Inc., 375 Hudson Street, New York, New York 10014, USA
Penguin Group (Canada), 10 Alcorn Avenue, Toronto, Ontario, Canada M4V 3B2
(a division of Pearson Penguin Canada Inc.)
Penguin Ireland, 25 St Stephen's Green, Dublin 2, Ireland (a division of Penguin Books Ltd)
Penguin Group (Australia), 250 Camberwell Road, Camberwell, Victoria 3124, Australia
(a division of Pearson Australia Group Pty Ltd)
Penguin Books India Pvt Ltd, 11 Community Centre, Panchsheel Park, New Delhi – 110 017, India
Penguin Group (NZ), cnr Airborne and Rosedale Roads, Albany, Auckland 1310, New Zealand
(a division of Pearson New Zealand Ltd)
Penguin Books (South Africa) (Pty) Ltd, 24 Sturdee Avenue, Rosebank 2196, South Africa

Penguin Books Ltd, Registered Offices: 80 Strand, London WC2R ORL, England

www.penguin.com

This edition first published in Penguin Books 1972
Reprinted with revised Further Reading and Account of the Text 1996
Reissued in the Penguin Shakespeare series 2005

8

Account of the Text and Commentary copyright © George Hunter, 1972, 1996
General Introduction and Chronology copyright © Stanley Wells, 2005
Introduction, The Play in Performance and Further Reading copyright © Kiernan Ryan, 2005

Printed in England by Clays Ltd, St Ives plc
Typeset in 11.5/12.5 pt PostScript Monotype Fournier
by Palimpsest Book Production Limited, Polmont, Stirlingshire

ISBN-13: 978-0-14-101229-2

www.greenpenguin.co.uk

Penguin Books is committed to a sustainable future
for our business, our readers and our planet.
The book in your hands is made from paper
certified by the Forest Stewardship Council.

PENGUIN SHAKESPEARE

Contents

General Introduction

Every play by Shakespeare is unique. This is part of his greatness. A restless and indefatigable experimenter, he moved with a rare amalgamation of artistic integrity and dedicated professionalism from one kind of drama to another. Never shackled by convention, he offered his actors the alternation between serious and comic modes from play to play, and often also within the plays themselves, that the repertory system within which he worked demanded, and which provided an invaluable stimulus to his imagination. Introductions to individual works in this series attempt to define their individuality. But there are common factors that underpin Shakespeare's career.

Nothing in his heredity offers clues to the origins of his genius. His upbringing in Stratford-upon-Avon, where he was born in 1564, was unexceptional. His mother, born Mary Arden, came from a prosperous farming family. Her father chose her as his executor over her eight sisters and his four stepchildren when she was only in her late teens, which suggests that she was of more than average practical ability. Her husband John, a glover, apparently unable to write, was nevertheless a capable businessman and loyal townsfellow, who seems to have fallen on relatively hard times in later life. He would have been brought up as a Catholic, and may have retained

Catholic sympathies, but his son subscribed publicly to Anglicanism throughout his life.

The most important formative influence on Shakespeare was his school. As the son of an alderman who became bailiff (or mayor) in 1568, he had the right to attend the town's grammar school. Here he would have received an education grounded in classical rhetoric and oratory, studying authors such as Ovid, Cicero and Quintilian, and would have been required to read, speak, write and even think in Latin from his early years. This classical education permeates Shakespeare's work from the beginning to the end of his career. It is apparent in the self-conscious classicism of plays of the early 1590s such as the tragedy of *Titus Andronicus*, *The Comedy of Errors*, and the narrative poems *Venus and Adonis* (1592–3) and *The Rape of Lucrece* (1593–4), and is still evident in his latest plays, informing the dream visions of *Pericles* and *Cymbeline* and the masque in *The Tempest*, written between 1607 and 1611. It inflects his literary style throughout his career. In his earliest writings the verse, based on the ten-syllabled, five-beat iambic pentameter, is highly patterned. Rhetorical devices deriving from classical literature, such as alliteration and antithesis, extended similes and elaborate wordplay, abound. Often, as in *Love's Labour's Lost* and *A Midsummer Night's Dream*, he uses rhyming patterns associated with lyric poetry, each line self-contained in sense, the prose as well as the verse employing elaborate figures of speech. Writing at a time of linguistic ferment, Shakespeare frequently imports Latinisms into English, coining words such as abstemious, addiction, incarnadine and adjunct. He was also heavily influenced by the eloquent translations of the Bible in both the Bishops' and the Geneva versions. As his experience grows, his verse and prose become more supple,

the patterning less apparent, more ready to accommo-
date the rhythms of ordinary speech, more colloquial in
diction, as in the speeches of the Nurse in *Romeo and
Juliet*, the characterful prose of Falstaff and Hamlet's
soliloquies. The effect is of increasing psychological
realism, reaching its greatest heights in *Hamlet*, *Othello*,
King Lear, *Macbeth* and *Antony and Cleopatra*. Gradually
he discovered ways of adapting the regular beat of the
pentameter to make it an infinitely flexible instrument for
matching thought with feeling. Towards the end of his
career, in plays such as *The Winter's Tale*, *Cymbeline* and
The Tempest, he adopts a more highly mannered style,
in keeping with the more overtly symbolical and emblem-
atical mode in which he is writing.

So far as we know, Shakespeare lived in Stratford till
after his marriage to Anne Hathaway, eight years his
senior, in 1582. They had three children: a daughter,
Susanna, born in 1583 within six months of their marriage,
and twins, Hamnet and Judith, born in 1585. The next
seven years of Shakespeare's life are virtually a blank.
Theories that he may have been, for instance, a schoolmaster, or a lawyer, or a soldier, or a sailor, lack evidence
to support them. The first reference to him in print, in
Robert Greene's pamphlet *Greene's Groatsworth of Wit*
of 1592, parodies a line from *Henry VI, Part III*, implying
that Shakespeare was already an established playwright.
It seems likely that at some unknown point after the birth
of his twins he joined a theatre company and gained
experience as both actor and writer in the provinces and
London. The London theatres closed because of plague
in 1593 and 1594; and during these years, perhaps recog-
nizing the need for an alternative career, he wrote and
published the narrative poems *Venus and Adonis* and *The
Rape of Lucrece*. These are the only works we can be

certain that Shakespeare himself was responsible for putting into print. Each bears the author's dedication to Henry Wriothesley, Earl of Southampton (1573–1624), the second in warmer terms than the first. Southampton, younger than Shakespeare by ten years, is the only person to whom he personally dedicated works. The Earl may have been a close friend, perhaps even the beautiful and adored young man whom Shakespeare celebrates in his *Sonnets*.

The resumption of playing after the plague years saw the founding of the Lord Chamberlain's Men, a company to which Shakespeare was to belong for the rest of his career, as actor, shareholder and playwright. No other dramatist of the period had so stable a relationship with a single company. Shakespeare knew the actors for whom he was writing and the conditions in which they performed. The permanent company was made up of around twelve to fourteen players, but one actor often played more than one role in a play and additional actors were hired as needed. Led by the tragedian Richard Burbage (1568–1619) and, initially, the comic actor Will Kemp (d. 1603), they rapidly achieved a high reputation, and when King James I succeeded Queen Elizabeth I in 1603 they were renamed as the King's Men. All the women's parts were played by boys; there is no evidence that any female role was ever played by a male actor over the age of about eighteen. Shakespeare had enough confidence in his boys to write for them long and demanding roles such as Rosalind (who, like other heroines of the romantic comedies, is disguised as a boy for much of the action) in *As You Like It*, Lady Macbeth and Cleopatra. But there are far more fathers than mothers, sons than daughters, in his plays, few if any of which require more than the company's normal complement of three or four boys.

The company played primarily in London's public playhouses – there were almost none that we know of in the rest of the country – initially in the Theatre, built in Shoreditch in 1576, and from 1599 in the Globe, on Bankside. These were wooden, more or less circular structures, open to the air, with a thrust stage surmounted by a canopy and jutting into the area where spectators who paid one penny stood, and surrounded by galleries where it was possible to be seated on payment of an additional penny. Though properties such as cauldrons, stocks, artificial trees or beds could indicate locality, there was no representational scenery. Sound effects such as flourishes of trumpets, music both martial and amorous, and accompaniments to songs were provided by the company's musicians. Actors entered through doors in the back wall of the stage. Above it was a balconied area that could represent the walls of a town (as in *King John*), or a castle (as in *Richard II*), and indeed a balcony (as in *Romeo and Juliet*). In 1609 the company also acquired the use of the Blackfriars, a smaller, indoor theatre to which admission was more expensive, and which permitted the use of more spectacular stage effects such as the descent of Jupiter on an eagle in *Cymbeline* and of goddesses in *The Tempest*. And they would frequently perform before the court in royal residences and, on their regular tours into the provinces, in non-theatrical spaces such as inns, guildhalls and the great halls of country houses.

Early in his career Shakespeare may have worked in collaboration, perhaps with Thomas Nashe (1567–c. 1601) in *Henry VI, Part I* and with George Peele (1556–96) in *Titus Andronicus*. And towards the end he collaborated with George Wilkins (*fl.* 1604–8) in *Pericles*, and with his younger colleagues Thomas Middleton (1580–1627), in *Timon of Athens*, and John Fletcher (1579–1625), in *Henry*

VIII, *The Two Noble Kinsmen* and the lost play *Cardenio*.
Shakespeare's output dwindled in his last years, and he
died in 1616 in Stratford, where he owned a fine house,
New Place, and much land. His only son had died at the
age of eleven, in 1596, and his last descendant died in
1670. New Place was destroyed in the eighteenth century
but the other Stratford houses associated with his life are
maintained and displayed to the public by the Shakespeare
Birthplace Trust.

One of the most remarkable features of Shakespeare's
plays is their intellectual and emotional scope. They span
a great range from the lightest of comedies, such as *The
Two Gentlemen of Verona* and *The Comedy of Errors*, to
the profoundest of tragedies, such as *King Lear* and
Macbeth. He maintained an output of around two plays
a year, ringing the changes between comic and serious.
All his comedies have serious elements: Shylock, in *The
Merchant of Venice*, almost reaches tragic dimensions, and
Measure for Measure is profoundly serious in its examin-
ation of moral problems. Equally, none of his tragedies
is without humour: Hamlet is as witty as any of his comic
heroes, *Macbeth* has its Porter, and *King Lear* its Fool.
His greatest comic character, Falstaff, inhabits the history
plays and *Henry V* ends with a marriage, while *Henry
VI, Part III*, *Richard II* and *Richard III* culminate in the
tragic deaths of their protagonists.

Although in performance Shakespeare's characters can
give the impression of a superabundant reality, he is not
a naturalistic dramatist. None of his plays is explicitly
set in his own time. The action of few of them (except
for the English histories) is set even partly in England
(exceptions are *The Merry Wives of Windsor* and the
Induction to *The Taming of the Shrew*). Italy is his
favoured location. Most of his principal story-lines derive

from printed writings; but the structuring and translation of these narratives into dramatic terms is Shakespeare's own, and he invents much additional material. Most of the plays contain elements of myth and legend, and many derive from ancient or more recent history or from romantic tales of ancient times and faraway places. All reflect his reading, often in close detail. Holinshed's *Chronicles* (1577, revised 1587), a great compendium of English, Scottish and Irish history, provided material for his English history plays. The *Lives of the Noble Grecians and Romans* by the Greek writer Plutarch, finely translated into English from the French by Sir Thomas North in 1579, provided much of the narrative material, and also a mass of verbal detail, for his plays about Roman history. Some plays are closely based on shorter individual works: *As You Like It*, for instance, on the novel *Rosalynde* (1590) by his near-contemporary Thomas Lodge (1558–1625), *The Winter's Tale* on *Pandosto* (1588) by his old rival Robert Greene (1558–92) and *Othello* on a story by the Italian Giraldi Cinthio (1504–73). And the language of his plays is permeated by the Bible, the Book of Common Prayer and the proverbial sayings of his day.

Shakespeare was popular with his contemporaries, but his commitment to the theatre and to the plays in performance is demonstrated by the fact that only about half of his plays appeared in print in his lifetime, in slim paperback volumes known as quartos, so called because they were made from printers' sheets folded twice to form four leaves (eight pages). None of them shows any sign that he was involved in their publication. For him, performance was the primary means of publication. The most frequently reprinted of his works were the non-dramatic poems – the erotic *Venus and Adonis* and the more moralistic *The Rape of Lucrece*. The *Sonnets*, which appeared in 1609, under his name but possibly without his consent, were less successful, perhaps because the vogue for sonnet sequences, which peaked in the 1590s, had passed by then. They were not reprinted until 1640, and then only in garbled form along with poems by other writers. Happily, in 1623, seven years after he died, his colleagues John Heminges (1556–1630) and Henry Condell (d. 1627) published his collected plays, including eighteen that had not previously appeared in print, in the first Folio, whose name derives from the fact that the printers' sheets were folded only once to produce two leaves (four pages). Some of the quarto editions are badly printed, and the fact that some plays exist in two, or even three, early versions creates problems for editors. These are discussed in the Account of the Text in each volume of this series.

Shakespeare's plays continued in the repertoire until the Puritans closed the theatres in 1642. When performances resumed after the Restoration of the monarchy in 1660 many of the plays were not to the taste of the times, especially because their mingling of genres and failure to meet the requirements of poetic justice offended against the dictates of neoclassicism. Some, such as *The Tempest* (changed by John Dryden and William Davenant in 1667 to suit contemporary taste), *King Lear* (to which Nahum Tate gave a happy ending in 1681) and *Richard III* (heavily adapted by Colley Cibber in 1700 as a vehicle for his own talents), were extensively rewritten; others fell into neglect. Slowly they regained their place in the repertoire, and they continued to be reprinted, but it was not until the great actor David Garrick (1717–79) organized a spectacular jubilee in Stratford in 1769 that Shakespeare began to be regarded as a transcendental genius. Garrick's idolatry prefigured the enthusiasm of critics such as Samuel Taylor Coleridge (1772–1834) and William Hazlitt (1778–1830). Gradually Shakespeare's reputation spread abroad, to Germany, America, France and to other European countries.

During the nineteenth century, though the plays were generally still performed in heavily adapted or abbreviated versions, a large body of scholarship and criticism began to amass. Partly as a result of a general swing in education away from the teaching of Greek and Roman texts and towards literature written in English, Shakespeare became the object of intensive study in schools and universities. In the theatre, important turning points were the work in England of two theatre directors, William Poel (1852–1934) and his disciple Harley Granville-Barker (1877–1946), who showed that the application of knowledge, some of it newly acquired, of early staging conditions to performance of the plays could render the original texts viable in terms of the modern theatre. During the twentieth century appreciation of Shakespeare's work, encouraged by the availability of audio, film and video versions of the plays, spread around the world to such an extent that he can now be claimed as a global author.

The influence of Shakespeare's works permeates the English language. Phrases from his plays and poems – 'a tower of strength', 'green-eyed jealousy', 'a foregone conclusion' – are on the lips of people who may never have read him. They have inspired composers of songs, orchestral music and operas; painters and sculptors; poets, novelists and film-makers. Allusions to him appear in pop songs, in advertisements and in television shows. Some of his characters – Romeo and Juliet, Falstaff, Shylock and Hamlet – have acquired mythic status. He is valued for his humanity, his psychological insight, his wit and humour, his lyricism, his mastery of language, his ability to excite, surprise, move and, in the widest sense of the word, entertain audiences. He is the greatest of poets, but he is essentially a dramatic poet. Though his plays have much to offer to readers, they exist fully only in performance. In these volumes we offer individual introductions, notes on language and on specific points of the text, suggestions for further reading and information about how each work has been edited. In addition we include accounts of the ways in which successive generations of interpreters and audiences have responded to challenges and rewards offered by the plays. The Penguin Shakespeare series aspires to remove obstacles to understanding and to make pleasurable the reading of the work of the man who has done more than most to make us understand what it is to be human.

Stanley Wells

The Chronology of
Shakespeare's Works

A few of Shakespeare's writings can be fairly precisely dated. An allusion to the Earl of Essex in the chorus to Act V of *Henry V*, for instance, could only have been written in 1599. But for many of the plays we have only vague information, such as the date of publication, which may have occurred long after composition, the date of a performance, which may not have been the first, or a list in Francis Meres's book *Palladis Tamia*, published in 1598, which tells us only that the plays listed there must have been written by that year. The chronology of the early plays is particularly difficult to establish. Not everyone would agree that the first part of *Henry VI* was written after the third, for instance, or *Romeo and Juliet* before *A Midsummer Night's Dream*. The following table is based on the 'Canon and Chronology' section in *William Shakespeare: A Textual Companion*, by Stanley Wells and Gary Taylor, with John Jowett and William Montgomery (1987), where more detailed information and discussion may be found.

The Two Gentlemen of Verona	1590–91
The Taming of the Shrew	1590–91
Henry VI, Part II	1591
Henry VI, Part III	1591

Introduction

I

It is difficult not to be daunted by the prospect of tackling the tragedy widely revered as Shakespeare's supreme achievement and a towering masterpiece of world literature. To study or to stage *King Lear* today, in the wake of the countless theatrical productions, critical commentaries and works of scholarship it has engendered over the last four centuries – to say nothing of the plethora of films, novels, plays, poetry, music and paintings it has spawned across the globe – is bound to seem a formidable task.

Some comfort can be squeezed from the fact that the task of squaring up to *King Lear* seemed just as formidable 200 years ago to the poets and critics of the Romantic age who shared Percy Bysshe Shelley's conviction that it was 'the most perfect specimen of the dramatic art existing in the world' (*A Defence of Poetry*, 1821) and who deserve much of the credit for raising the play to the position of pre-eminence it occupies to this day. John Keats had to steel his nerves before rereading the tragedy by rehearsing the experience in a sonnet:

> Adieu! for, once again, the fierce dispute
> Betwixt damnation and impassioned clay
> Must I burn through; once more humbly assay
> The bitter-sweet of this Shakespearian fruit.
> ('On Sitting Down to Read *King Lear* Once Again', 1818)

William Hazlitt threw in the towel before his critical bout with 'the best of all Shakespeare's plays' had even begun: 'We wish that we could pass this play over, and say nothing about it,' he wrote in *Characters of Shakespeare's Plays* (1817). 'All that we can say must fall far short of the subject; or even of what we ourselves conceive of it. To attempt to give a description of the play itself or of its effect upon the mind, is mere impertinence.' And a few years before that, in his essay 'On the Tragedies of Shakespeare' (1811), Charles Lamb had argued that to mount a production of the play was equally impertinent, since only in the theatre of the mind could its awesome effect be fully realized: 'the Lear of Shakespeare', he concluded, 'cannot be acted', because it is 'essentially impossible to be represented on a stage'.

Fortunately, theatre directors and acting companies from Lamb's time to our own have paid no heed to his strictures, and at their best have proved him wrong over and over again. One can see, of course, what Lamb was driving at. Even the most inspired performance of *King Lear* cannot hope to encompass the vast imaginative scope of the script, or bring every facet of its fierce poetry to life upon the stage, while pedestrian productions are prone to shrink Shakespeare's titanic tragedy into an interminable domestic melodrama, leaking pathos from every pore. Yet it is also true that seeing *King Lear* acted with skill and understanding, not only in the theatre, but also in film versions viewed in the cinema or on TV, animates aspects of the play and discloses dramatic possibilities that would never strike the mind confined to perusing it on the page. To see the tragedy transfigured on stage or screen by visionary directors such as Peter Brook, Grigori Kozintsev or Akira Kurosawa is to learn things about *King Lear* that cannot be taught in the classroom or the lecture hall.

That modern critics have paid as little mind to Hazlitt's qualms about commenting on *King Lear* as modern directors have to Lamb's disdain for staging it is not, it must be confessed, quite so fortunate. Far from hesitating to impose interpretations on a play that seems to defy definition and analysis, critics of every camp have vied tirelessly to recruit *King Lear* to their cause. Nor is this surprising, when one considers the prize that is at stake. As the keystone of the canon and the gold standard of literary value, *King Lear* is the prime target of every critical approach intent on proving its supremacy and confounding its rivals. The most compelling account of Shakespeare's masterpiece captures the flagship of the entire discipline.

For much of the twentieth century *King Lear* was in thrall to a variety of Christian readings, which obliged it to serve as a parable of sin, suffering, sacrifice and redemption, despite the scant support for such readings furnished by the text itself. In the 1960s, however, this critical consensus caved in, and interpretations of an emphatically secular, humanist cast took hold. For some, this meant treating the tragedy as a grim witness to the absurdity of life in a heartless universe; for others, it meant hailing it as proof that human dignity can be salvaged from the most unspeakable agony and despair.

These views of *King Lear* surrendered in turn in the
1980s to a new regime of politicized criticism, whose
chief aim was to work out whether the play endorsed or
attacked the assumptions governing society in Shakespeare's day and our own. As a result, *King Lear* is
currently overrun by a bewildering array of poststruc-
turalist, new-historicist, cultural-materialist, feminist and
psychoanalytic approaches, all of which claim to have
their finger on the pulse of the play.

To make things even more confusing, recent scholarship has made the definition of the text of *King Lear* a
matter for heated dispute, on the grounds that interpretations of the play will vary according to which version
of it is used. Should we base our reading of the play on
the Quarto edition published in 1608? Or should we base
it on the text published in the Folio edition of Shakespeare's plays in 1623, which differs from the Quarto in
a number of important respects? Or should we base it
on a text which, like this Penguin Shakespeare edition,
weaves the Folio and the Quarto together in an attempt
to combine the virtues of both?

Such questions certainly deserve to be discussed at
some point in the study of *King Lear*, as do the conflicting
critical responses it has provoked, the theatrical and
cultural contexts that shaped it, its performance history
on stage and screen, and much else besides. Too often,
however, the discussion of these matters at the outset
intrudes between the reader and the play, muffling its
immediate impact on us and obstructing our engagement
with the only questions that really count: what is *King
Lear* about and why does it matter? This introduction
proposes, therefore, to confront the play head-on, as the
reader encounters it in this edition, with the minimum
preamble. Its aim is to address the issues that *King Lear*

raises, and the problems that it poses, as they emerge from direct reflection on the tragedy itself.

2

The story *King Lear* sets out to dramatize is relatively simple and the basic facts are quickly told. It is the tale of two fathers and their families whose destinies are fatally entwined. In one plot an aged king's foolish rejection of the daughter who loves him, and his misplaced trust in her malevolent sisters, strips him of his power and strands him in a wasteland of anguish and insanity. From this plight death at last releases him, but not before the wicked sisters have met their deaths as well and the corpse of his devoted daughter, with whom he has just been reunited, lies cold in his arms. In a parallel plot a nobleman in the service of the king is duped by his ruthless, illegitimate son into fearing that his legitimate son means to murder him, and the latter is forced to flee in the guise of a demented beggar. The nobleman suffers the horror of being blinded following his betrayal by his bastard and, like the king, is turned out to wander in despair, at the mercy of the elements. Death finally terminates his suffering too, after he has been reconciled with his loyal and loving son, who dispatches his evil sibling in a climactic chivalric duel. At the end of the story all but three of the principal characters are dead, and the dazed survivors see no clear way forward.

The effect of Shakespeare's transmutation of this story into tragedy, however, is anything but simple. Whether he knew that he was about to grapple with matters of great moment and intractable complexity when he sat down to write *King Lear* is impossible to say. Circumstantial evidence suggests that he penned the play somewhere between late 1605 and early 1606. So we do know that he was writing at the height of his imaginative and expressive powers, with over two dozen comedies, histories and tragedies to his credit, and some of these plays clearly paved the way for *King Lear*.

During the previous decade he had already explored the fall of kings and the deposition of the powerful in the tragedies of *Richard III* (1592–3), *Richard II* (1595) and *Julius Caesar* (1599). In one of his earliest plays, *Titus Andronicus* (1592), he had tackled the derangement and destruction of a tyrannical patriarch, bereft of his beloved daughter. More recently, in *Hamlet* (1600–1601), the first of the great, mature tragedies, he had transmuted tragedy itself into a form flexible enough to sustain the fearless philosophical speculation that electrifies *King Lear*. *Othello* (1603–4), written a couple of years before *Lear*, and the play he wrote immediately after it, *Macbeth* (1606), saw Shakespeare probing further into the darkest reaches of domestic intimacy opened up by *Hamlet*, which shares *Lear*'s fear of what lurks at the heart of the family, in the sacrosanct bond between parent and child. *Timon of Athens* (1605), the bizarre, abortive tragedy that Shakespeare was working on around the same time as he was writing *King Lear*, centres likewise on a man of wealth and power, who recoils from the brazen ingratitude of those close to him into outraged exile and manic invective. And after his last great tragedy, *Antony and Cleopatra* (1606), Shakespeare returned, at the close of his career, to rework in romances such as *Pericles* (1607) and *The Winter's Tale* (1609) the theme of a father reunited with the daughter he thought he had lost for ever – this time, however, with the joyful ending so cruelly denied to Lear.

In fact, Shakespeare had already given a festive twist
to that theme several years before *King Lear* in his pastoral
romantic comedy *As You Like It*, whose family resem-
blance to the tragedy it prefigures is uncanny. In both
plays a ruler is cast out of civilized society and placed
at nature's mercy in a wilderness, where his exiled
daughter is at last restored to him; in both plays, too, a
good son is compelled by the malice of his brother to
flee into the same inhospitable domain, where he cares
for a vulnerable old man. Countless more parallels could
be drawn, not only between *Lear* and *As You Like It*, but
also between *Lear* and many more of Shakespeare's plays
than there is room to mention here. But even a cursory
review of the most blatant echoes and affinities confirms
how long the ingredients of *King Lear* had been brewing
in its author's mind, and how deeply rooted the concerns
of the play must have been to make him return to them
so obsessively throughout his theatrical career.

A further clue to Shakespeare's chief preoccupations
and creative design in *King Lear* can be found in the use
he made of his sources in constructing the play. *Lear* is
the only one of the tragedies to employ a fully developed double plot, whose twinned tales are crafted to illu-
minate each other at every stage. For the story of Lear
he relied primarily on an anonymous older play, which
was published in 1605 as *The True Chronicle History of
King Leir and his three daughters, Gonorill, Ragan, and
Cordella*, but which had been performed over a decade
earlier in 1594, by a cast that may have included
Shakespeare himself. To this narrative Shakespeare made
a number of crucial alterations and additions. He devised
new characters, including, most notably, the Fool and
Oswald; he inflated Lear's folly into full-blown madness
and supplied in the storm scene the perfect setting for

its eruption; and he erased virtually every trace of his source's Christian vision, leaving his characters marooned in an altogether bleaker, pagan universe.

Shakespeare's most drastic departure from *The True Chronicle History*, however, was to destroy its benign conclusion. The tragicomedy of *King Leir* winds up with the aged monarch back on his throne, Cordella safely restored, and every single character surviving. Shakespeare's *King Lear* concludes in unmitigated tragedy, with the shattered sovereign, all three of his daughters and almost everyone else killed off, and not a crumb of consolation in sight. There were other Elizabethan versions of the Lear story that Shakespeare undoubtedly knew, especially the ones he would have read in John Higgins's *Mirror for Magistrates* (1574), Raphael Holinshed's *Chronicles of England* (1577), and Book II, Canto 10 of Edmund Spenser's epic poem, *The Faerie Queene* (1590). From Spenser, indeed, he seems to have lifted the spelling of Cordelia's name and the idea that she died by hanging. But in all these versions, as in earlier renditions, the story ends with Lear reinstated and continuing for a time as king, while Cordelia lives on to meet her death much later, years after her father's natural demise. The brutal, comfortless denouement that Shakespeare inflicts on his audience is without precedent in the transmission of the tale, and plainly the result of a deliberate decision by the playwright to confound the expectations it was apt to arouse.

The inspiration for the parallel plot, which traces the fate of Gloucester and his two sons, Edgar and Edmund, came directly from another late Elizabethan work, the first edition of Sir Philip Sidney's prose romance *Arcadia*, published in 1590. Book II, Chapter 10 of *Arcadia* relates the story of the King of Paphlagonia, who has been deposed and blinded by his wicked, bastard son, Plexirtus, after being gulled into seeking the death of his elder, legitimate son, Leonatus. A homeless outcast, shunned by his former subjects and obliged to live by begging, the blind king is discovered and led on his way by Leonatus, just as Edgar leads his blind father, Gloucester, on the road to Dover in *King Lear*. Like Edgar, too, Leonatus frustrates his father's plan to commit suicide by plunging headlong to his death from a great height, and his father dies later instead, his heart torn between sorrow and joy, exactly as Gloucester does in Edgar's report of his passing:

> But his flawed heart –
> Alack, too weak the conflict to support –
> 'Twixt two extremes of passion, joy and grief,
> Burst smilingly. (V.3.194–7)

Once again, though, the disparities between Shakespeare's and his source's treatment of the tale shed light on the dramatist's more complex vision. Foremost among these is the fact that, unlike Leonatus, Edgar adopts the role of the mad mendicant, Poor Tom, and conceals his true identity from his father until the very end of their journey together. The episode in which Leonatus refuses to bring his father to the top of the rock from which he intends to fling himself is also developed by Shakespeare into the extraordinary Dover Cliff scene, in which Edgar fools Gloucester into falling from a purely imaginary precipice conjured out of words. In *Arcadia*, moreover, the father's death occurs only after his virtuous son has been enthroned in his place, while the latter forgives his villainous sibling on condition that he mend his ways. That Shakespeare contrives to have Edgar mortally

wound Edmund, and that he denies both the dying
Gloucester and the audience the certain knowledge that
Edgar will reign after Lear, is further evidence of his
desire to deepen the darkness of the tragedy by snuffing
out any solace that might flicker in its closing moments.

There are two other significant sources on which
Shakespeare drew in the composition of *King Lear*:
Samuel Harsnet's *A Declaration of Egregious Popish
Impostures* (1603), a polemical attack on the Catholic
practice of exorcism, and John Florio's translation of
Michel de Montaigne's *Essays*, published in the same
year as Harsnet's diatribe. From Harsnet's vivid, quirky
vocabulary Shakespeare filched a host of words and turns
of phrase that crop up all over the play, and especially
in the litany of demons and lunatic patter that enliven
Edgar's impression of a possessed Bedlamite. The pains
he took to make the speech and demeanour of Poor Tom
as authentic as possible testify to the intensity of Shakespeare's absorption in Edgar's alter ego and the importance he attached to the creature's part in the play. The
devils' names Flibberdigibbet, Smulkin, Modo and Mahu
all hark back to Harsnet. So does the word 'corky', which
Cornwall enlists to describe the aged arms of Gloucester
as he commands him to be bound (III.7.29); the word
'ruffle' in Gloucester's rebuke to Regan later in the same
scene: 'my hospitable favours | You should not ruffle
thus' (40–41); and Lear's use of the term 'hysterica
passio' to diagnose the malady that assails him in Act II,
scene 4.

To Florio's Montaigne *King Lear* is likewise indebted
for a clutch of idiosyncratic words that he had never used
before, words such as 'goatish' (I.2.127), 'marble-hearted'
(I.4.256), 'disnatured' (I.4.280) and 'handy-dandy'
(IV.6.154), which stuck in his mind as he read, and cried

out to be used again. Shakespeare's avidity for new or rare words is by no means confined to *King Lear*, but his raids on Harsnet and Florio converge with this play's palpable urge to reach beyond the limits of the language. Apart from expanding his vocabulary, Montaigne's essay 'Of the Affection of Fathers to Their Children' must have struck as many chords with Shakespeare while he worked on *Lear* as the French philosopher's likening of the nature of man to the nature of beasts in his 'Apologie of Raymond Sebond' – the echoes of the latter as Lear contemplates Poor Tom in the storm are unmistakable. But the tragedy may well owe a subtler, pervasive debt to Montaigne's radical scepticism about the unquestioned assumptions and values of the early modern world, and his readiness to ride roughshod over its most cherished pieties. At the very least, Shakespeare clearly encountered in Montaigne a kindred spirit, who would have understood his compulsion to force *King Lear* to the edge of the imaginable.

3

It is impossible to exaggerate the breathtaking boldness of the central idea of *King Lear* as Shakespeare dramatizes it. A mighty monarch, accustomed from birth to believe himself innately superior to his subjects by virtue of his royal blood, is robbed not only of his royalty but also of the roof over his head, and compelled to feel what the poor, naked wretches of his kingdom feel: hunger, cold and despair. A ruler who regards himself as divinely appointed to command and be obeyed is disobeyed by his own daughters, and driven as a consequence out of his mind with anger and grief. His insanity estranges him from a whole way of life he had taken for granted, making him question the very basis of his sovereign authority and power, and the justness of the society over which he had presided so thoughtlessly for so long. His recognition of the wrongs for which he is responsible as both a king and a father is not enough, however, to absolve or redeem him. From his punitive humiliation and protracted torment he reaps at the end of the play neither relief nor release, but only more intolerable pain and a pitiless death.

At the start of his tragic journey, in the opening scene of the play, Lear is the epitome of wilful, imperious majesty. He announces his decision to abdicate the throne and divide his kingdom between his three daughters, Gonerill, Regan and Cordelia, while he continues to enjoy 'The name and all th'addition to a king' (I.1.136) without the responsibility. He demands, furthermore, that each daughter compete for the choicest third of the kingdom by declaring in public how much more than her sisters she loves him. And when his favourite, youngest child, Cordelia, declines to demonstrate that she loves him most of all, thwarting his 'darker purpose' (I.1.36) by refusing to take part in the charade he has sprung on them, Lear throws a regal tantrum of cosmic proportions. His pride wounded, his authority flouted, he reasserts his supremacy by divorcing himself from the child he adores in a blaze of portentous rhetoric:

> For by the sacred radiance of the sun,
> The mysteries of Hecat and the night,
> By all the operation of the orbs
> From whom we do exist, and cease to be,
> Here I disclaim all my paternal care,
> Propinquity and property of blood,

And as a stranger to my heart and me
Hold thee from this for ever. (I.1.109–16)

Minutes later, having failed to heed Lear's equally bombastic warning 'Come not between the dragon and his wrath' (122), the king's most faithful servant, Kent, finds himself irrevocably banished with the same impetuous abruptness.

Three scenes later, however, when Kent rejoins his liege lord in the guise of the plain-spoken servant, Caius, the authority in Lear's countenance that Kent 'would fain call master' (I.4.28) is already on the wane. Divested of both property and power, Lear must endure the insolence of Gonerill's servant, Oswald, and the frosty remonstrations of Gonerill herself. Having reduced himself through his own rashness, as the Fool points out, from an omnipotent ruler to 'an 0 without a figure' (I.4.188–9), his grandiloquent histrionics and prodigious curses cut no ice with those who perceive in him merely 'Lear's shadow' (227). He rails in vain against ingratitude, the 'marble-hearted fiend' (256), and his prayer to Nature to 'convey sterility' into his eldest daughter's womb and 'Dry up in her the organs of increase' (275–6) only underscores his impotence. Before Act I is over he realizes that he has wronged Cordelia and feels the first stirrings of derangement as the appalling implications of his folly dawn on him: 'O let me not be mad, not mad, sweet heaven!' (I.5.42).

The second act soon confirms the Fool's prediction that Regan's reception of her father will more than match her sister's: 'She will taste as like this as a crab [i.e. a sour crab-apple] does to a crab' (I.5.18). The contempt she and Cornwall show for Lear's royalty by putting his messenger, Caius, in the stocks, and her collusion with Gonerill to whittle his retinue of knights down to zero ('What need one?' (II.4.258)), push the old king over the edge. Devastated by his daughters' display of 'Sharp-toothed unkindness' (II.4.130) and brazen disdain for 'The offices of nature, bond of childhood, | Effects of courtesy, dues of gratitude' (173–4), Lear heads out into the gathering storm 'To wage against the enmity o'th'air, | To be a comrade with the wolf and owl' and feel 'Necessity's sharp pinch' (204–6). His parting fulmination against the 'unnatural hags' (273) he has nurtured makes pathetically plain how feeble the once-feared potentate has become, as even the resources of hyperbole fail him:

> I will have such revenges on you both
> That all the world shall – I will do such things –
> What they are yet I know not; but they shall be
> The terrors of the earth. (274–7)

Lear recovers his phenomenal powers of invocation and malediction in the superb arias of wrath he declaims at the beginning of Act III. When he stands bareheaded in the storm and summons the elemental forces of nature to do his bidding, he fleetingly regains his stature as a superhuman sovereign on a cosmic stage, notwith-standing the futility of his appeal:

> And thou all-shaking thunder,
> Strike flat the thick rotundity o'the world,
> Crack Nature's moulds, all germens spill at once
> That makes ingrateful man! (III.2.6–9)

But this is merely a prelude to the profound metamorphosis this astounding act has in store for him. Within a few lines King Lear has cut himself down to size by acknowledging that he is no more than 'A poor, infirm, weak, and despised old man' (20). As his 'wits begin to turn' (III.2.67) and the cold begins to bite, he shows concern for the Fool's discomfort instead of his own, and ushers him into the hovel ahead of himself. Before he follows, however, Lear pauses to deliver this heartfelt prayer:

> Poor naked wretches, wheresoe'er you are,
> That bide the pelting of this pitiless storm,
> How shall your houseless heads and unfed sides,
> Your looped and windowed raggedness, defend you
> From seasons such as these? O, I have ta'en
> Too little care of this! Take physic, pomp;
> Expose thyself to feel what wretches feel,
> That thou mayst shake the superflux to them
> And show the heavens more just. (III.4.28–36)

The capricious, egotistical despot of the opening scene has been transformed by his children's cruelty and 'The tyranny of the open night' (III.4.2) into a man who feels compassion for the most despised of his fellow human beings, and suddenly comprehends the callous iniquity of his own regime.

Nor has Shakespeare finished with King Lear yet. The enforced enlightenment of the hapless monarch has only just begun. The sight of Edgar as Tom o'Bedlam later in the same scene moves Lear to exclaim: 'Thou art the thing itself! Unaccommodated man is no more but such a poor, bare, forked animal as thou art. Off, off, you lendings! Come, unbutton here' (III.4.103–5). It is a remarkable moment, whose implications cut far deeper than Lear's prayer for the homeless and starving. The dramatist whose company was called the King's Men, and whose livelihood depended on the patronage of the absolutist monarch, James I, stages a scene in which a king *physically enacts* his recognition that the same 'poor, bare, forked animal' shivers beneath his royal robes and a beggar's rags. Lear's prayer on the threshold of the hovel presupposes the same stratified society, in which 'pomp' would persist, but would treat those at its mercy with greater sympathy and generosity. But when Lear tears off his 'lendings', the tawdry fancy dress of majesty, to expose the 'unaccommodated man' it masks, he acts out the understanding that monarchy itself, and the unequal distribution of power and property it entails, have no warrant in nature. On the contrary: our shared physical constitution as human animals, and the shared needs, vulnerability and mortality that attend it, refute the rationale that divides us into the rulers and the ruled, the sated and the starving, making a mockery of hierarchy.

Nor does the fact that Lear is depicted as unhinged at this point diminish the impact of this revelation, whose consequences Shakespeare pursues into the following act. In the exchange between the crazed king and the sightless Gloucester in Act IV, scene 6 Lear returns to the question of justice left hanging in Act III, scene 6, the surreal scene in which the Fool and Edgar joined him to arraign an invisible Gonerill and Regan. But by now his disenchantment with the very idea of dominion is complete. When Gloucester asks, 'Is't not the King?' Lear replies sarcastically, 'Ay, every inch a king. | When I do stare see how the subject quakes' (IV.6.107–8). And his disenchantment does not stop there. Although you are blind, Lear says to Gloucester, 'you see how this world goes', and Gloucester's response, 'I see it feelingly' (IV.6.148–50), unleashes this stunning speech, which Edgar's subsequent aside prompts us to hear as 'matter and impertinency mixed, | Reason in madness!' (IV.6.175–6):

LEAR What, art mad? A man may see how this world goes with no eyes. Look with thine ears. See how yon justice rails upon yon simple thief. Hark in thine ear – change places and, handy-dandy, which is the justice, which is the thief? Thou hast seen a farmer's dog bark at a beggar?

GLOUCESTER Ay, sir.

LEAR And the creature run from the cur? There thou mightst behold the great image of authority: a dog's obeyed in office.

Thou rascal beadle, hold thy bloody hand.

Why dost thou lash that whore? Strip thy own back.

Thou hotly lusts to use her in that kind

For which thou whipp'st her. The usurer hangs the cozener.

Thorough tattered clothes great vices do appear;

Robes and furred gowns hide all. Plate sins with gold,

And the strong lance of justice hurtless breaks;

Arm it in rags, a pigmy's straw does pierce it.

None does offend, none, I say none; I'll able 'em. (151–69)

From 'Come not between the dragon and his wrath' to 'a dog's obeyed in office': Lear has travelled an immense distance at terrifying speed. But in the last line quoted he takes a further quantum leap in the conclusion he draws from the injustice and hypocrisy of his society. 'None does offend' because everyone offends when inequality and exploitation are institutionalized, when the whole culture is intrinsically culpable. Lear has left the sentimental exhortation to 'Take physic, pomp' far behind. For what is a summons to charity worth that comes from the lips of a king? How can the moral refinement of those who rule provide the solution, when the fact of their existence is the source of the problem? At this moment the tragedy breaks through to the awareness that its causes lie beyond the delinquencies of individuals, in the system that creates the poor and subjects them to the powerful in the first place.

The Lear whom Cordelia is reunited with shortly after this, the Lear who kneels to her for forgiveness, is a very different king from the irate tyrant who cast her off in the opening scene. Indeed, he no longer thinks of himself as a king at all and has no more use for magniloquence:

> I am a very foolish fond old man,
> Four score and upward, not an hour more nor less,
> And, to deal plainly,
> I fear I am not in my perfect mind. (IV.7.60–63)

Unlike the protagonist of *King Leir*, the last thing on Lear's mind is reclaiming his crown and resuming a reign whose inherent immorality he cannot disown. When he and Cordelia are captured, the prospect of imprisonment with her strikes him as infinitely preferable, because it means liberation from the relentless power-struggles of the court, which he now views with Olympian bemusement:

>   . . . so we'll live,
> And pray, and sing, and tell old tales, and laugh
> At gilded butterflies, and hear poor rogues
> Talk of court news; and we'll talk with them too –
> Who loses and who wins, who's in, who's out –
> And take upon's the mystery of things
> As if we were God's spies; and we'll wear out,

In a walled prison, packs and sects of great ones
That ebb and flow by the moon. (V.3.11–19)

Unfortunately for Lear and Cordelia, Shakespeare has no intention of letting them off that lightly. Far from finding respite at last from his afflictions, despite the revolution of consciousness he has undergone, Lear is compelled to watch his daughter hanged in the prison he had hoped would be their haven, and then to give up the ghost himself as he gazes in bewildered grief upon her lifeless face.

Shakespeare goes out of his way, moreover, to amplify the impact of Lear's story by having Gloucester's story describe the same arc of agony, insight and oblivion. Gloucester's folly is the credulity that severs him from Edgar, places him in the hands of Edmund, and leads to his eyes being gouged out by Cornwall and Regan. But, just as the metaphorical madness of Lear's actions in the opening scene mutates into the actual madness through which he acquires wisdom, so Gloucester's blindness to the true nature of his sons morphs into the real blindness which allows him to see feelingly the way the world goes. As Gloucester himself says to the old man who protests that he cannot see his way to Dover: 'I have no way and therefore want no eyes; | I stumbled when I saw' (IV.1.18–19). Like Lear's derangement, Gloucester's traumatic blinding dislocates him from the culture that has shaped his assumptions and values. His speech to Poor Tom as they set out for Dover both echoes Lear's plea for the poor, naked wretches of his realm and anticipates, in the last two lines, the levelling thrust of Lear's 'reason in madness' speech:

Here, take this purse, thou whom the heavens' plagues
Have humbled to all strokes. That I am wretched

Makes thee the happier. Heavens deal so still!
Let the superfluous and lust-dieted man
That slaves your ordinance, that will not see
Because he does not feel, feel your power quickly!
So distribution should undo excess
And each man have enough. (IV.1.63–70)

The trauma of sudden dislocation and degradation is
not restricted to Lear and Gloucester. Both Edgar and,
to a lesser degree, Kent undergo transmutations that
mirror those inflicted on the former's father and the
latter's master. Having lost his identity like Lear ('Edgar
I nothing am' (II.3.21)), Edgar adopts 'the basest and
most poorest shape | That ever penury, in contempt of
man, | Brought near to beast' (II.3.7–9). As Poor Tom
he becomes the appalling incarnation of the lesson Lear
and Gloucester learn, and his own capacity for compassion expands as a result of witnessing the misery the king
and his father must endure. When he drops the persona
of Tom to lead Gloucester on after the Dover Cliff
scene, he introduces himself to his father afresh as 'A
most poor man made tame to fortune's blows, | Who,
by the art of known and feeling sorrows, | Am preg-
nant to good pity' (IV.6.221–3). Unlike Gloucester and
Lear, of course, Edgar survives, having triumphed over
Edmund, but only to become the presumptive king of a
ravaged kingdom. The Earl of Kent declines to share
the rule of the realm with him, preferring to follow his
beloved master to the grave rather than stay in a world
where 'All's cheerless, dark, and deadly' (V.3.288). He,
too, has just abandoned the alter ego he has sustained
throughout the play. As the rough-spoken Caius, 'A very
honest-hearted fellow, and as poor as the King'
(I.4.19–20), he has suffered the shame of the stocks and

shared Lear's nightmare in the storm, only to behold both his king and Cordelia 'dead as earth' (V.3.259).

By multiplying the monarch's fate in this way, by replicating its trajectory in the fates of prominent noblemen like Gloucester, Edgar and Kent, Shakespeare makes it clear that the tragedy has a bigger quarry than the king in its sights. Given the deaths not only of Lear, Cordelia and Gloucester but also of Gonerill, Regan, Edmund and Cornwall, not to mention the presumed death of the Fool and the imminent death of Kent, it is as if an entire dispensation has been undone and destroyed.

We know that in 1606 *King Lear* 'was played before the King's Majesty at Whitehall upon St Stephen's night in Christmas holidays', as the title page of the 1608 Quarto puts it. What King James and his court made of his company's play is not recorded. As the Feast of St Stephen (now better known as Boxing Day) was traditionally associated with hospitality and giving alms to the poor, it is hard to imagine how the scandalous import of Lear's ordeal could have escaped them, or failed to leave them chastened. On the other hand, there is no reason to suppose that James and the aristocrats about him were any less adept at deflecting the implications of art away from themselves than the audiences of our own day are. Even so, to write and perform a play for the monarch, in which a king spurns his royal robes as mere 'lendings', calls upon 'pomp' to 'take physic', and declares that 'a dog's obeyed in office', takes some nerve, especially when such irreverence is expressly endorsed as 'reason in madness'. And to ditch the happy ending of the old *Leir* play in order to deny the king restoration and consign him to an excruciating death is to push one's luck to the limit. James himself may well have remained oblivious to the seditious dimension of *King Lear*, but it is worth recalling that just a few decades later, in 1649, 'the great image of authority' in the shape of his son, Charles I, was put to death by Parliament and his kingdom replaced by a Commonwealth. It is perhaps not entirely fanciful to suppose that *King Lear*, more than most of Shakespeare's history plays and tragedies, played a part in creating the climate that made that revolution possible.

Nothing confirms this supposition more strongly than Nahum Tate's adaptation of *King Lear* to suit the tastes of the post-revolutionary Restoration world of Charles II. Tate cut the character of the Fool altogether, deleting his insubordinate satire and riddling prophecies in the process; he changed Edgar and Cordelia into virtuous lovers, to whom Lear bequeaths his restored kingdom; and he spared the lives of Lear, Gloucester and Kent, who retire to a 'cool Cell' to ruminate in peace on 'Fortunes past'. Tate's aim was, in his own words, 'to rectify what was wanting in the regularity and probability of the tale', by constraining it to 'conclude in a success to the innocent distressed persons' rather than in their annihilation. In order to make the tragedy tolerable, in other words, Tate turned it back into the tragicomedy that Shakespeare set out to demolish. That Tate's emasculated travesty displaced Shakespeare's *King Lear* on the English stage from 1681 until 1838 is a powerful testimony to the subversive potential of the play that Shakespeare wrote.

The tragedy still has the potential, moreover, to disturb and disconcert its audience today. Absolute monarchs may be a dying breed in the twenty-first century, but autocratic rulers and despotic regimes are far from extinct, social divisions and economic injustices thrive, and hunger and poverty persist on a scale beyond even Shakespeare's imagination. To such a world the tragedy

of a king who confesses his kinship with a beggar, the
tragedy of an earl who perceives that 'distribution should
undo excess | And each man have enough' (IV.1.69–70),
has more to say than ever.

4

But that is far from being all it has to say. Any account
of *King Lear* that fails to confront the tragic conflict it
dramatizes between hierarchy and humanity, between the
destructive imperatives of division and domination incar-
nate in a king, and the need for equality, compassion and
community embodied by a naked beggar, cannot begin
to do justice to the play today. Yet it is also the domestic
double tragedy of two fathers and their children, which
has troubling home truths to tell about the family and
about patriarchy that are not the sole preserve of royalty
and the ruling class in Jacobean Britain. If we look at
the play afresh from this perspective, we are forced to
wrestle with contradictions and ambiguities that compli-
cate our response to it.

Consider, first of all, the relationship between King
Lear and his daughters. On the face of it, the moral
oppositions and distinctions could scarcely be more clear-
cut. Lear is 'a very foolish fond old man', the victim of
'Filial ingratitude' (III.4.14), who is 'More sinned against
than sinning' (III.2.59); Gonerill and Regan swiftly reveal
themselves to be pitiless predators, 'Tigers not daughters' (IV.2.40); while Cordelia, the 'unprized-precious
maid' (I.1.259), is the radiant epitome of selfless filial
love, the 'one daughter | Who redeems nature from the
general curse' (IV.6.206), whose 'smiles and tears' are
'like a better way' (IV.3.18–19).

But Lear's 'darker purpose' in carving up the kingdom is unmasked at the outset as a self-serving fantasy of paternal munificence, designed to leave all three children beholden to him and secure the 'kind nursery' (I.1.124) of Cordelia for the rest of his days. His public trial of his daughters' love betrays not only his monumental vanity, but also his view of the love between parent and child as a commodity that can be quantified and priced. He rewards Gonerill and Regan for sharing that view and excelling in the 'glib and oily art' (I.1.224) of flattering their father, and he punishes Cordelia for rejecting the language of calculation, loving in silence, and speaking the unvarnished truth about their relationship. 'I loved her most' (I.1.123), laments Lear, clinging still to the computation of love; yet the speed with which he converts that love into its monstrous antithesis, and the cannibalistic imagery he conscripts to express his loathing for Cordelia, make one wonder what kind of love it must have been to begin with:

> The barbarous Scythian,
> Or he that makes his generation messes
> To gorge his appetite, shall to my bosom
> Be as well neighboured, pitied, and relieved
> As thou my sometime daughter. (I.1.116–20)

What is more, after the heart-stopping reconciliation of 'this child-changèd father' (IV.7.17) with Cordelia, whom he begs to 'forget and forgive' (83–4), Lear's attitude to his dearest daughter remains uncomfortably exclusive, indeed just as proprietorial as it was in his dream of committing his last years to 'her kind nursery'. When the captive Cordelia asks, 'Shall we not see these daughters and these sisters?', her father cries, 'No, no,

no, no! Come, let's away to prison. | We two alone will
sing like birds i'the cage' (V.3.7–9). Even the unbearable climax of the tragedy, when Lear enters with
Cordelia's corpse in his arms and dies looking desperately for life in her lips, is clouded by the uneasy feeling
that his quest to possess her has finally been fulfilled.

The treatment meted out to the aged patriarch by 'his
dog-hearted daughters' (IV.3.45), Gonerill and Regan,
becomes all too explicable, though no less unforgivable,
when judged as a response to their father's treatment of
them. He has reared all three siblings to regard each
other as rivals for his affections, and has made it plain
that 'He always loved our sister most' (I.1.289–90), as
Gonerill reminds Regan. Indeed, the extension of their
rivalry into their contest for Edmund's love proves to
be literally the death of the elder sisters. Their conviction that their father 'hath ever but slenderly known
himself', and that 'The best and soundest of his time hath
been but rash' (I.1.292–5), is borne out by his disowning
of Cordelia, and makes their fear of what they can expect
from 'the infirmity of his age' as well as 'the imperfections of long-ingraffed condition' (292, 296) entirely
justifiable. Their vindictive humiliation of their father is
obviously not justifiable, but there is a fiendish poetic
justice in the way Gonerill and Regan crush Lear by
bargaining the number of his knights down to none. The
minds that could stage such a ruthless Dutch auction are
mirror-images of the mind that demanded a public reckoning of their love and put a price-tag on their hearts.
The truth of the old saying that the fruit does not fall
far from the tree is brought home with a vengeance to
Lear, who acknowledges Gonerill to be 'a disease that's
in my flesh, | Which I must needs call mine' (II.4.217–18).

It would be sheer sentimentality, moreover, to pretend

that Cordelia has escaped contamination by her father's example, and to cast her as the angelic antithesis of her demonized sisters. By her decision to 'Love, and be silent' (I.1.62), because, as she puts it, 'I cannot heave | My heart into my mouth' (91–2), she becomes without question a living symbol of the 'better way' that lies beyond the world as it stands, and beyond the tainted language that keeps that world in place. But her blank refusal to indulge her father's ploy to bestow on her 'A third more opulent' (I.1.86) than her sisters' also evinces an inflexible obstinacy and a presumption of moral superiority that bear the unmistakable stamp of her progenitor. Cordelia's blunt insistence on saying 'Nothing' gives way under pressure to the dispassionate precision of 'I love your majesty | According to my bond, no more nor less' (I.1.92–3), and finally succumbs to her father's discourse of calculation – but with a hurtful twist worthy of Gonerill and Regan:

> That lord whose hand must take my plight shall carry
> Half my love with him, half my care and duty.
> Sure I shall never marry like my sisters,
> To love my father all. (101–4)

There is a steely glint of spite in these clinical words, whose truthfulness cannot disguise their barbed intent to wound. It is difficult to dismiss the inference that Cordelia's brave act of non-compliance is at the same time an act of retaliation against her father and a perverse proof of her superiority to her sisters after all. It is a proof, however, purchased at the cost of her father's desolation, the disintegration of the kingdom, and her own complicity.

Lear and his three daughters are caught in a vicious

family circle of mutual punishment, which Lear's moral enlightenment and transcendent reunion with Cordelia cannot completely eclipse. In Lear's case, indeed, there is no escaping the suspicion that, deep down, he is not simply lashing out at his children for breaking his heart, seeking to hurt them by exposing himself to anguish and insanity in the storm. It may be that, by punishing his daughters for their lack of love, he is fulfilling an unconscious urge to punish himself, because he does not deserve to be loved. The ferocious speech in the storm that concludes 'I am a man | More sinned against than sinning' certainly suggests that unacknowledged culpability is preying on his mind:

> Tremble, thou wretch
> That hast within thee undivulgèd crimes
> Unwhipped of justice. Hide thee, thou bloody hand,
> Thou perjured, and thou simular of virtue
> That art incestuous. Caitiff, to pieces shake,
> That under covert and convenient seeming
> Has practised on man's life. Close pent-up guilts,
> Rive your concealing continents, and cry
> These dreadful summoners grace. (III.2.51–9)

If this speech is subliminally addressed to himself, and those 'close pent-up guilts' include his own, then part of Lear's 'darker purpose' in staging the love-test and dividing his kingdom is to precipitate the calamity that brings judgement upon him, to provoke the very suffering he bewails.

To impute such convoluted psychological motives to Lear may seem far-fetched, but they find a striking parallel in the characterization of Edgar, which suggests that Shakespeare's exploration of these matters is anything but unwitting. Edgar sums up his kinship with the king succinctly: 'He childed as I fathered' (III.6.108). The title page of the 1608 Quarto underlines their affinity by giving second billing, after the life and death of Lear and his daughters, not to the life of Gloucester, but to 'the unfortunate life of Edgar, son and heir to the Earl of Gloucester, and his sullen and assumed humour of Tom of Bedlam'.

Edgar is an extremely enigmatic figure, the chief puzzle being why he needs 't'assume a semblance | That very dogs disdained' (V.3.185–6) at all, let alone why he sustains it long after the pretext of disguise has become implausible. What pent-up guilt is being expiated by inflicting on himself such a protracted physical and mental penance? The clue lies in his equally baffling failure to reveal himself to his blind father when Gloucester gives him the perfect cue:

> O dear son Edgar,
> The food of thy abusèd father's wrath!
> Might I but live to see thee in my touch
> I'd say I had eyes again. (IV.1.21–4)

Edgar continues to deny his remorseful father the solace that is in his gift right up to the latter's death, which is triggered by the shock of his son's belated revelation. En route to that lethal disclosure, moreover, Edgar engineers the mock-suicide of the man who sired him, exploiting his blindness to make him believe he has leapt in vain 'From the dread summit of this chalky bourn' (IV.6.57). It seems reasonable to conclude that Edgar's anger at his father's credulous distrust of him finds circuitous satisfaction in these ways. Even as he guides him, begs for him and comforts him, Edgar is also making him pay, as surely as his brother Edmund makes him pay for the stigma of being a bastard. What Edgar's self-laceration as Poor Tom implies, however, is that he shares Lear's secret desire to punish himself as well. Poor Tom serves as the scapegoat for the filial aggression the virtuous Edgar must repress, and perhaps for Edgar's fear that his true feelings for his father merited his father's mistrust. As for Gloucester, his mortification at the blame he must shoulder for the fate of his sons and himself dogs him to the grave.

To expose the antagonisms that conspire in the tragedy of Lear's and Gloucester's families is not to dispute the reality of the love that Lear and Cordelia, Gloucester and Edgar, learn to feel for each other. Lear's description of himself as an 'old kind father, whose frank heart gave all' (III.4.20) is not untrue, nor is the compassion that Edgar and Cordelia show for their fathers faked. To Cordelia's uncompromising mind, 'Love's not love | When it is mingled with regards that stands | Aloof from th'entire point' (I.1.238–40). But *King Lear* makes it clear that love within the patriarchal family, however pure it seems, is doomed to be infected by domination, dependency, resentment and guilt. Rose-tinted accounts of the tragedy that see Lear and Gloucester as redeemed by love cannot face the fact that love is placed in the dock by the play as an accomplice in the catastrophe.

The closely related question of gender is subjected to an equally unsettling appraisal. *King Lear* offers ample corroboration for feminist interpretations of the play as a seductive misogynistic fantasy. From this critical perspective, the conspicuous absence of mothers from both families in the sources plays right into Shakespeare's hands. Lear's tragic agony as a victim of his own folly and filial ingratitude is seen as a smokescreen for what really drives the drama: the male desire not merely to

supplant the mother and smother maternal urges, but to
extirpate every female trait that threatens the sway of
men. "Twas this flesh begot | Those pelican daughters'
(III.4.71–2), declares Lear, displacing the woman who
bore them. Yet he fears the feminine tears that would
impugn his masculinity: 'let not women's weapons, water
drops, | Stain my man's cheeks' (II.4.272–3). By the
same token, the strident masculinity of Gonerill and
Regan serves to vilify them, in contrast to Cordelia,
whose 'voice was ever soft, | Gentle and low – an excel-
lent thing in woman' (V.3.270–71). The curse Lear begs
Nature to inflict on Gonerill speaks for itself: 'Into her
womb convey sterility, | Dry up in her the organs of
increase' (I.4.275–6). In the very scene in which he
displays such trenchant 'reason in madness', he vents a
venomous horror of female sexuality:

> Down from the waist they are centaurs,
> Though women all above;
> But to the girdle do the gods inherit,
> Beneath is all the fiends' –
> There's hell, there's darkness, there is the sulphurous
>   pit – burning, scalding, stench, consumption! (IV.6.124–9)

Nor can it be denied that all three of Lear's daughters
– the entire female populace of the play – end up being
eliminated along with him, leaving an exclusively masculine world at the close.

This idea of the epitome of patriarchy hogging the
tragic spotlight as he dies on a stage purged of women
may sound cynical, but the view of *King Lear* that gives
rise to it can find plenty of footholds in the text. That
said, a full account of the gender factor would have to
find room for feminist readings that point in a quite

different direction. Such readings would not dispute the virulent misogyny that mars Lear's speech and is stitched into the fabric of the plot. But they would contest the conclusion that the play underwrites the patriarchal prejudices and stereotypes by which its protagonists are gripped. For it is equally possible to argue that Lear's tragedy shows the appalling human cost of those prejudices and stereotypes to both women and men, and the desirability of redefining masculinity to embrace qualities whose repression leaves men emotionally maimed. From this standpoint, Lear's suffocating fit of 'Hysterica passio' – 'O, how this mother swells up toward my heart!' (II.4.54) – is a symptom, like the tears he fights in vain, of his emotional emancipation. The upsurge of maternal impulses and feminine empathy within him is inseparable from his discovery of compassion for the hungry and homeless in the storm, and his questioning of the basis of sovereignty itself. Lear is at the centre, moreover, of a group of male figures – Gloucester, Kent, Edgar, the Fool and Albany – who are, or who become, like Edgar, 'pregnant to good pity' (IV.6.223), and who form an outcast community within the play of nurturing, tender-hearted men, in sharp contrast to Edmund, Cornwall, Gonerill and Regan. Far from condoning patriarchal conceptions of gender, in other words, *King Lear* exposes their collusion in the tragedy, and portrays men moving beyond them.

5

Yet, however well founded such views of *King Lear* may be, the full scope of the play remains beyond their reach. There is no doubt that what happens to the families of

Lear and Gloucester, and consequently to the kingdom of Britain, is inextricable from the structures of subjection that warp relationships within society, within the family and between the sexes. In this respect, Gloucester's belief that people's fates are forged by 'spherical predominance', that we are what we are 'by an enforced obedience of planetary influence' (I.2.123–5), is rebutted not merely by Edmund but by the play as a whole. The play bears out Edmund's contention that 'men | Are as the time is' (V.3.31–2), the creatures of the epoch and culture in which they find themselves. But it also demonstrates that they have the potential to be other than the time is, to swim against the tide of history. *King Lear* shows what hierarchy and patriarchy make humans do to each other and to themselves. Yet in the same breath, through the transformations of Lear and Gloucester, through the silent love of Cordelia, through the beggar that Edgar discovers within himself, it affirms the human capacity to live and love on terms quite different from those that destroy its protagonists. To that extent, *King Lear* can be seen as a radical, forward-looking tragedy, whose cruelties and horrors are unmasked as the man-made creations of a society that men and women can question, and that men and women can change.

Shakespeare, however, is not content to let matters rest there. This conception of *King Lear* may be true as far as it goes, but the problem is that it does not go far enough, and nowhere near as far as the play's author is prepared to go. For, as *King Lear* proceeds, Shakespeare becomes increasingly troubled by the possibility that the cause of the tragedy is housed not in history, in explicable human conflicts of interest, but in the inhuman imperatives of natural law, whose ultimate rationale remains unfathomable.

What if Edmund, who prides himself on being conceived 'in the lusty stealth of nature' (I.2.11), and who holds 'the plague of custom' (I.2.3) in contempt, is closer to the truth than Cordelia, whose filial piety 'redeems nature from the general curse' (IV.6.206)? What if the daughters Lear excoriates as 'unnatural hags' (II.4.273) are simply being true to their nature as 'she-foxes' (III.6.22), at home in the realm of the tigers, wolves, serpents and vultures to which they are constantly compared? Nurture may go some way towards explaining the 'Sharp-toothed unkindness' (II.4.130) and merciless rapacity of Gonerill and Regan, but it founders on the fact that their younger sister, reared in the same family, under the same circumstances, turned out otherwise. 'The stars above us govern our conditions', reflects Kent, clutching like Gloucester at astrological straws, 'Else one self mate and make could not beget | Such different issues' (IV.3.33–5). Laying his daughters' dispositions to the charge of a star will not do, however, for Lear, who wonders whether the real reason resides in the flesh itself: 'Then let them anatomize Regan, see what breeds about her heart. Is there any cause in nature that makes these hard hearts?' (III.6.75–7).

In the storm scenes, fired by the spectacle of Poor Tom's 'uncovered body' (III.4.99), Lear confronts the stark physiological fact of our animal nature and asks an equally basic and perplexing question: 'Is man no more than this? Consider him well. Thou owest the worm no silk, the beast no hide, the sheep no wool, the cat no perfume. Ha! Here's three on's are sophisticated. Thou art the thing itself!' (III.4.99–103). Once the façade of cultivation and the accretions of convention have been stripped away, the human animal is revealed as a very vulnerable creature, driven by the same primal needs and appetites as its fellow creatures. The distinction between the human and the animal had already been put under stress in the previous act, when Lear sought to defend his right to his entourage against the cold rationality of Gonerill and Regan:

> O, reason not the need! Our basest beggars
> Are in the poorest things superfluous.
> Allow not nature more than nature needs –
> Man's life is cheap as beast's. (II.4.259–62)

In the face of cold, hunger, and the onslaught of 'The to-and-fro conflicting wind and rain' (III.1.11), the distinction collapses, and Lear finds himself 'a comrade with the wolf and owl' indeed, classed with 'the cub-drawn bear . . . | The lion and the belly-pinchèd wolf' (12–13), just like his predatory daughters. In this light, Albany's fear that 'Humanity must perforce prey on itself | Like monsters of the deep' (IV.2.49–50) appears all too plausible.

'Here's a night', observes the Fool to Lear, 'pities neither wise men nor fools' (III.2.12–13). A storm, like the need for food, warmth and shelter, is no respecter of rank, desert or species. The liberating implication of the storm scenes is that the system of social differences on which hierarchy depends has no basis in nature, which views all human beings as bare, forked animals. But to accept that implication is also to acknowledge the extent of humanity's subjection to forces of nature which are indifferent to its fate, and over which human beings have no control.

Nothing hammers home nature's cruel impartiality more emphatically than the ending of *King Lear*, in which good and bad perish alike, regardless of merit. Edgar,

Edmund and Albany queue up in the closing scene to impose poetic justice with a platitude: 'The gods are just, and of our pleasant vices | Make instruments to plague us' (V.3.168–9), Edgar concludes; 'The wheel is come full circle' (172), concurs Edmund; 'All friends shall taste | The wages of their virtue, and all foes | The cup of their deservings' (300–302), declares Albany. But Shakespeare is having none of this conventional cant, and the words have hardly left Albany's mouth when Lear dashes any hope of self-delusion with the terrible monosyllabic question he asks Cordelia in his final speech:

> Why should a dog, a horse, a rat have life,
> And thou no breath at all? Thou'lt come no more;
> Never, never, never, never, never. (V.3.304–6)

Samuel Johnson, who found the dying moments of *King Lear* unbearable to read, famously complained in his editorial notes on the play that 'Shakespeare has suffered the virtue of Cordelia to perish in a just cause, contrary to the natural ideas of justice, to the hope of the reader, and, what is yet more strange, to the faith of the chronicles' (*The Plays of William Shakespeare*, 1765). But Cordelia's death demonstrates that there is nothing natural about the idea of justice, which is the invention of human culture. The answer to Lear's question is that in nature's eyes Cordelia's life is indeed worth no more than the life of a rat, and its termination is equally insignificant. Nature's laws are neutral and amoral: they dictate that 'The younger rises when the old doth fall' (III.3.23), and that the stronger young will prevail over the weaker, making some hearts hard and some hearts kind, whether human beings like it or not. But the deeper question of why nature should be like that at all, and why humankind should be at the mercy of its implacable indifference, echoes unanswered throughout the play.

Shakespeare's violation of precedent and expectation at the end of *King Lear* betrays a streak of cruelty that mimics the pitilessness of nature itself. There is something sadistic about the way the spectator's hopes are played with right down to Lear's last line, making the final impact of the play – its conclusion as a tragedy or a tragicomedy – turn on a mere breath. It would be dishonest, moreover, to deny that an icy current of nihilism courses through *King Lear*. Lear's revulsion from the ubiquitous brute fact of procreation ('The wren goes to't, and the small gilded fly | Does lecher in my sight' (IV.6.112–13)) and his eagerness to annihilate the very springs of life ('Crack Nature's moulds, all germens spill at once' (III.2.8)) goes beyond mere misogyny. It is a symptom of the hunger for oblivion that he shares with the eyeless Gloucester ('Away, and let me die' (IV.6.48)), a hunger that can be stilled only by death itself. 'You do me wrong to take me out o'the grave' (IV.7.45) is Lear's gentle rebuke to Cordelia when he sees her again for the first time; and when Edgar tries to revive Lear as he dies, Kent checks him with: 'O, let him pass. He hates him | That would upon the rack of this tough world | Stretch him out longer' (V.3.311–13).

Lear's craving for death is much more than a response to his own dire predicament. It is a craving to escape the common fate inflicted on the human animal by the blind will of nature. 'Thou knowest the first time that we smell the air | We wawl and cry', says Lear to Gloucester, 'we cry that we are come | To this great stage of fools' (IV.6.180–81, 183–4). As for the last time that we smell the air, 'Men must endure | Their going hence even as their coming hither' (V.2.9–10), as Edgar admonishes his world-weary father. In between, the simplest sensations alone seem real, and only plain statements of bare fact ring true: 'I am cold myself' (III.2.69); 'I feel this pinprick' (IV.7.56); 'She's gone for ever' (V.3.257).

The tragedy of *King Lear* begins with Cordelia's 'nothing', the word that haunts every act like a baleful refrain, and ends with Lear's 'never', whose harrowing repetition reverberates in the mind long after the last speech of the play has faded. But, although it would be wrong to ignore the undertow of nihilism that pulls *King Lear* towards the void, it would be a mistake to confuse it with the final vision of the tragedy, which cannot be boiled down to misanthropic despair at the futility of human existence. By placing the social tragedy of Lear's and Gloucester's families in the wider, natural perspective of an enigmatic universe, Shakespeare exposes the fragility of the views humans take of life, but he does not discount them as worthless. The effect is rather to disengage us from the characters' plight and pull us back to a point from which we can judge it not only with empathy, but also with profound detachment.

6

It is not just from the plight of the characters, however, that Shakespeare seeks to detach us. He is no less concerned to distance us from the entire play *as a play*, to throw into question the validity of *King Lear* as a work of verbal and theatrical art. Whether the source of the suffering and death it depicts is to be found in human history or in natural history, or at the point where nature and culture converge, it is the dramatic and rhetorical skill of a playwright that has crafted *King Lear* in these terms and compelled us to ponder such matters, and Shakespeare never lets us lose sight of this fact. However mesmerizing the poetry of the play may be, however overpowering the spectacle of doom it stages, *King Lear*'s account of human life should not be regarded as complete or definitive. It is one version of the world, woven out of words on the loom of tragic form, by a dramatist writing within the constraints of his time and place. This qualification is built into the design and wording of the play, which prompts us repeatedly to treat the vision it is forging with circumspection.

Act II, scene 1 provides some striking examples of *King Lear*'s self-conscious theatricality and keenness to advertise its verbal artifice. When Edgar enters, interrupting his brother's caustic soliloquy on astrological superstition, Edmund breaks off to draw the audience even more closely into his confidence: 'pat he comes, like the catastrophe of the old comedy. My cue is villainous melancholy, with a sigh like Tom o'Bedlam' (I.2.134–5). The stage-villain's *sotto voce* aside, delivered within a direct address which is already at one remove from the play's world, sharpens the spectator's awareness of that world's debt to dramatic conventions and traditions. But it does more than that. Edmund's invocation of Tom o'Bedlam serves as a subconscious cue for Edgar's creation of the character in Act II, scene 3. It is as if the mere utterance of the name summons the beggar into being out of nowhere. An equally uncanny prefiguring occurs a few dozen lines later, when Edmund clinches his deception of the gullible Edgar by assuring him: 'I have told you what I have seen and heard but faintly, nothing like the image and horror of it' (I.2.170–2). Four acts later that last phrase is echoed with a vengeance, and with a twist, by Edgar himself. 'Is this the promised end?' asks Kent, aghast at the entrance of Lear with Cordelia's lifeless body; 'Or image of that horror?' (V.3.261–2) wonders Edgar, turning Edmund's words round to lay the stress on representation rather than reality.

The second scene of Act I harbours a further instance of verbal anticipation, of words predicting and procuring deeds, in Gloucester's earlier exchange with Edmund. Asked by his father what paper he has put away so hastily, Edmund replies, in a verbatim echo of Cordelia's fateful reply to Lear, 'Nothing, my lord'; to which Gloucester responds, with a black irony that resonates only in retrospect: 'If it be nothing I shall not need spectacles' (I.2.32, 35–6). For the letter is indeed nothing, in as much as it is a baseless fabrication, and soon Gloucester will never see anything again. Lear's diction plays its part in producing Gloucester's blinding too. In Act I, scene 4, struggling to suppress his tears, he cries 'Old fond eyes, | Beweep this cause again, I'll pluck ye out' (298–9). Gloucester picks up this buried prompt two acts later as Regan and Cornwall prepare to torture him. When Regan demands why he has sent the king to Dover, Gloucester retorts, 'Because I would not see thy cruel nails| Pluck out his poor old eyes' (III.7.55–6), which in turn gives his tormentors their cue to pluck out his own eyes instead. The cumulative impact of such premonitions and echoes, which become fully apparent through close reading, is to reveal the shaping hand of the dramatist at work. Through a subtle web of intimations and allusions, *King Lear* calls its nature as a scripted artefact continually to our attention.

At the centre of that web is the Dover Cliff scene, one of the most disconcerting scenes Shakespeare ever

wrote. Vocally disguised at this point as a peasant, Edgar
assures Gloucester that, despite the evidence of his
surviving senses, they are labouring uphill towards a cliff-
top and the sea can be clearly heard. And now, Edgar
announces, they have arrived at the summit from which
his father plans to pitch himself:

> Come on, sir; here's the place. Stand still! How fearful
> And dizzy 'tis to cast one's eyes so low!
> The crows and choughs that wing the midway air
> Show scarce so gross as beetles. Halfway down
> Hangs one that gathers sampire – dreadful trade!
> Methinks he seems no bigger than his head.
> The fishermen that walk upon the beach
> Appear like mice, and yon tall anchoring bark
> Diminished to her cock; her cock, a buoy
> Almost too small for sight. The murmuring surge
> That on th'unnumbered idle pebble chafes
> Cannot be heard so high. I'll look no more,
> Lest my brain turn, and the deficient sight
> Topple down headlong. (IV.6.11–24)

Setting aside Edgar's dubious motives for deluding his
father, what is so arresting about this passage is
Shakespeare's brazen display of the art of illusion. For
a start, it is delivered by a character whose identity
consists of a succession of impostures, the most blatant
being his impersonation of a Bedlam beggar, whom Lear
mistakes for 'the thing itself. Through Edgar, Shakespeare shows how the imagination can carve out of words
a three-dimensional prospect as solid, detailed and
convincing as it would be if it were meant to be
real, and not just a figment of Edgar's fantasy. What
Gloucester is induced to envisage is credible enough not

only to make him 'topple down headlong', but also to make the audience unsure for a moment which way to take it themselves.

The scene brings home the fact that the whole of *King Lear* – what we accept as the reality of its world – is a verbal fabrication as baseless and insubstantial as the one Edgar foists on his father, and conscripts us to collude in: '(*aside*) Why I do trifle thus with his despair | Is done to cure it' (IV.6.33–4). Only a conjuror as confident of his powers as Shakespeare could afford to show the audience exactly how the trick is done. But this virtuoso display of wizardry with words is put on to do more than dazzle us. By framing an illusion within a reality that is itself an illusion, it blurs the border between imaginary and real within the world of the play, and between the play-world and the real world in which we are watching or reading it. It suspends us between engrossment in the dramatic fiction of *King Lear* and vigilant distrust of the virtual reality it creates.

King Lear itself, in other words, is not immune to Shakespeare's scepticism. The authority of the play's tragic perspective is as vulnerable as the lives of the characters it destroys. Yet to describe the stance that Shakespeare adopts in *King Lear*, and that we are invited to share, as one of sceptical detachment scarcely does justice to the sublime strangeness of this tragedy. If anyone is privy to the secret of this strangeness, it is the Fool, that mercurial figure who shuttles between the world of the play and the world of the audience, and who melts away without explanation, once his theatrical task is done, with the riddling, topsy-turvy quip, 'And I'll go to bed at noon' (III.6.83). For the Fool comes as close as a character could to personifying the dispassionate perspective of the play itself. Reflecting on the role of the Fool in

Shakespeare in 1811, Samuel Taylor Coleridge remarked:
'We meet with characters who are, as it were, unfeeling
spectators of the most passionate situations, constantly
in life. The Fool serves to supply the place of some such
uninterested person where all the characters besides have
interest.' And 'the most genuine and real' of Shakespeare's
Fools, Coleridge added, 'is in *Lear*'.

It is to the Fool that Shakespeare entrusts the delivery
of his most cryptic clue to the source of *King Lear*'s
sublimity. At the close of Act III, scene 2, at the turning
point of the tragedy, as Kent leads his mad master off to
shelter from the storm, the Fool hangs back, steps out
of the play and addresses the audience directly:

This is a brave night to cool a courtesan. I'll speak a
prophecy ere I go:
    When priests are more in word than matter,
    When brewers mar their malt with water,
    When nobles are their tailors' tutors,
    No heretics burned but wenches' suitors –
    Then shall the realm of Albion
    Come to great confusion.

    When every case in law is right,
    No squire in debt nor no poor knight;
    When slanders do not live in tongues,
    Nor cutpurses come not to throngs,
    When usurers tell their gold i'the field,
    And bawds and whores do churches build –
    Then comes the time, who lives to see't,
    That going shall be used with feet.
This prophecy Merlin shall make; for I live before his
time. (79–96)

'This is one of the Shakespearian shocks or blows that take the breath away', wrote G. K. Chesterton of that final line ('The Tragedy of *King Lear*', 1930). It takes the breath away because of the sudden sense of temporal vertigo it induces. The Fool's teasing prophecy juxtaposes utopian possibilities with dystopian actualities, encapsulating the battle between the way things are and the way they could be that rages at the core of the tragedy. It pans back from the immediate action, estranging the play from its spectators by compressing it into a conundrum, delivered in outdated doggerel. And its parting shot, with its bamboozling prophecy of a prophecy, catapults us forward in time to a point beyond the past in which *King Lear* is set *and* the present in which it is being performed. The Fool's speech scrambles our normal perception of time in order to place us, for one dizzying moment, in an unknown future far ahead of our time too.

Coleridge might well have had *King Lear* in mind when he contended that Shakespeare is as unlike his contemporaries as he is unlike us. Shakespeare's imagination is out of sync with his epoch and ours, Coleridge maintained, because 'He writes not for past ages but for that in which he lives and that which is to follow'; while he 'registers what is past, he projects the future in a wonderful degree', and in this sense 'shakes off the iron bondage of space and time'. As the Fool's eerie prophecy intimates, not the least astonishing thing about *King Lear* is its ability to imagine its world and time from the standpoint of an era that is yet to come, and in the sure knowledge that one day, when that era too is long gone, 'This great world | Shall so wear out to naught' (IV.6.135–6). *King Lear*'s disengagement from its time frees it not merely to strike at the foundations of early modern society, but even to anticipate the extinction of that

society in the guise of ancient Britain. How prophetic
the play will prove about the fate of society in the twenty-
first century remains to be seen. The sole certainty is
that *King Lear* will stay one step ahead of us, constantly
disclosing, through the dialogue it stages between the
future and the past, compelling new perspectives on the
present.

Kiernan Ryan

The Play in Performance

In his essay 'On the Tragedies of Shakespeare' (1811) Charles Lamb protested that *King Lear* is impossible to stage satisfactorily, because its cosmic scope and sublime vision dwindle into banality in performance:

To see Lear acted, to see an old man tottering about the stage with a walking-stick, turned out of doors by his daughters in a rainy night, has nothing in it but what is painful and disgusting. We want to take him into shelter and relieve him. That is all the feeling which the acting of Lear ever produced in me. But the Lear of Shakespeare cannot be acted. The contemptible machinery by which they mimic the storm which he goes out in, is not more inadequate to represent the horrors of the real elements, than any actor can be to represent Lear: they might more easily propose to personate the Satan of Milton upon a stage, or one of Michael Angelo's terrible figures.

The early nineteenth-century productions of *King Lear* that provoked Lamb's protest may well have deserved his disgust. But since that time, and especially since the Second World War, both the stage and the screen have produced ample evidence that the play can be performed with a power and intensity that might lead even Lamb to recant.

That is not to say, of course, that anyone setting out to stage or film *King Lear* today does not have to face up to fundamental problems and make difficult decisions in order to bring Shakespeare's script effectively to life. The risk of the play floundering in a slough of sentimental bathos remains just as high as it was in Lamb's time, and the text has all sorts of traps to spring on unwary directors and casts.

At the most basic, practical level, however, *King Lear* is surprisingly straightforward to stage. When Shakespeare's all-male company, the King's Men, first performed the play, in late 1605 or early 1606 at their regular public theatre, the Globe, and when they put it on at court for King James, as the title page of the Quarto tells us they did, on St Stephen's night in 1606, sixteen actors (including three boys to play Lear's daughters) would have sufficed to cover all the parts with the aid of some adroit doubling. Four centuries later the Old Vic mounted its 2003 production of *King Lear*, directed by Stephen Unwin and starring Timothy West, with a cast of seventeen actors handling all the roles by means of doubling, exactly as their Jacobean counterparts had – the only major casting difference being that Gonerill, Regan and Cordelia were played by women. The Old Vic production, moreover, required as few props as Shakespeare's company to perform *King Lear* on a stage as bare of scenery as the Globe's would have been. All the script calls for are commonplace items such as chairs (one of which may serve as Lear's throne), a set of stocks for Kent, a map to indicate the divisions of the kingdom, a coronet for Cornwall and Albany to 'part between' them (I.1.139), weapons, torches, purses and letters.

The music and sound effects demanded by the play are equally simple and, thanks to modern technology, even

easier to supply today than in 1605: thunder and lightning have to be simulated during the storm scenes of
Acts II and III, and the background noise of battle in
Act V, scene 2; soothing music must be played offstage
in Act IV, scene 7 to heal Lear's mind; and a variety of
drum-rolls and trumpet-blasts are needed to signal formal
entrances, exits and events, such as Edgar's summoning
of Edmund to combat in the final scene. *King Lear* is a
long, complicated play, packed with incident and spectacle designed to enthral the eye, including fights, torture,
deaths, disguises, processions and an imaginary leap from
a cliff. But, apart from Act II, scene 1, when Edmund
calls on Edgar to 'descend' (19), the entire tragedy can
be played out, as it was at the Old Vic in 2003, on the
floor of the main stage, without employing an upper
level or an inner recess. A curtained alcove (the 'discovery space') at the back of the stage and a gallery or
balcony above it were structural features of the Globe,
but Shakespeare patently considered neither indispensable to the staging of *King Lear*.

Deciding which version of the tragedy to stage, and
how much of that version to include, is a trickier matter.
Should the production be based on the 1608 Quarto text,
the 1623 first Folio text, or a script that splices Folio and
Quarto together to make the most of both of them, as
this edition seeks to do? The Folio text has a different
title from the Quarto, describing *King Lear* as a '*Tragedy*'
rather than a '*True Chronicle History*'; it lacks nearly 300
lines contained in the Quarto; it adds over 100 lines that
the Quarto does not include; and between the two texts
there are over 800 minor verbal discrepancies, many of
which are significant. (See An Account of the Text,
below, for a detailed analysis.) To stick dogmatically to
the later Folio version, which represents Shakespeare's

own revision of the play in the view of some modern
scholars, is to lose the hallucinatory trial of Lear's daughters in Act III, scene 6; to return to the Quarto, on the
other hand, to restore the lines omitted by the Folio, is
to sacrifice the uncanny prophecy the Fool delivers to
the audience at the end of Act III, scene 2, and Lear's
enigmatic dying lines: 'Do you see this? Look on her!
Look, her lips! | Look there! Look there!' (V.3.308–9).

Small wonder, therefore, that modern theatrical practice has tended to favour a conflated text, which gives
the production the option of using whatever seems to
work best on stage. Most recent productions, including
Nicholas Hytner's for the Royal Shakespeare Company
(RSC) in 1990, which favoured the Folio text, have opted
to keep Lear's delirious mock-trial of Gonerill and
Regan, because it is so dramatically powerful, and
because of its resonance with his trial of his children's
love in Act I and the configuration of their corpses on
stage in the final scene. At the same time, if the Quarto
had never survived and Act III, scene 6 had disappeared
with it, no one would ever have thought that a scene was
missing from *King Lear*, and it is equally possible to
argue that Lear's searing indictment of the judicial system
in Act IV, scene 6 is all the more potent for not being
pre-empted in the previous act.

Act IV, scene 3, which consists of a conversation
between Kent and a Gentleman, also occurs solely in the
Quarto, but is commonly cut or drastically abridged with
few qualms, since the case for retaining it on grounds of
theatrical impact or dramatic coherence is far weaker.
Even so, scrapping this scene means losing lines about
Cordelia that contribute much to the exalted view of her
that circulates in *King Lear*, the most striking being: 'You
have seen | Sunshine and rain at once; her smiles and

tears | Were like a better way' (IV.3.17–19). Much less
defensible is the decision that is sometimes taken to omit
the Fool's prophecy, as the 1974 New York production
starring James Earl Jones, and directed by Edwin Sherin,
did. The reason usually given for cutting this startling
speech is that it is too arcane and alien for modern
audiences, and the same reason sanctions further contrac-
tions of the Fool's riddling discourse and the extem-
porized gibberish of Poor Tom. But what the performed
script gains in clarity from these cuts has to be set against
the resulting impoverishment of the play's vision, which
cultivates obscurity and baffles communication for its
own dark purposes. No one who witnessed Antony Sher's
voicing of the Fool's prophecy, in the RSC's 1982 production directed by Adrian Noble, will forget the spine-
tingling impact of Sher's seeming to speak from a place
and a time beyond the world of the play.

The question of where and when to set the action of
King Lear is as complex as the question of which version
of the text to perform. According to Holinshed's
Chronicles, King Lear reigned in Britain around 800 BC,
before the founding of Rome. The period in which the
play's events take place, however, is neither clearly nor
consistently established by the text. On the contrary,
King Lear creates a fluid theatrical timescape, in which
the prehistoric, Anglo-Saxon, Roman and medieval eras
mingle anachronistically with Jacobean Britain, and with
apocalyptic and utopian premonitions of the future. The
drawback of pinning the play down to a specific era
through costume, props and scenery may thus be to
forfeit much of its strange, elusive quality, which is
rooted in its reluctance to be historically fixed and
circumscribed.

This is certainly true of the long tradition of setting

King Lear in the archaic epoch of Stonehenge, a tradition which stretches back to William Macready's seminal restaging of the play in 1838, and which can still be seen, alive and well, in the 1983 Granada TV production, directed by Michael Elliott and starring Laurence Olivier. But the same charge of trapping the play in time could be levelled at Jonathan Miller's 1982 version for BBC TV, starring Michael Hordern, which set the tragedy in the Jacobean era in which it was written, or at Giorgio Strehler's 1972 Milan production, which was performed by actors clad in black leather in a bleak modern wasteland. However, siting *King Lear* in a deliberately abstract, timeless milieu and clothing the cast in costumes redolent of no particular era does not seem to be the answer either, at least not if the reception given to George Devine's notorious 1955 production, starring John Gielgud and designed by Isamu Noguchi, is anything to go by. To prescribe appropriate settings for *Lear* is plainly as foolish as it is undesirable, but if doing justice to the text is a criterion, there is a lot to be said for the time-traversing approach adopted, for example, by the National Theatre's acclaimed 1997 production, directed by Richard Eyre, which commuted discreetly between diverse periods, just like *King Lear* itself.

The *mise-en-scène* on which a production settles cannot be divorced, of course, from the conception of the tragedy it is designed to house. It makes an enormous difference, for instance, if Lear is actually dressed as a monarch, as he was in all the classic performances of the role between the mid eighteenth century and the end of the nineteenth. From David Garrick to Edmund Kean to Macready to Edwin Forrest, Lear was played in the ermine-trimmed scarlet robes of a king. So, when he strove in the storm to tear off his royal 'lendings' and expose the same 'poor, bare, forked animal' (III.4.104–5) visible beneath Poor Tom's rags, his costume under- scored the levelling implications of the scene and increased the impact of the monarch's moral transfor- mation in the course of the third and fourth acts. Scarlet and ermine, needless to say, are not the sole means of signalling the gulf of rank and power that divides the ruler from the ruled or the rich from the wretched, as the Russian director Grigori Kozintsev's superb black- and-white film of *King Lear* (1970) demonstrates. And in Peter Brook's trail-blazing stage production in 1962 (a film version of which appeared in 1971) Paul Scofield's austere, brooding, bare-headed Lear proved that regality could be evoked without relying on regalia at all.

Nonetheless, Brook's revolutionary reinterpretation of the tragedy heralded a tendency in modern produc- tions to dilute, blur or even erase the outward signs of Lear's royalty. When Brook staged Act IV, scene 6 with the mad Lear, the blind Gloucester and the disguised Edgar all dressed in the same ragged sackcloth, he enhanced the impression of an archetypal human condi- tion, but thereby obscured the tragedy's origin in a social order that can be challenged and changed. When the distinction between society's 'poor naked wretches' and those who keep them poor and wretched is masked in this manner, *King Lear*'s assault on authority and injus- tice collapses. In recent decades it has become common- place to portray Lear from the start as an ailing old man rather than a fearsome sovereign surrounded by the trap- pings of majesty. Thus in Deborah Warner's National Theatre production in 1990 a geriatric Lear played by Brian Cox made his first appearance bundled up in a wheelchair with a rug over his knees; while in the produc- tion directed by Nicholas Hytner in the same year at the

RSC John Wood played the unhinged king in the ill-assorted, cast-off clothes a charity might dispense to the homeless.

The appeal of playing Lear like this is clear: it speaks directly to a modern Western culture in which the neglect of the aged and the proliferation of 'houseless heads and unfed sides' (III.4.30) on city streets have become chronic problems. There is no doubt that the politics of the family and the politics of philanthropy are right at the heart of Shakespeare's tragedy. But to privilege these aspects of the play at the expense of the more fundamental political questions *King Lear* poses, and the demise of hierarchy and domination that it foreshadows, may be to purchase immediate relevance at too high a price.

All too often, productions in this style merely succeed in reducing *King Lear* to exactly the kind of domestic melodrama Lamb was complaining about 200 years ago. Nor is it difficult to see why the temptation to cut *King Lear* down to size persists. In the same essay Lamb decries the sentimentalized travesty of the tragedy that had held the stage since 1681, in the shape of Nahum Tate's more palatable adaptation. The trouble with Shakespeare's *King Lear*, Lamb observes, is that for Tate and his ilk

it is too hard and stony; it must have love scenes and a happy ending. It is not enough that Cordelia is a daughter, she must shine as a lover too. Tate has put his hook in the nostrils of this Leviathan, for Garrick and his followers, the showmen of the scene, to draw the mighty beast about more easily.

Lamb is absolutely right. There is indeed something 'hard and stony', even monstrous, about the vision of *King Lear* as Shakespeare wrote it that critics since Dr Johnson, and productions from Tate's time to ours, have flinched from, even after Shakespeare's text was restored to the stage by Macready in 1838. The tragedy displays a cruelty towards its characters that resembles the cruelty of nature itself, and it shows no mercy to the hopes of the audience either. It puts a whole dispensation to death, systematically exterminating all but three of its ruling-class protagonists, without a flicker of remorse. It is hardly surprising that modern productions still choose to play it for pathos, as the tale of a rejected father redeemed too late by his daughter's love, rather than meet the tragedy's chilling, implacable gaze.

To regain a sense of the qualities of *Lear* that recent stage productions have been prone to repress, one need only turn to the remarkable films of the play made by Brook and Kozintsev. Both directors make telling use of the advantages their medium gives them over the stage. They exploit to the full in particular the stark, barren landscapes in which they set the outdoor action, and bring home the vicious hostility of the weather to humans when the heavens open in the storm scenes. Brook's version looks, at times, as though it is set in the aftermath of an arctic Armageddon; Kozintsev's protagonists seem, at times, to be marooned beneath endless skies on the rock-strewn surface of some alien planet. In the storm scenes of both films the characters are almost obliterated by sheets of sweeping rain. The fragility of the 'poor, bare, forked animal' among the elements, at the mercy of nature's blind will, is visually expressed with a force that even the most resourceful theatre company would be hard put to match. In both films, too, the blank animosity of the earth and the elements conveys the unsparing severity of Shakespeare's play.

Unlike Brook, however, Kozintsev succeeds in dramatizing, through the destruction of Lear's and Gloucester's families, the destruction of a whole society and the end of an epoch. His film is densely populated in many scenes with peasants, courtiers and soldiers, which expands the world of the tragedy and reminds us how much is riding on the fates of its protagonists. Cost and convention conspire in the theatre to narrow the play's focus to the family conflicts that set parent against child, sibling against sibling. But in Kozintsev's *King Lear* the broader political and historical dimensions of Shakespeare's tragedy are inescapable. In one of the most memorable scenes of the film Lear's prayer to the homeless and destitute, who 'bide the pelting of this pitiless storm' (III.4.29), is addressed not in soliloquy to an imaginary abstraction, but to flesh-and-blood beggars, huddling together for warmth in the hovel before the eyes of their mortified king.

But if Brook's film, like the stage production on which it was based, is guilty of blunting the play's political point in some respects, it more than makes up for it in others. Indeed, it offers a wealth of insights into Shakespeare's text that future stage productions and screen versions of the play might do well to take on board. Brook's grasp of *King Lear*'s impassive view of its characters' suffering and extinction has already been touched on. At the end of the film, in rapid succession, Edgar buries an axe in Edmund with one brutal blow, Gonerill dashes her brains out on a rock after dashing out Regan's, Cordelia is hanged, and Lear enters howling with her corpse in his arms. The speed of the sequence and the abruptness of the cutting leave no purchase for the spectator's empathy. Not a drop of pathos is milked from Lear's dying words over his daughter's body on a deserted shore. Instead of allowing us, like so many productions, to relax into the customary compassionate response,

Brook keeps us at a distance and obliges us to confront
something more disturbing, something that Shakespeare's
King Lear confronts us with by other means.

It is the recognition of our complicity as spectators
in the tragedy performed for us on stage or screen: the
acknowledgement of our part in the spectacle of suffering
and death devised for our entertainment and edification.
From the outset, Brook's film is as self-consciously cinematic as Shakespeare's play is self-consciously theatrical.
We are continuously made aware of the camera at work
and of the film as an edited artefact. But at key moments
Brook goes further and pulls the viewer into the frame
too. When Gloucester is blinded in an act of savage
violence, the screen is blacked out as he screams in agony,
until our sight is restored with a shot of his mutilated
eyes. (In the stage production Brook created an unfor-
gettable *coup de théâtre* by bringing the houselights up
to signal the interval as the audience watched the sight-
less Gloucester grope his way towards the wings.) And
during the Dover Cliff scene the camera connives with
Edgar's deception of his father's mind's eye right up to
the moment when he falls, deliberately duping the audience as well by manipulating its gaze, just as Edgar's
words manipulate Gloucester's imagination.

Most disconcerting of all, however, is the way the
dying Lear, in the closing seconds of the film, looks
directly into the camera at the audience to address the
corpse of Cordelia. As he utters his cryptic last words
in full close-up – 'Do you see this? Look on her! Look,
her lips! | Look there! Look there!' – he looks and points
straight at the viewer, turning each silent witness of his
death into his lifeless daughter. Then he slides slowly
down and out of shot into oblivion, leaving us staring
into the void of a pure white screen. The effect is deeply

troubling, because it leaves us feeling that we have been victims of the tragedy too, that *King Lear* numbers us amongst its dead.

From Tate's day to our day too many productions of Shakespeare's most harrowing and uncompromising tragedy have sought, in Lamb's splendid phrase, to put their hook 'in the nostrils of this Leviathan' so as 'to draw the mighty beast about more easily'. The truly great productions of *King Lear*, like those caught for ever on film by Kozintsev and Brook, are the ones that show us what happens when the mighty beast is unleashed.

Kiernan Ryan

Further Reading

EDITIONS AND EDITORIAL PROBLEMS

Recent decades have witnessed intense scholarly debate about the status and relationship of the Quarto (1608) and the first Folio (1623) versions of the text of *King Lear*. That debate has generated in turn a plethora of modern editions. Accessible accounts of what is at stake in the debate – what difference it makes to use one text rather than another – can be found in the introductions to Stanley Wells's Oxford World's Classics edition (2000), which is based on the Quarto; Jay L. Halio's edition (1992) for the New Cambridge Shakespeare, which is based on the Folio; and R. A. Foakes's Arden edition (1997), which conflates the Folio and Quarto texts. Michael Warren's *The Parallel 'King Lear'* (1989) prints facsimiles of the original Quarto and Folio versions side by side on facing pages for comparison; the Quarto and Folio texts can also be compared in modernized form in *'King Lear': A Parallel Text Edition* (1993), edited by René Weis. Jay L. Halio has edited a separate, modern-spelling edition of the 1608 Quarto (New Cambridge Shakespeare, 1994). The 1986 Oxford edition of the *Complete Works*, edited by Stanley Wells and Gary Taylor, includes both the Quarto and the Folio texts; the 1997

Norton Shakespeare (general editor Stephen Greenblatt), which is based on the Oxford edition, furnishes a conflated text in addition to the Quarto and Folio versions. *The Riverside Shakespeare* (2nd edn 1997, general editor G. Blakemore Evans), settles for a single, conflated text of the tragedy.

SOURCES

The anonymous old *King Leir* play is available as a Malone Society reprint (1907; 1956); in modernized form in Joseph Satin's *Shakespeare and His Sources* (1966); and, most accessibly, in Geoffrey Bullough's *Narrative and Dramatic Sources of Shakespeare*, volume VII (1973), which also includes the relevant chapters of Sidney's *Arcadia* and other source materials on which Shakespeare drew. Wilfred Perrett has traced *The Story of King Lear from Geoffrey of Monmouth to Shakespeare* (1904). F. W. Brownlow provides an edition of *A Declaration of Egregious Popish Impostures* in *Shakespeare, Harsnett, and the Devils of Denham* (1993), which considers the relationship of Harsnet's work to Shakespeare's at length. Harsnet's *Declaration* plays a key role in Stephen Greenblatt's influential essay 'Shakespeare and the Exorcists', in *Shakespearean Negotiations* (1988). *King Lear*'s debts to its various sources are discussed in the single-volume editions of the play by Wells, Halio and Foakes cited above.

CRITICISM

Critical responses to *King Lear* from 1623 to 1801 can be tracked through the six volumes of Brian Vickers's

Shakespeare: The Critical Heritage (1974–81). For Johnson's comments on the play, see *Samuel Johnson on Shakespeare*, ed. H. R. Woudhuysen (1989). Jonathan Bate's anthology, *The Romantics on Shakespeare* (1992), contains substantial selections from Coleridge and Hazlitt on *Lear* and the core of Lamb's essay 'On the Tragedies of Shakespeare', which contends that *King Lear* is unstageable. There is also a section on *Lear* in *Coleridge on Shakespeare*, ed. Terence Hawkes (1969).

In the twentieth century, up until the 1960s, criticism of *King Lear* was dominated by overtly or implicitly Christian interpretations, the most influential of which may be found in A. C. Bradley's *Shakespearean Tragedy* (1904); G. Wilson Knight's *The Wheel of Fire* (1930; revised edn 1949); and J. F. Danby's *Shakespeare's Doctrine of Nature* (1949). In the 1960s, however, readings of this kind came under attack, most notably from Barbara Everett in her essay 'The New *King Lear*' (in Kermode's anthology, listed below) and W. R. Elton's *'King Lear' and the Gods* (1966). For the next two decades, critics generally divided into two opposing camps: on the one hand were those who, like Maynard Mack in *'King Lear' in Our Time* (1966), took a stoical view of the tragedy as vindicating human values in the face of a hostile universe; on the other were those more in tune with Jan Kott's essay *'King Lear*, or Endgame' in *Shakespeare our Contemporary* (1964), which saluted the play's nihilistic vision of life as a brutal, pointless joke. Kott's account of *Lear* as foreshadowing Samuel Beckett's Theatre of the Absurd strongly influenced Peter Brook's landmark staging of the play in 1962 and his 1971 film of the tragedy.

With the advent of the 1980s these views of *King Lear* were supplanted by the current regime of readings, which consider its meaning to be inseparable from questions of language, gender, power and the unconscious. Stimulating deconstructive accounts of the play, which revolve round its problematizing of language and representation, are provided by Malcolm Evans in _Signifying Nothing_ (1986) and by Jonathan Goldberg and Jackson Cope in _Shakespeare and Deconstruction_, ed. G. D. Atkins and D. M. Bergeron (1988). Two feminist interpretations of _Lear_, both of which draw heavily on psychoanalytic ideas, stand out as especially illuminating: Coppélia Kahn's 'The Absent Mother in _King Lear_', in _Rewriting the Renaissance_, ed. M. W. Ferguson et al. (1986); and Janet Adelman's chapter on the tragedy in _Suffocating Mothers: Fantasies of Maternal Origin in Shakespeare's Plays_ (1992). Harry Berger's essays on the psychological subtext of relationships in the Lear and Gloucester families in _Making Trifles of Terrors_ (1997) are equally rewarding. The seminal cultural-materialist reading of _Lear_ as 'a play about power, property and inheritance' can be found in Jonathan Dollimore's _Radical Tragedy_ (1984). Power is crucial to the new historicists' take on _King Lear_ too, although critics of this stamp differ widely in their judgements of the play's relationship to the Jacobean state. Stephen Greenblatt, for example, in 'Shakespeare and the Exorcists' (cited above) and 'The Cultivation of Anxiety: King Lear and His Heirs' (in _Learning to Curse_, 1990), sees the tragedy as subtly enforcing the subjection of the audience to authority; in _Shakespeare and the Popular Voice_ (1989), however, Annabel Patterson insists that _King Lear_ speaks for the dispossessed victims of power; while Leah Marcus's essay, 'Retrospective: _King Lear_ on St Stephen's Night, 1606' (_Puzzling Shakespeare_, 1988), concludes that the play's political stance is intractably ambiguous.

Three of the most valuable studies of *King Lear* to have appeared in this period have little in common with the approaches at present in vogue. John Bayley's chapter 'The King's Ship' in *Shakespeare and Tragedy* (1981) and Stephen Booth's *'King Lear', 'Macbeth', Indefinition and Tragedy* (1983) afford brilliant insights into the form and style of the play. The full measure of Joseph Wittreich's groundbreaking book, *'Image of That Horror': History, Prophecy, and Apocalypse in 'King Lear'* (1984), still remains to be taken.

Frank Kermode has edited *'King Lear': A Casebook* (1969; revised edn 1992), which includes extracts from Johnson and the Romantics as well as key twentieth-century critics from Bradley to Greenblatt. *'King Lear': Contemporary Critical Essays*, ed. Kiernan Ryan (1993), is a compendium of recent essays by leading new-historicist, feminist and deconstructive critics, including Greenblatt, Patterson, Marcus, Kahn and Goldberg. Useful collections of essays on *Lear* have also been edited by Lawrence Danson (*On 'King Lear'*, 1981), by Kenneth Muir (*'King Lear': Critical Essays*, 1984), and by Muir and Stanley Wells (*Aspects of 'King Lear'*, 1982). The changing critical perception of *King Lear* is charted in Ann Thompson's *'King Lear': The Critics Debate* (1988); R. A. Foakes's *From 'Hamlet' to 'Lear'* (1993); and Kiernan Ryan's *'King Lear*: A Retrospect, 1980–2000', in *Shakespeare Survey 55*: '*King Lear* and Its Afterlife' (2002).

PERFORMANCE

Nahum Tate's *The History of 'King Lear'* has been edited by James Black for Regents Restoration Drama series (1975), and is included in *Shakespeare Made Fit*, ed.

Sandra Clark (1997), which has suggestions for further reading on Tate's version. For the stage history of the play from Tate to the present day, see Marvin Rosenberg's *The Masks of 'King Lear'* (1972); J. S. Bratton's annotated edition for the Plays in Performance series (1987); Alexander Leggatt's *King Lear* in the Shakespeare in Performance series (1990); and the richly illustrated, fully searchable text and performance archive available on the *Cambridge 'King Lear' CD-ROM* (2000). The most notable modern dramatic reworkings of the Lear story are Edward Bond's *Lear* (1971); *Lear's Daughters* by Elaine Feinstein and the Women's Theatre Group (1987); and Howard Barker's *Seven Lears* (1990).

The films of *King Lear* directed by Grigori Kozintsev (1970) and Peter Brook (1971) are available on video, as is the televised version of Joseph Papp's 1974 New York production, starring James Earl Jones; the 1982 BBC TV production, starring Michael Hordern and directed by Jonathan Miller; and the 1983 Granada TV production, starring Laurence Olivier and directed by Michael Elliott. The Lear story has been recycled in a host of films, including the Hollywood movies *House of Strangers* (1949), *Broken Lance* (1954) and *The Big Show* (1961); Jean-Luc Godard's bizarre, postmodern *King Lear* with Woody Allen (1987); *A Thousand Acres* (1997), based on Jane Smiley's 1991 novel; and *My Kingdom* (2002), starring Richard Harris as a Liverpool gang-boss. All these cinematic offshoots are overshadowed, however, by Akira Kurosawa's 1985 film *Ran* ('chaos, war'), which transforms Shakespeare's play into a stunning samurai epic.

For critical accounts of Kozintsev's and Brook's films, see Jack Jorgens, *Shakespeare on Film* (1977); Anthony Davies, *Filming Shakespeare's Plays* (1988); Kenneth S.

Rothwell, *A History of Shakespeare on Screen* (1999); and *The Cambridge Companion to Shakespeare on Film*, ed. Russell Jackson (2000). Kozintsev's own book, *'King Lear': The Space of Tragedy* (1977), is full of insights into the director's vision of his film. Commentary on the TV productions by Jonathan Miller and Michael Elliott can be found in James P. Lusardi and June Schlueter, *Reading Shakespeare in Performance: 'King Lear'* (1991).

THE TRAGEDY OF
KING LEAR

The Characters in the Play

LEAR, King of Britain
GONERILL, Lear's eldest daughter
REGAN, Lear's second daughter
CORDELIA, Lear's youngest daughter
Duke of ALBANY, husband of Gonerill
Duke of CORNWALL, husband of Regan
King of FRANCE
Duke of BURGUNDY

Earl of KENT, later disguised as Caius
Earl of GLOUCESTER
EDGAR, son of Gloucester, later disguised as Poor Tom
EDMUND, bastard son of Gloucester

OSWALD, Gonerill's steward
Lear's FOOL
Three KNIGHTS
CURAN, gentleman of Gloucester's household
GENTLEMEN
Three SERVANTS
OLD MAN, a tenant of Gloucester
Three MESSENGERS
DOCTOR, attendant on Cordelia
A CAPTAIN, follower of Edmund

A HERALD
Two OFFICERS

Knights of Lear's train, servants, soldiers, attendants, gentlemen

Enter Kent, Gloucester, and Edmund

KENT I thought the King had more affected the Duke of
Albany than Cornwall.

GLOUCESTER It did always seem so to us. But now in the
division of the kingdom it appears not which of the
Dukes he values most, for qualities are so weighed that
curiosity in neither can make choice of either's moiety.

KENT Is not this your son, my lord?

GLOUCESTER His breeding, sir, hath been at my charge.
I have so often blushed to acknowledge him that now I
am brazed to it.

KENT I cannot conceive you.

GLOUCESTER Sir, this young fellow's mother could;
whereupon she grew round-wombed, and had indeed,
sir, a son for her cradle ere she had a husband for her
bed. Do you smell a fault?

KENT I cannot wish the fault undone, the issue of it being
so proper.

GLOUCESTER But I have a son, sir, by order of law, some
year elder than this, who yet is no dearer in my account.
Though this knave came something saucily to the world,
before he was sent for, yet was his mother fair; there
was good sport at his making, and the whoreson must be

acknowledged. Do you know this noble gentleman, Edmund?

EDMUND No, my lord.

GLOUCESTER My lord of Kent. Remember him hereafter as my honourable friend.

EDMUND My services to your lordship.

KENT I must love you and sue to know you better.

30   EDMUND Sir, I shall study deserving.

GLOUCESTER He hath been out nine years, and away he shall again. The King is coming.

Sound a sennet. Enter one bearing a coronet
Enter King Lear, Cornwall, Albany, Gonerill,
Regan, Cordelia, and attendants

LEAR Attend the lords of France and Burgundy, Gloucester.

GLOUCESTER I shall, my liege.

Exeunt Gloucester and Edmund

LEAR

Meantime we shall express our darker purpose.
Give me the map there. Know, that we have divided
In three our kingdom; and 'tis our fast intent
To shake all cares and business from our age,
40   Conferring them on younger strengths, while we
Unburdened crawl toward death. Our son of Cornwall –
And you, our no less loving son of Albany –
We have this hour a constant will to publish
Our daughters' several dowers, that future strife
May be prevented now. The princes, France and Burgundy,
Great rivals in our youngest daughter's love,
Long in our court have made their amorous sojourn,
And here are to be answered. Tell me, my daughters,
Since now we will divest us both of rule,
50   Interest of territory, cares of state,
Which of you shall we say doth love us most,

That we our largest bounty may extend
Where nature doth with merit challenge. Gonerill,
Our eldest born, speak first.

GONERILL

Sir, I love you more than word can wield the matter,
Dearer than eyesight, space, and liberty,
Beyond what can be valued rich or rare,
No less than life, with grace, health, beauty, honour,
As much as child e'er loved or father found;
A love that makes breath poor and speech unable;   60
Beyond all manner of 'so much' I love you.

CORDELIA (*aside*)

What shall Cordelia speak? Love, and be silent.

LEAR

Of all these bounds, even from this line to this,
With shadowy forests and with champains riched,
With plenteous rivers and wide-skirted meads,
We make thee lady. To thine and Albany's issues
Be this perpetual. – What says our second daughter,
Our dearest Regan, wife of Cornwall?

REGAN

I am made of that self mettle as my sister
And price me at her worth. In my true heart   70
I find she names my very deed of love;
Only she comes too short, that I profess
Myself an enemy to all other joys
Which the most precious square of sense possesses,
And find I am alone felicitate
In your dear highness' love.

CORDELIA (*aside*)   Then poor Cordelia!

And yet not so, since I am sure my love's
More ponderous than my tongue.

LEAR

To thee and thine hereditary ever

80   Remain this ample third of our fair kingdom,
      No less in space, validity, and pleasure
      Than that conferred on Gonerill. – Now, our joy,
      Although our last and least, to whose young love
      The vines of France and milk of Burgundy
      Strive to be interested: what can you say to draw
      A third more opulent than your sisters'? Speak!
CORDELIA Nothing, my lord.
LEAR Nothing?
CORDELIA Nothing.
LEAR
90   Nothing will come of nothing. Speak again.
CORDELIA
      Unhappy that I am, I cannot heave
      My heart into my mouth. I love your majesty
      According to my bond, no more nor less.
LEAR
      How, how, Cordelia! Mend your speech a little
      Lest you may mar your fortunes.
CORDELIA   Good my lord,
      You have begot me, bred me, loved me.
      I return those duties back as are right fit,
      Obey you, love you, and most honour you.
      Why have my sisters husbands, if they say
100   They love you all? Haply when I shall wed,
      That lord whose hand must take my plight shall carry
      Half my love with him, half my care and duty.
      Sure I shall never marry like my sisters,
      To love my father all.
LEAR
      But goes thy heart with this?
CORDELIA   Ay, my good lord.
LEAR So young, and so untender?
CORDELIA So young, my lord, and true.

LEAR

    Let it be so! Thy truth then be thy dower!
    For by the sacred radiance of the sun,
    The mysteries of Hecat and the night,   110
    By all the operation of the orbs
    From whom we do exist, and cease to be,
    Here I disclaim all my paternal care,
    Propinquity and property of blood,
    And as a stranger to my heart and me
    Hold thee from this for ever. The barbarous Scythian,
    Or he that makes his generation messes
    To gorge his appetite, shall to my bosom
    Be as well neighboured, pitied, and relieved
    As thou my sometime daughter.

KENT   Good my liege –   120

LEAR

    Peace, Kent!
    Come not between the dragon and his wrath.
    I loved her most, and thought to set my rest
    On her kind nursery. (*To Cordelia*) Hence and avoid
        my sight! –
    So be my grave my peace as here I give
    Her father's heart from her. Call France! Who stirs?
    Call Burgundy! Cornwall and Albany,
    With my two daughters' dowers digest the third.
    Let pride, which she calls plainness, marry her.
    I do invest you jointly with my power,   130
    Pre-eminence, and all the large effects
    That troop with majesty. Ourself by monthly course,
    With reservation of an hundred knights,
    By you to be sustained, shall our abode
    Make with you by due turn. Only we shall retain
    The name and all th'addition to a king; the sway,
    Revenue, execution of the rest,

Beloved sons, be yours; which to confirm,
This coronet part between you.

KENT   Royal Lear,
140   Whom I have ever honoured as my king,
Loved as my father, as my master followed,
As my great patron thought on in my prayers –

LEAR
The bow is bent and drawn; make from the shaft.

KENT
Let it fall rather, though the fork invade
The region of my heart. Be Kent unmannerly
When Lear is mad. What wouldst thou do, old man?
Think'st thou that duty shall have dread to speak
When power to flattery bows? To plainness honour's
      bound
When majesty stoops to folly. Reserve thy state,
150   And in thy best consideration check
This hideous rashness. Answer my life my judgement,
Thy youngest daughter does not love thee least,
Nor are those empty-hearted whose low sounds
Reverb no hollowness.

LEAR   Kent, on thy life, no more!

KENT
My life I never held but as a pawn
To wage against thine enemies; nor fear to lose it,
Thy safety being motive.

LEAR   Out of my sight!

KENT
See better, Lear, and let me still remain
The true blank of thine eye.

LEAR
160   Now by Apollo –

KENT   Now by Apollo, King,
Thou swear'st thy gods in vain.

LEAR   O vassal, miscreant!
  He makes to strike him
ALBANY *and* CORNWALL Dear sir, forbear!
KENT
  Kill thy physician and thy fee bestow
  Upon the foul disease. Revoke thy gift,
  Or whilst I can vent clamour from my throat
  I'll tell thee thou dost evil.
LEAR   Hear me, recreant,
  On thine allegiance hear me!
  That thou hast sought to make us break our vow,
  Which we durst never yet, and, with strained pride,
  To come betwixt our sentence and our power,   170
  Which nor our nature nor our place can bear,
  Our potency made good, take thy reward.
  Five days we do allot thee for provision
  To shield thee from disasters of the world,
  And on the sixth to turn thy hated back
  Upon our kingdom. If on the tenth day following
  Thy banished trunk be found in our dominions
  The moment is thy death. Away! By Jupiter,
  This shall not be revoked!
KENT
  Fare thee well, King, sith thus thou wilt appear,   180
  Freedom lives hence and banishment is here.
  (*To Cordelia*)
  The gods to their dear shelter take thee, maid,
  That justly think'st and hast most rightly said.
  (*To Gonerill and Regan*)
  And your large speeches may your deeds approve
  That good effects may spring from words of love. –
  Thus Kent, O princes, bids you all adieu;
  He'll shape his old course in a country new.   *Exit*

Flourish. Enter Gloucester with France and Bur-
gundy, and attendants

GLOUCESTER

Here's France and Burgundy, my noble lord.

LEAR

My lord of Burgundy,

190   We first address toward you, who with this king
Hath rivalled for our daughter: what in the least
Will you require in present dower with her
Or cease your quest of love?

BURGUNDY   Most royal majesty,
I crave no more than hath your highness offered,
Nor will you tender less.

LEAR   Right noble Burgundy,
When she was dear to us we did hold her so;
But now her price is fallen. Sir, there she stands;
If aught within that little-seeming substance,
Or all of it, with our displeasure pieced,

200   And nothing more, may fitly like your grace,
She's there and she is yours.

BURGUNDY   I know no answer.

LEAR

Will you with those infirmities she owes,
Unfriended, new-adopted to our hate,
Dowered with our curse and strangered with our oath,
Take her or leave her?

BURGUNDY   Pardon me, royal sir,
Election makes not up in such conditions.

LEAR

Then leave her, sir, for, by the power that made me,
I tell you all her wealth. (*To France*) For you, great king,
I would not from your love make such a stray

210   To match you where I hate; therefore beseech you
T'avert your liking a more worthier way

Than on a wretch whom Nature is ashamed
Almost t'acknowledge hers.

FRANCE   This is most strange,
That she whom even but now was your best object,
The argument of your praise, balm of your age,
The best, the dearest, should in this trice of time
Commit a thing so monstrous to dismantle
So many folds of favour. Sure her offence
Must be of such unnatural degree
That monsters it; or your fore-vouched affection   220
Fall into taint; which to believe of her
Must be a faith that reason without miracle
Should never plant in me.

CORDELIA   I yet beseech your majesty –
If for I want that glib and oily art
To speak and purpose not, since what I well intend
I'll do't before I speak – that you make known
It is no vicious blot, murder or foulness,
No unchaste action or dishonoured step
That hath deprived me of your grace and favour,
But even for want of that for which I am richer: 230
A still-soliciting eye and such a tongue
That I am glad I have not, though not to have it
Hath lost me in your liking.

LEAR   Better thou
Hadst not been born than not t'have pleased me better.

FRANCE
Is it but this, a tardiness in nature
Which often leaves the history unspoke
That it intends to do? My lord of Burgundy,
What say you to the lady? Love's not love
When it is mingled with regards that stands
Aloof from th'entire point. Will you have her?   240
She is herself a dowry.

BURGUNDY   Royal Lear,
Give but that portion which yourself proposed
And here I take Cordelia by the hand,
Duchess of Burgundy.

LEAR
Nothing! I have sworn; I am firm.

BURGUNDY (*to Cordelia*)
I am sorry then you have so lost a father
That you must lose a husband.

CORDELIA   Peace be with Burgundy!
Since that respect and fortunes are his love,
I shall not be his wife.

FRANCE
250   Fairest Cordelia, that art most rich, being poor,
Most choice, forsaken, and most loved, despised,
Thee and thy virtues here I seize upon.
Be it lawful I take up what's cast away.
Gods, gods! 'Tis strange that from their cold'st neglect
My love should kindle to inflamed respect.
Thy dowerless daughter, King, thrown to my chance,
Is queen of us, of ours, and our fair France.
Not all the dukes of waterish Burgundy
Can buy this unprized-precious maid of me.
260   Bid them farewell, Cordelia, though unkind.
Thou losest here, a better where to find.

LEAR
Thou hast her, France; let her be thine, for we
Have no such daughter, nor shall ever see
That face of hers again. Therefore begone,
Without our grace, our love, our benison!
Come, noble Burgundy.
        Flourish. Exeunt Lear, Burgundy, Cornwall, Albany,
        Gloucester, and attendants

FRANCE Bid farewell to your sisters.

CORDELIA

    The jewels of our father, with washed eyes
    Cordelia leaves you. I know you what you are;
    And, like a sister, am most loath to call   270
    Your faults as they are named. Love well our father!
    To your professèd bosoms I commit him.
    But yet, alas, stood I within his grace,
    I would prefer him to a better place.
    So farewell to you both.

REGAN

    Prescribe not us our duty.

GONERILL   Let your study

    Be to content your lord, who hath received you
    At Fortune's alms. You have obedience scanted,
    And well are worth the want that you have wanted.

CORDELIA

    Time shall unfold what plighted cunning hides;   280
    Who covers faults, at last with shame derides.
    Well may you prosper!

FRANCE   Come, my fair Cordelia.

Exeunt France and Cordelia

GONERILL Sister, it is not little I have to say of what most
nearly appertains to us both. I think our father will
hence tonight.

REGAN That's most certain, and with you; next month
with us.

GONERILL You see how full of changes his age is. The
observation we have made of it hath not been little. He
always loved our sister most; and with what poor judge-   290
ment he hath now cast her off appears too grossly.

REGAN 'Tis the infirmity of his age. Yet he hath ever but
slenderly known himself.

GONERILL The best and soundest of his time hath been
but rash. Then must we look from his age to receive not

alone the imperfections of long-ingraffed condition, but
therewithal the unruly waywardness that infirm and
choleric years bring with them.

REGAN Such unconstant starts are we like to have from
300   him as this of Kent's banishment.

GONERILL There is further compliment of leave-taking
between France and him. Pray you, let us hit together.
If our father carry authority with such disposition as he
bears, this last surrender of his will but offend us.

REGAN We shall further think of it.

GONERILL We must do something, and i'th'heat.

                                 Exeunt

I.2   *Enter Edmund*

EDMUND

Thou, Nature, art my goddess; to thy law
My services are bound. Wherefore should I
Stand in the plague of custom and permit
The curiosity of nations to deprive me,
For that I am some twelve or fourteen moonshines
Lag of a brother? Why bastard? Wherefore base?
When my dimensions are as well-compact,
My mind as generous, and my shape as true
As honest madam's issue? Why brand they us
10 With 'base'? with 'baseness'? 'bastardy'? 'base, base'?
Who in the lusty stealth of nature take
More composition and fierce quality
Than doth within a dull, stale, tired bed
Go to the creating a whole tribe of fops
Got 'tween asleep and wake? Well then,
Legitimate Edgar, I must have your land.
Our father's love is to the bastard Edmund
As to the legitimate. Fine word 'legitimate'!

Well, my 'legitimate', if this letter speed
And my invention thrive, Edmund the base   20
Shall top the legitimate. I grow. I prosper.
Now gods stand up for bastards!
   Enter Gloucester

GLOUCESTER
  Kent banished thus? and France in choler parted?
  And the King gone tonight? prescribed his power?
  Confined to exhibition? All this done
  Upon the gad? Edmund, how now? What news?

EDMUND So please your lordship, none.

GLOUCESTER Why so earnestly seek you to put up that
  letter?

EDMUND I know no news, my lord.   30

GLOUCESTER What paper were you reading?

EDMUND Nothing, my lord.

GLOUCESTER No? What needed then that terrible dispatch of it into your pocket? The quality of nothing
  hath not such need to hide itself. Let's see! Come! If it
  be nothing I shall not need spectacles.

EDMUND I beseech you, sir, pardon me. It is a letter from
  my brother that I have not all o'er-read; and for so much
  as I have perused, I find it not fit for your o'erlooking.

GLOUCESTER Give me the letter, sir.   40

EDMUND I shall offend either to detain or give it. The
  contents, as in part I understand them, are to blame.

GLOUCESTER Let's see, let's see!

EDMUND I hope for my brother's justification he wrote
  this but as an essay or taste of my virtue.

GLOUCESTER (*reading*) *This policy and reverence of age*
  makes the world bitter to the best of our times, keeps our
  fortunes from us till our oldness cannot relish them. I begin
  to find an idle and fond bondage in the oppression of aged
  tyranny, who sways not as it hath power but as it is   50

suffered. Come to me that of this I may speak more. If our
father would sleep till I waked him, you should enjoy half
his revenue for ever, and live the beloved of your brother,
                                                    Edgar.

Hum! Conspiracy! 'Sleep till I waked him, you should
enjoy half his revenue'. My son Edgar, had he a hand to
write this? a heart and brain to breed it in? When came
you to this? Who brought it?

EDMUND It was not brought me, my lord. There's the
60   cunning of it. I found it thrown in at the casement of my
closet.

GLOUCESTER You know the character to be your
brother's?

EDMUND If the matter were good, my lord, I durst swear
it were his; but in respect of that I would fain think it
were not.

GLOUCESTER It is his!

EDMUND It is his hand, my lord; but I hope his heart is
not in the contents.

70   GLOUCESTER Has he never before sounded you in this
business?

EDMUND Never, my lord. But I have heard him oft maintain it to be fit that, sons at perfect age and fathers
declined, the father should be as ward to the son, and
the son manage his revenue.

GLOUCESTER O villain, villain! His very opinion in the
letter! Abhorred villain! Unnatural, detested, brutish
villain! worse than brutish! Go, sirrah, seek him. I'll
apprehend him. Abominable villain! Where is he?

80   EDMUND I do not well know, my lord. If it shall please
you to suspend your indignation against my brother till
you can derive from him better testimony of his intent,
you should run a certain course; where, if you violently
proceed against him, mistaking his purpose, it would

make a great gap in your own honour and shake in
pieces the heart of his obedience. I dare pawn down my
life for him that he hath writ this to feel my affection to
your honour and to no other pretence of danger.

GLOUCESTER Think you so?

EDMUND If your honour judge it meet I will place you   90
where you shall hear us confer of this and by an
auricular assurance have your satisfaction, and that
without any further delay than this very evening.

GLOUCESTER He cannot be such a monster –

EDMUND Nor is not, sure.

GLOUCESTER To his father that so tenderly and entirely
loves him. Heaven and earth! Edmund, seek him out.
Wind me into him, I pray you. Frame the business after
your own wisdom. I would unstate myself to be in a due
resolution.   100

EDMUND I will seek him, sir, presently, convey the business as I shall find means, and acquaint you withal.

GLOUCESTER These late eclipses in the sun and moon
portend no good to us. Though the wisdom of nature
can reason it thus and thus, yet nature finds itself
scourged by the sequent effects: love cools, friendship
falls off, brothers divide. In cities, mutinies; in countries,
discord; in palaces, treason; and the bond cracked 'twixt
son and father. This villain of mine comes under the
prediction: there's son against father; the King falls   110
from bias of nature: there's father against child. We
have seen the best of our time. Machinations, hollowness, treachery, and all ruinous disorders follow us dis-
quietly to our graves – find out this villain, Edmund;
it shall lose thee nothing; do it carefully – and the noble
and true-hearted Kent banished! His offence, honesty!
'Tis strange.   *Exit*

EDMUND This is the excellent foppery of the world, that

when we are sick in fortune – often the surfeits of our
own behaviour – we make guilty of our disasters the sun,
the moon, and stars, as if we were villains on necessity,
fools by heavenly compulsion, knaves, thieves, and
treachers by spherical predominance, drunkards, liars,
and adulterers by an enforced obedience of planetary
influence; and all that we are evil in by a divine
thrusting-on. An admirable evasion of whoremaster
man, to lay his goatish disposition to the charge of a
star. My father compounded with my mother under the
Dragon's tail, and my nativity was under Ursa Major, so
that it follows I am rough and lecherous. Fut! I should
have been that I am had the maidenliest star in the
firmament twinkled on my bastardizing. Edgar –

 (*enter Edgar*)

pat he comes, like the catastrophe of the old comedy.
My cue is villainous melancholy, with a sigh like Tom
o'Bedlam. (*Aloud*) O these eclipses do portend these
divisions: (*he sings*) Fa, sol, la, mi.

EDGAR How now, brother Edmund! What serious con-
templation are you in?

EDMUND I am thinking, brother, of a prediction I read
this other day, what should follow these eclipses.

EDGAR Do you busy yourself with that?

EDMUND I promise you, the effects he writes of succeed
unhappily, as of unnaturalness between the child and the
parent, death, dearth, dissolutions of ancient amities,
divisions in state, menaces and maledictions against king
and nobles, needless diffidences, banishment of friends,
dissipation of cohorts, nuptial breaches, and I know not
what.

EDGAR How long have you been a sectary astronomical?

EDMUND When saw you my father last?

EDGAR The night gone by.

EDMUND Spake you with him?

EDGAR Ay, two hours together.

EDMUND Parted you in good terms? Found you no displeasure in him by word nor countenance?

EDGAR None at all.

EDMUND Bethink yourself wherein you may have offended him, and at my entreaty forbear his presence until some little time hath qualified the heat of his displeasure, which at this instant so rageth in him that with   160 the mischief of your person it would scarcely allay.

EDGAR Some villain hath done me wrong.

EDMUND That's my fear. I pray you have a continent forbearance till the speed of his rage goes slower; and, as I say, retire with me to my lodging, from whence I will fitly bring you to hear my lord speak. Pray ye, go! There's my key. If you do stir abroad, go armed.

EDGAR Armed, brother?

EDMUND Brother, I advise you to the best. I am no honest man if there be any good meaning toward you. I have   170 told you what I have seen and heard but faintly, nothing like the image and horror of it. Pray you, away!

EDGAR Shall I hear from you anon?

EDMUND I do serve you in this business.

                                                    Exit Edgar

A credulous father and a brother noble,
Whose nature is so far from doing harms
That he suspects none; on whose foolish honesty
My practices ride easy – I see the business:
Let me, if not by birth, have lands by wit;
All with me's meet that I can fashion fit.   *Exit*   180

1.3   *Enter Gonerill and Oswald, her steward*

GONERILL Did my father strike my gentleman for chid-
ing of his Fool?

OSWALD Ay, madam.

GONERILL

By day and night he wrongs me; every hour
He flashes into one gross crime or other
That sets us all at odds. I'll not endure it!
His knights grow riotous, and himself upbraids us
On every trifle. When he returns from hunting
I will not speak with him. Say I am sick.
10   If you come slack of former services
You shall do well; the fault of it I'll answer.

OSWALD He's coming, madam; I hear him.

GONERILL

Put on what weary negligence you please,
You and your fellows. I'd have it come to question.
If he distaste it let him to my sister,
Whose mind and mine I know in that are one,
Not to be overruled. Idle old man,
That still would manage those authorities
That he hath given away! Now, by my life,
20   Old fools are babes again, and must be used
With checks, as flatteries, when they are seen abused.
Remember what I have said.

OSWALD   Well, madam.

GONERILL

And let his knights have colder looks among you.
What grows of it, no matter. Advise your fellows so.
I would breed from hence occasions, and I shall,
That I may speak. I'll write straight to my sister
To hold my very course. Prepare for dinner.   *Exeunt*

Enter Kent in disguise   I.4

KENT

If but as well I other accents borrow
That can my speech diffuse, my good intent
May carry through itself to that full issue
For which I razed my likeness. Now, banished Kent,
If thou canst serve where thou dost stand condemned,
So may it come thy master whom thou lovest
Shall find thee full of labours.

Horns within. Enter Lear and Knights

LEAR Let me not stay a jot for dinner! Go, get it ready!

Exit First Knight

How now? What art thou?

KENT A man, sir.   10

LEAR What dost thou profess? What wouldst thou with
us?

KENT I do profess to be no less than I seem: to serve him
truly that will put me in trust, to love him that is honest,
to converse with him that is wise and says little, to fear
judgement, to fight when I cannot choose, and to eat no
fish.

LEAR What art thou?

KENT A very honest-hearted fellow, and as poor as the
King.   20

LEAR If thou be'st as poor for a subject as he's for a king
thou art poor enough. What wouldst thou?

KENT Service.

LEAR Who wouldst thou serve?

KENT You.

LEAR Dost thou know me, fellow?

KENT No, sir; but you have that in your countenance
which I would fain call master.

LEAR What's that?

KENT Authority.   30

LEAR What services canst thou do?

KENT I can keep honest counsel, ride, run, mar a curious
tale in telling it, and deliver a plain message bluntly.
That which ordinary men are fit for I am qualified in,
and the best of me is diligence.

LEAR How old art thou?

KENT Not so young, sir, to love a woman for singing, nor
so old to dote on her for anything. I have years on my
back forty-eight.

40 LEAR Follow me; thou shalt serve me if I like thee no
worse after dinner. I will not part from thee yet. Dinner,
ho, dinner! Where's my knave, my Fool? Go you and
call my Fool hither.   *Exit Second Knight*

    Enter Oswald

You! You, sirrah! Where's my daughter?

OSWALD So please you –   *Exit*

LEAR What says the fellow there? Call the clotpoll back.

                       Exit Third Knight

Where's my Fool? Ho, I think the world's asleep.

    Enter Third Knight

How now? Where's that mongrel?

THIRD KNIGHT He says, my lord, your daughter is not
50 well.

LEAR Why came not the slave back to me when I called
him?

THIRD KNIGHT Sir, he answered me in the roundest
manner he would not.

LEAR He would not!

THIRD KNIGHT My lord, I know not what the matter is,
but to my judgement your highness is not entertained
with that ceremonious affection as you were wont.
There's a great abatement of kindness appears as well
60 in the general dependants as in the Duke himself also
and your daughter.

LEAR Ha! Sayest thou so?

THIRD KNIGHT I beseech you pardon me, my lord, if I
be mistaken; for my duty cannot be silent when I think
your highness wronged.

LEAR Thou but rememberest me of mine own conception. I have perceived a most faint neglect of late,
which I have rather blamed as mine own jealous
curiosity than as a very pretence and purpose of unkindness. I will look further into't. But where's my   70
Fool? I have not seen him this two days.

THIRD KNIGHT Since my young lady's going into
France, sir, the Fool hath much pined away.

LEAR No more of that! I have noted it well. Go you and
tell my daughter I would speak with her.

                                     Exit Third Knight

Go you, call hither my Fool.   *Exit another Knight*
    Enter Oswald

O, you, sir, you! Come you hither, sir. Who am I, sir?

OSWALD My lady's father.

LEAR 'My lady's father', my lord's knave! You whoreson
dog! You slave! You cur!   80

OSWALD I am none of these, my lord, I beseech your
pardon.

LEAR Do you bandy looks with me, you rascal?
    He strikes him

OSWALD I'll not be strucken, my lord.

KENT Nor tripped neither, you base football-player?
    He trips him

LEAR I thank thee, fellow. Thou servest me and I'll love
thee.

KENT (*to Oswald*) Come, sir, arise, away! I'll teach you
differences. Away, away! If you will measure your
lubber's length again, tarry; but away, go to! Have you 90
wisdom?

He pushes Oswald out
So.

LEAR Now, my friendly knave, I thank thee. There's earnest of thy service.
He gives him money
Enter the Fool

FOOL Let me hire him too. Here's my coxcomb.

LEAR How now, my pretty knave! How dost thou?

FOOL Sirrah, you were best take my coxcomb.

KENT Why, Fool?

FOOL Why? For taking one's part that's out of favour. Nay, and thou canst not smile as the wind sits, thou'lt catch cold shortly. There, take my coxcomb! Why, this fellow has banished two on's daughters, and did the third a blessing against his will. If thou follow him, thou must needs wear my coxcomb. How now, nuncle! Would I had two coxcombs and two daughters!

LEAR Why, my boy?

FOOL If I gave them all my living, I'd keep my coxcombs myself. There's mine. Beg another of thy daughters.

LEAR Take heed, sirrah, the whip!

FOOL Truth's a dog must to kennel; he must be whipped out when the Lady Brach may stand by the fire and stink.

LEAR A pestilent gall to me!

FOOL Sirrah, I'll teach thee a speech.

LEAR Do.

FOOL Mark it, nuncle:
Have more than thou showest,
Speak less than thou knowest,
Lend less than thou owest,
Ride more than thou goest,
Learn more than thou trowest,
Set less than thou throwest;

    Leave thy drink and thy whore
    And keep in-a-door,
    And thou shalt have more
    Than two tens to a score.

KENT This is nothing, Fool.

FOOL Then 'tis like the breath of an unfee'd lawyer: you gave me nothing for't. Can you make no use of nothing, nuncle?   130

LEAR Why, no, boy. Nothing can be made out of nothing.

FOOL (*to Kent*) Prithee tell him; so much the rent of his land comes to. He will not believe a fool.

LEAR A bitter fool!

FOOL Dost thou know the difference, my boy, between a bitter fool and a sweet one?

LEAR No, lad; teach me.

FOOL

    That lord that counselled thee
      To give away thy land,
    Come place him here by me;   140
      Do thou for him stand.
    The sweet and bitter fool
      Will presently appear:
    The one in motley here,
      The other found out – there.

LEAR Dost thou call me fool, boy?

FOOL All thy other titles thou hast given away; that thou wast born with.

KENT This is not altogether fool, my lord.

FOOL No, faith; lords and great men will not let me. If I   150 had a monopoly out they would have part on't; and ladies too – they will not let me have all the fool to myself; they'll be snatching. Nuncle, give me an egg and I'll give thee two crowns.

LEAR What two crowns shall they be?

FOOL Why, after I have cut the egg i'the middle and eat
up the meat, the two crowns of the egg. When thou
clovest thy crown i'the middle, and gavest away both
parts, thou borest thine ass on thy back o'er the dirt.
160   Thou hadst little wit in thy bald crown when thou
gavest thy golden one away. If I speak like myself in
this, let him be whipped that first finds it so.

    Fools had ne'er less grace in a year,
        For wise men are grown foppish
    And know not how their wits to wear,
        Their manners are so apish.

LEAR When were you wont to be so full of songs, sirrah?
FOOL I have used it, nuncle, e'er since thou madest thy
daughters thy mothers; for when thou gavest them the
170   rod and puttest down thine own breeches,
    (sings)

        Then they for sudden joy did weep,
           And I for sorrow sung,
        That such a king should play bo-peep
           And go the fools among.

Prithee, nuncle, keep a schoolmaster that can teach thy
fool to lie; I would fain learn to lie.
LEAR And you lie, sirrah, we'll have you whipped.
FOOL I marvel what kin thou and thy daughters are.
They'll have me whipped for speaking true; thou'lt
180   have me whipped for lying; and sometimes I am
whipped for holding my peace. I had rather be any kind
o'thing than a fool. And yet I would not be thee, nuncle.
Thou hast pared thy wit o'both sides and left nothing
i'the middle. Here comes one o'the parings.
    Enter Gonerill
LEAR How now, daughter! What makes that frontlet on?
You are too much of late i'the frown.
FOOL Thou wast a pretty fellow when thou hadst no need

to care for her frowning. Now thou art an 0 without a
figure. I am better than thou art now; I am a fool; thou
art nothing. (*To Gonerill*) Yes, forsooth, I will hold my   190
tongue. So your face bids me, though you say nothing.
    Mum, mum!
    He that keeps nor crust nor crumb,
    Weary of all, shall want some.
      He points to Lear
That's a shelled peascod.

GONERILL

Not only, sir, this your all-licensed fool
But other of your insolent retinue
Do hourly carp and quarrel, breaking forth
In rank and not-to-be-endurèd riots. Sir,
I had thought by making this well known unto you   200
To have found a safe redress; but now grow fearful
By what yourself too late have spoke and done
That you protect this course and put it on
By your allowance; which if you should, the fault
Would not 'scape censure, nor the redresses sleep;
Which in the tender of a wholesome weal
Might in their working do you that offence
Which else were shame, that then necessity
Will call discreet proceeding.

FOOL For you know, nuncle,   210
    The hedge-sparrow fed the cuckoo so long
    That it's had it head bit off by it young.
So out went the candle and we were left darkling.

LEAR Are you our daughter?

GONERILL

I would you would make use of your good wisdom,
Whereof I know you are fraught, and put away
These dispositions which of late transport you
From what you rightly are.

FOOL May not an ass know when the cart draws the
220   horse?

  Whoop, Jug, I love thee!

LEAR

 Does any here know me? This is not Lear.
 Does Lear walk thus, speak thus? Where are his eyes?
 Either his notion weakens, his discernings
 Are lethargied – Ha! Waking? 'Tis not so!
 Who is it that can tell me who I am?

FOOL Lear's shadow.

LEAR I would learn that; for by the marks of sovereignty,
 knowledge, and reason, I should be false persuaded I
230   had daughters.

FOOL Which they will make an obedient father.

LEAR Your name, fair gentlewoman?

GONERILL

 This admiration, sir, is much o'the savour
 Of other your new pranks. I do beseech you
 To understand my purposes aright:
 As you are old and reverend, should be wise.
 Here do you keep a hundred knights and squires,
 Men so disordered, so deboshed and bold,
 That this our court, infected with their manners,
240   Shows like a riotous inn; epicurism and lust
 Makes it more like a tavern or a brothel
 Than a graced palace. The shame itself doth speak
 For instant remedy. Be then desired,
 By her that else will take the thing she begs,
 A little to disquantity your train,
 And the remainders that shall still depend
 To be such men as may besort your age,
 Which know themselves and you.

LEAR   Darkness and devils!
 Saddle my horses! Call my train together!

Degenerate bastard, I'll not trouble thee.   250
Yet have I left a daughter.

GONERILL

You strike my people, and your disordered rabble
Make servants of their betters.

Enter Albany

LEAR

Woe that too late repents! – O, sir, are you come?
Is it your will? Speak, sir! – Prepare my horses.
Ingratitude, thou marble-hearted fiend,
More hideous when thou showest thee in a child
Than the sea-monster!

ALBANY   Pray, sir, be patient.

LEAR (*to Gonerill*)

Detested kite, thou liest!
My train are men of choice and rarest parts,   260
That all particulars of duty know
And in the most exact regard support
The worships of their name. O most small fault,
How ugly didst thou in Cordelia show!
Which, like an engine, wrenched my frame of nature
From the fixed place, drew from my heart all love,
And added to the gall. O Lear, Lear, Lear!
Beat at this gate that let thy folly in
  (*he strikes his head*)
And thy dear judgement out! Go, go, my people.

Exeunt Kent and Knights

ALBANY

My lord, I am guiltless as I am ignorant   270
Of what hath moved you.

LEAR   It may be so, my lord.

He kneels

Hear, Nature, hear! Dear goddess, hear!
Suspend thy purpose if thou didst intend

To make this creature fruitful.
Into her womb convey sterility,
Dry up in her the organs of increase,
And from her derogate body never spring
A babe to honour her. If she must teem,
Create her child of spleen, that it may live
280 And be a thwart disnatured torment to her.
Let it stamp wrinkles in her brow of youth,
With cadent tears fret channels in her cheeks,
Turn all her mother's pains and benefits
To laughter and contempt, that she may feel
How sharper than a serpent's tooth it is
To have a thankless child! Away, away!   *Exit*

ALBANY

Now gods that we adore, whereof comes this?

GONERILL

Never afflict yourself to know more of it;
But let his disposition have that scope
290 As dotage gives it.
    Enter Lear

LEAR

What, fifty of my followers at a clap?
Within a fortnight?

ALBANY   What's the matter, sir?

LEAR

I'll tell thee – (*to Gonerill*) life and death! I am
    ashamed
That thou hast power to shake my manhood thus,
That these hot tears which break from me perforce
Should make thee worth them. Blasts and fogs upon thee!
Th'untented woundings of a father's curse
Pierce every sense about thee! – Old fond eyes,
Beweep this cause again, I'll pluck ye out
300 And cast you with the waters that you loose

To temper clay. Yea, is't come to this?
Let it be so. I have another daughter,
Who, I am sure, is kind and comfortable.
When she shall hear this of thee, with her nails
She'll flay thy wolvish visage. Thou shalt find
That I'll resume the shape which thou dost think
I have cast off for ever.   *Exit*

GONERILL   Do you mark that?

ALBANY
I cannot be so partial, Gonerill,
To the great love I bear you –

GONERILL
Pray you, content – What, Oswald, ho!   310
(*To the Fool*) You, sir, more knave than fool, after your
    master!

FOOL Nuncle Lear, nuncle Lear, tarry! Take the Fool
    with thee.
        A fox, when one has caught her,
        And such a daughter
        Should sure to the slaughter,
        If my cap would buy a halter –
        So the fool follows after.   *Exit*

GONERILL
This man hath had good counsel! A hundred knights!
'Tis politic and safe to let him keep   320
At point a hundred knights! Yes, that on every dream,
Each buzz, each fancy, each complaint, dislike,
He may enguard his dotage with their powers
And hold our lives in mercy. – Oswald, I say!

ALBANY
Well, you may fear too far.

GONERILL   Safer than trust too far.
Let me still take away the harms I fear,
Not fear still to be taken. I know his heart.

What he hath uttered I have writ my sister;
If she sustain him and his hundred knights
330   When I have showed th'unfitness –

    Enter Oswald

                             How now, Oswald!
What, have you writ that letter to my sister?

OSWALD Ay, madam.

GONERILL
Take you some company and away to horse.
Inform her full of my particular fear,
And thereto add such reasons of your own
As may compact it more. Get you gone,
And hasten your return.   *Exit Oswald*
                No, no, my lord,
This milky gentleness and course of yours,
Though I condemn not, yet, under pardon,
340   You are much more a-taxed for want of wisdom
Than praised for harmful mildness.

ALBANY
How far your eyes may pierce I cannot tell;
Striving to better, oft we mar what's well.

GONERILL Nay then –

ALBANY Well, well – th'event!   *Exeunt*

I.5   *Enter Lear, Kent, Knight, and the Fool*

LEAR (*to Kent*) Go you before to Gloucester with these
letters. Acquaint my daughter no further with anything
you know than comes from her demand out of the letter.
If your diligence be not speedy I shall be there afore
you.

KENT I will not sleep, my lord, till I have delivered your
letter.   *Exit*

FOOL If a man's brains were in's heels, were't not in

danger of kibes?

LEAR Ay, boy.   10

FOOL Then I prithee be merry. Thy wit shall not go slipshod.

LEAR Ha, ha, ha!

FOOL Shalt see thy other daughter will use thee kindly;
for though she's as like this as a crab's like an apple, yet
I can tell what I can tell.

LEAR What canst tell, boy?

FOOL She will taste as like this as a crab does to a crab.
Thou canst tell why one's nose stands i'the middle on's
face?   20

LEAR No.

FOOL Why, to keep one's eyes of either side's nose; that
what a man cannot smell out he may spy into.

LEAR I did her wrong.

FOOL Canst tell how an oyster makes his shell?

LEAR No.

FOOL Nor I neither. But I can tell why a snail has a house.

LEAR Why?

FOOL Why, to put's head in; not to give it away to his
daughters, and leave his horns without a case.   30

LEAR I will forget my nature. So kind a father! – Be my
horses ready?

FOOL Thy asses are gone about 'em. The reason why the
seven stars are no more than seven is a pretty reason.

LEAR Because they are not eight?

FOOL Yes, indeed. Thou wouldst make a good fool.

LEAR To take't again perforce! Monster ingratitude!

FOOL If thou wert my fool, nuncle, I'd have thee beaten
for being old before thy time.

LEAR How's that?   40

FOOL Thou shouldst not have been old till thou hadst
been wise.

LEAR

O let me not be mad, not mad, sweet heaven!
Keep me in temper; I would not be mad!
How now! Are the horses ready?

KNIGHT Ready, my lord.

LEAR Come, boy.   *Exeunt all except the Fool*

FOOL

She that's a maid now, and laughs at my departure,
Shall not be a maid long, unless things be cut shorter.

                                                    Exit

*

II.I   *Enter Edmund and Curan by opposite doors*

EDMUND Save thee, Curan.

CURAN And you, sir. I have been with your father and
given him notice that the Duke of Cornwall and Regan
his Duchess will be here with him this night.

EDMUND How comes that?

CURAN Nay, I know not. You have heard of the news
abroad – I mean the whispered ones, for they are yet but
ear-kissing arguments?

EDMUND Not I. Pray you what are they?

10   CURAN Have you heard of no likely wars toward 'twixt
the Dukes of Cornwall and Albany?

EDMUND Not a word.

CURAN You may do, then, in time. Fare you well, sir. *Exit*

EDMUND

The Duke be here tonight! The better! best!
This weaves itself perforce into my business.
My father hath set guard to take my brother,
And I have one thing of a queasy question
Which I must act. Briefness and fortune work! –

Brother, a word! Descend! Brother, I say!

   Enter Edgar

My father watches. O, sir, fly this place;   20

Intelligence is given where you are hid.

You have now the good advantage of the night.

Have you not spoken 'gainst the Duke of Cornwall?

He's coming hither now i'the night, i'th'haste,

And Regan with him. Have you nothing said

Upon his party 'gainst the Duke of Albany?

Advise yourself.

EDGAR   I am sure on't, not a word.

EDMUND

I hear my father coming. Pardon me;

In cunning I must draw my sword upon you.

Draw! Seem to defend yourself! Now quit you well.   30

(*Aloud*) Yield! Come before my father! Light, ho, here!

(*Aside*) Fly, brother! (*Aloud*) Torches, torches! (*Aside*)

   So farewell.   *Exit Edgar*

Some blood drawn on me would beget opinion

Of my more fierce endeavour. I have seen drunkards

Do more than this in sport.

   He wounds himself in the arm

           (*Aloud*) Father, father! –

Stop, stop! – No help?

   Enter Gloucester and servants with torches

GLOUCESTER   Now, Edmund, where's the villain?

EDMUND

Here stood he in the dark, his sharp sword out,

Mumbling of wicked charms, conjuring the moon

To stand auspicious mistress.

GLOUCESTER   But where is he?

EDMUND

Look, sir, I bleed.

GLOUCESTER   Where is the villain, Edmund?   40

EDMUND

Fled this way, sir, when by no means he could –

GLOUCESTER

Pursue him, ho! Go after.   *Exeunt some servants*

'By no means' what?

EDMUND

Persuade me to the murder of your lordship;
But that I told him the revenging gods
'Gainst parricides did all the thunder bend,
Spoke with how manifold and strong a bond
The child was bound to the father – sir, in fine,
Seeing how loathly opposite I stood
To his unnatural purpose, in fell motion

50   With his preparèd sword he charges home
My unprovided body, latched mine arm;
But when he saw my best alarumed spirits
Bold in the quarrel's right, roused to th'encounter,
Or whether gasted by the noise I made,
Full suddenly he fled.

GLOUCESTER   Let him fly far,
Not in this land shall he remain uncaught;
And found – dispatch. The noble Duke, my master,
My worthy arch and patron, comes tonight.
By his authority I will proclaim it

60   That he which finds him shall deserve our thanks,
Bringing the murderous coward to the stake;
He that conceals him, death.

EDMUND

When I dissuaded him from his intent,
And found him pight to do it, with curst speech
I threatened to discover him. He replied,
'Thou unpossessing bastard, dost thou think,
If I would stand against thee, would the reposal
Of any trust, virtue, or worth in thee

Make thy words faithed? No, what I should deny –
As this I would; ay, though thou didst produce   70
My very character – I'd turn it all
To thy suggestion, plot, and damnèd practice;
And thou must make a dullard of the world
If they not thought the profits of my death
Were very pregnant and potential spurs
To make thee seek it.'

GLOUCESTER   O strange and fastened villain!
Would he deny his letter, said he? I never got him.
     Tucket within
Hark, the Duke's trumpets! I know not why he comes. –
All ports I'll bar; the villain shall not 'scape.
The Duke must grant me that. Besides, his picture   80
I will send far and near, that all the kingdom
May have due note of him; and of my land,
Loyal and natural boy, I'll work the means
To make thee capable.
     Enter Cornwall, Regan, and attendants

CORNWALL
How now, my noble friend? Since I came hither –
Which I can call but now – I have heard strange news.

REGAN
If it be true, all vengeance comes too short
Which can pursue th'offender. How dost, my lord?

GLOUCESTER
O madam, my old heart is cracked; it's cracked.

REGAN
What, did my father's godson seek your life?   90
He whom my father named? your Edgar?

GLOUCESTER
O lady, lady, shame would have it hid!

REGAN
Was he not companion with the riotous knights

That tended upon my father?

GLOUCESTER

I know not, madam. 'Tis too bad, too bad!

EDMUND

Yes, madam, he was of that consort.

REGAN

No marvel then though he were ill affected.
'Tis they have put him on the old man's death,
To have th'expense and waste of his revenues.

100 I have this present evening from my sister
Been well informed of them, and with such cautions
That if they come to sojourn at my house
I'll not be there.

CORNWALL   Nor I, assure thee, Regan.
Edmund, I hear that you have shown your father
A child-like office.

EDMUND   It was my duty, sir.

GLOUCESTER

He did bewray his practice, and received
This hurt you see, striving to apprehend him.

CORNWALL

Is he pursued?

GLOUCESTER   Ay, my good lord.

CORNWALL

If he be taken he shall never more

110 Be feared of doing harm. Make your own purpose
How in my strength you please. For you, Edmund,
Whose virtue and obedience doth this instant
So much commend itself, you shall be ours.
Natures of such deep trust we shall much need;
You we first seize on.

EDMUND   I shall serve you, sir,
Truly, however else.

GLOUCESTER   For him I thank your grace.

CORNWALL

You know not why we came to visit you –

REGAN

Thus out of season, threading dark-eyed night –
Occasions, noble Gloucester, of some price,
Wherein we must have use of your advice.   120
Our father he hath writ, so hath our sister,
Of differences, which I best thought it fit
To answer from our home. The several messengers
From hence attend dispatch. Our good old friend,
Lay comforts to your bosom, and bestow
Your needful counsel to our businesses,
Which craves the instant use.

GLOUCESTER   I serve you, madam.
Your graces are right welcome.   *Exeunt. Flourish*

Enter Kent and Oswald by opposite doors   II.2

OSWALD

Good dawning to thee, friend. Art of this house?

KENT Ay.

OSWALD Where may we set our horses?

KENT I'the mire.

OSWALD Prithee, if thou lovest me, tell me.

KENT I love thee not.

OSWALD Why then, I care not for thee.

KENT If I had thee in Lipsbury pinfold I would make thee
care for me.

OSWALD Why dost thou use me thus? I know thee not.   10

KENT Fellow, I know thee.

OSWALD What dost thou know me for?

KENT A knave, a rascal, an eater of broken meats, a base,
proud, shallow, beggarly, three-suited, hundred-pound,
filthy-worsted-stocking knave; a lily-livered, action-

taking, whoreson glass-gazing super-serviceable finical
rogue, one-trunk-inheriting slave; one that wouldst be a
bawd in way of good service, and art nothing but the
composition of a knave, beggar, coward, pander, and
20   the son and heir of a mongrel bitch; one whom I will
beat into clamorous whining if thou deniest the least
syllable of thy addition.

OSWALD Why, what a monstrous fellow art thou thus to
rail on one that is neither known of thee nor knows thee!

KENT What a brazen-faced varlet art thou, to deny thou
knowest me! Is it two days since I tripped up thy heels
and beat thee before the King? Draw, you rogue! For
though it be night, yet the moon shines. I'll make a sop
o'the moonshine of you, you whoreson cullionly barber-
30   monger! Draw!

He brandishes his sword

OSWALD Away! I have nothing to do with thee.

KENT Draw, you rascal! You come with letters against the
King, and take Vanity the puppet's part against the
royalty of her father. Draw, you rogue! or I'll so
carbonado your shanks – Draw, you rascal! Come your
ways!

OSWALD Help, ho! Murder! Help!

KENT Strike, you slave!

Oswald tries to escape

Stand, rogue! Stand, you neat slave! Strike!

He beats him

40   OSWALD Help, ho! Murder! Murder!

*Enter Edmund, Cornwall, Regan, Gloucester, and
servants*

EDMUND How now! What's the matter? Part!

KENT With you, goodman boy, and you please! Come, I'll
flesh ye; come on, young master.

GLOUCESTER Weapons? Arms? What's the matter here?

CORNWALL

Keep peace, upon your lives!

He dies that strikes again. What is the matter?

REGAN

The messengers from our sister and the King –

CORNWALL What is your difference? Speak.

OSWALD I am scarce in breath, my lord.

KENT No marvel, you have so bestirred your valour. You 50
cowardly rascal, nature disclaims in thee; a tailor made
thee.

CORNWALL Thou art a strange fellow. A tailor make a
man?

KENT A tailor, sir. A stone-cutter or a painter could not
have made him so ill, though they had been but two
years o'the trade.

CORNWALL (to Oswald) Speak yet, how grew your
quarrel?

OSWALD This ancient ruffian, sir, whose life I have 60
spared at suit of his grey beard –

KENT Thou whoreson zed, thou unnecessary letter! My
lord, if you will give me leave, I will tread this unbolted
villain into mortar and daub the wall of a jakes with him.
'Spare my grey beard', you wagtail!

CORNWALL Peace, sirrah!

You beastly knave, know you no reverence?

KENT

Yes, sir; but anger hath a privilege.

CORNWALL Why art thou angry?

KENT

That such a slave as this should wear a sword   70
Who wears no honesty. Such smiling rogues as these,
Like rats, oft bite the holy cords atwain,
Which are t' intrinse t'unloose; smooth every passion
That in the natures of their lords rebel,

Being oil to fire, snow to the colder moods,
Renege, affirm, and turn their halcyon beaks
With every gale and vary of their masters,
Knowing naught – like dogs – but following. –
A plague upon your epileptic visage!
80 Smile you my speeches as I were a fool?
Goose, if I had you upon Sarum Plain,
I'd drive ye cackling home to Camelot.

CORNWALL What, art thou mad, old fellow?

GLOUCESTER How fell you out? Say that.

KENT
No contraries hold more antipathy
Than I and such a knave.

CORNWALL
Why dost thou call him knave? What is his fault?

KENT His countenance likes me not.

CORNWALL
No more perchance does mine, nor his, nor hers.

KENT
90 Sir, 'tis my occupation to be plain.
I have seen better faces in my time
Than stands on any shoulder that I see
Before me at this instant.

CORNWALL   This is some fellow
Who, having been praised for bluntness, doth affect
A saucy roughness, and constrains the garb
Quite from his nature. He cannot flatter, he!
An honest mind and plain – he must speak truth!
And they will take it, so; if not, he's plain.
These kind of knaves I know, which in this plainness
100 Harbour more craft and more corrupter ends
Than twenty silly-ducking observants
That stretch their duties nicely.

KENT
    Sir, in good faith, in sincere verity,
    Under th'allowance of your great aspect
    Whose influence like the wreath of radiant fire
    On flickering Phoebus' front –

CORNWALL   What mean'st by this?

KENT To go out of my dialect which you discommend so
    much. I know, sir, I am no flatterer. He that beguiled
    you in a plain accent was a plain knave; which, for my
    part, I will not be, though I should win your displeasure   110
    to entreat me to't.

CORNWALL What was th'offence you gave him?

OSWALD I never gave him any.
    It pleased the King his master very late
    To strike at me upon his misconstruction,
    When he, compact, and flattering his displeasure,
    Tripped me behind; being down, insulted, railed,
    And put upon him such a deal of man
    That worthied him, got praises of the King
    For him attempting who was self-subdued;   120
    And in the fleshment of this dread exploit
    Drew on me here again.

KENT   None of these rogues and cowards
    But Ajax is their fool.

CORNWALL   Fetch forth the stocks!
    You stubborn ancient knave, you reverend braggart,
    We'll teach you –

KENT   Sir, I am too old to learn.
    Call not your stocks for me. I serve the King,
    On whose employment I was sent to you.
    You shall do small respect, show too bold malice
    Against the grace and person of my master,
    Stocking his messenger.   130

CORNWALL

    Fetch forth the stocks! As I have life and honour,
    There shall he sit till noon.

REGAN

    Till noon? Till night, my lord, and all night too.

KENT

    Why, madam, if I were your father's dog
    You should not use me so.

REGAN   Sir, being his knave, I will.

CORNWALL

    This is a fellow of the selfsame colour
    Our sister speaks of. Come, bring away the stocks.

     Stocks brought out

GLOUCESTER

    Let me beseech your grace not to do so.
    His fault is much, and the good King, his master,
140   Will check him for't. Your purposed low correction
    Is such as basest and contemned'st wretches
    For pilferings and most common trespasses
    Are punished with. The King must take it ill
    That he, so slightly valued in his messenger,
    Should have him thus restrained.

CORNWALL   I'll answer that.

REGAN

    My sister may receive it much more worse
    To have her gentleman abused, assaulted,
    For following her affairs. – Put in his legs.

     Kent is put in the stocks

    Come, my lord, away.

                Exeunt all but Gloucester and Kent

GLOUCESTER

150   I am sorry for thee, friend. 'Tis the Duke's pleasure,
    Whose disposition all the world well knows
    Will not be rubbed nor stopped. I'll entreat for thee.

KENT

 Pray do not, sir. I have watched and travelled hard.
 Some time I shall sleep out, the rest I'll whistle.
 A good man's fortune may grow out at heels.
 Give you good morrow!

GLOUCESTER   The Duke's to blame in this.
 'Twill be ill taken.   *Exit*

KENT

 Good King, that must approve the common saw,
 Thou out of Heaven's benediction comest
 To the warm sun.   160
 Approach, thou beacon to this under globe,
 That by thy comfortable beams I may
 Peruse this letter. Nothing almost sees miracles
 But misery. I know 'tis from Cordelia,
 Who hath most fortunately been informed
 Of my obscurèd course, and (*reading*) 'shall find time
 From this enormous state, seeking to give
 Losses their remedies'. All weary and o'erwatched,
 Take vantage, heavy eyes, not to behold
 This shameful lodging.   170
 Fortune, good night; smile once more; turn thy wheel.
  He sleeps

  Enter Edgar   II.3

EDGAR

 I heard myself proclaimed,
 And by the happy hollow of a tree
 Escaped the hunt. No port is free, no place
 That guard and most unusual vigilance
 Does not attend my taking. Whiles I may 'scape
 I will preserve myself; and am bethought
 To take the basest and most poorest shape

That ever penury, in contempt of man,
Brought near to beast. My face I'll grime with filth,
10 Blanket my loins, elf all my hairs in knots,
And with presented nakedness outface
The winds and persecutions of the sky.
The country gives me proof and precedent
Of Bedlam beggars, who, with roaring voices,
Strike in their numbed and mortified bare arms
Pins, wooden pricks, nails, sprigs of rosemary;
And with this horrible object, from low farms,
Poor pelting villages, sheepcotes, and mills
Sometimes with lunatic bans, sometime with prayers,
20 Enforce their charity: 'Poor Turlygod! Poor Tom!'
That's something yet; Edgar I nothing am.   *Exit*

II.4   *Kent still in the stocks*
            Enter Lear, the Fool, and a Gentleman

LEAR
  'Tis strange that they should so depart from home
  And not send back my messengers.

GENTLEMAN   As I learned,
  The night before there was no purpose in them
  Of this remove.

KENT   Hail to thee, noble master!

LEAR
  Ha!
  Makest thou this shame thy pastime?

KENT   No, my lord.

FOOL Ha, ha! He wears cruel garters. Horses are tied by
  the heads, dogs and bears by the neck, monkeys by the
  loins, and men by the legs. When a man's over-lusty at
10 legs, then he wears wooden nether-stocks.

LEAR
    What's he that hath so much thy place mistook
    To set thee here?
KENT   It is both he and she;
    Your son and daughter.
LEAR No.
KENT Yes.
LEAR No, I say.
KENT I say yea.
LEAR No, no, they would not.
KENT Yes, they have.
LEAR By Jupiter, I swear no!   20
KENT
    By Juno, I swear ay!
LEAR   They durst not do't;
    They could not, would not do't; 'tis worse than murder
    To do upon respect such violent outrage.
    Resolve me with all modest haste which way
    Thou mightst deserve or they impose this usage,
    Coming from us.
KENT   My lord, when at their home
    I did commend your highness' letters to them,
    Ere I was risen from the place that showed
    My duty kneeling, came there a reeking post,
    Stewed in his haste, half breathless, panting forth   30
    From Gonerill his mistress salutations;
    Delivered letters, spite of intermission,
    Which presently they read; on whose contents
    They summoned up their meiny, straight took horse,
    Commanded me to follow and attend
    The leisure of their answer, gave me cold looks;
    And meeting here the other messenger,
    Whose welcome I perceived had poisoned mine –
    Being the very fellow which of late

40   Displayed so saucily against your highness –
      Having more man than wit about me, drew.
      He raised the house with loud and coward cries.
      Your son and daughter found this trespass worth
      The shame which here it suffers.

FOOL Winter's not gone yet if the wild geese fly that way.
        Fathers that wear rags
            Do make their children blind,
        But fathers that bear bags
            Shall see their children kind.
50   Fortune, that arrant whore,
            Ne'er turns the key to the poor.
      But for all this thou shalt have as many dolours for thy
      daughters as thou canst tell in a year.

LEAR
      O, how this mother swells up toward my heart!
      Hysterica passio, down, thou climbing sorrow!
      Thy element's below. Where is this daughter?

KENT With the Earl, sir, here within.

LEAR Follow me not; stay here.   *Exit*

GENTLEMAN
      Made you no more offence but what you speak of?
60 KENT None.

      How chance the King comes with so small a number?

FOOL And thou hadst been set i'the stocks for that ques-
      tion, thou'dst well deserved it.

KENT Why, Fool?

FOOL We'll set thee to school to an ant to teach thee
      there's no labouring i'the winter. All that follow their
      noses are led by their eyes, but blind men; and there's
      not a nose among twenty but can smell him that's
      stinking. Let go thy hold when a great wheel runs down
70   a hill, lest it break thy neck with following. But the great
      one that goes upward, let him draw thee after. When a

wise man gives thee better counsel, give me mine again;
I would ha' none but knaves use it, since a fool gives it.
  That sir which serves and seeks for gain,
    And follows but for form,
  Will pack when it begins to rain,
    And leave thee in the storm;
  But I will tarry, the fool will stay,
    And let the wise man fly.
  The knave turns fool that runs away;   80
    The fool no knave, perdy.

KENT Where learned you this, Fool?

FOOL Not i'the stocks, fool.

  Enter Lear and Gloucester

LEAR
Deny to speak with me? They are sick; they are weary?
They have travelled all the night? Mere fetches,
The images of revolt and flying-off.
Fetch me a better answer.

GLOUCESTER   My dear lord,
You know the fiery quality of the Duke,
How unremovable and fixed he is
In his own course.

LEAR   Vengeance, plague, death, confusion!   90
'Fiery'? What 'quality'? Why, Gloucester, Gloucester,
I'd speak with the Duke of Cornwall and his wife.

GLOUCESTER
Well, my good lord, I have informed them so.

LEAR
'Informed them'! Dost thou understand me, man?

GLOUCESTER Ay, my good lord.

LEAR
The King would speak with Cornwall, the dear father
Would with his daughter speak, commands, tends,
    service.

Are they 'informed' of this? My breath and blood!
'Fiery'? The 'fiery' Duke? Tell the hot Duke that –
No, but not yet! Maybe he is not well.
Infirmity doth still neglect all office
Whereto our health is bound; we are not ourselves
When nature, being oppressed, commands the mind
To suffer with the body. I'll forbear;
And am fallen out with my more headier will
To take the indisposed and sickly fit
For the sound man. – Death on my state! Wherefore
Should he sit here? This act persuades me
That this remotion of the Duke and her
Is practice only. Give me my servant forth.
Go tell the Duke and's wife I'd speak with them –
Now presently! Bid them come forth and hear me,
Or at their chamber door I'll beat the drum
Till it cry sleep to death.

GLOUCESTER I would have all well betwixt you.   *Exit*

LEAR
O me, my heart, my rising heart! But down!

FOOL Cry to it, nuncle, as the cockney did to the eels
when she put 'em i'the paste alive. She knapped 'em
o'the coxcombs with a stick and cried 'Down, wantons,
down!' 'Twas her brother that in pure kindness to his
horse buttered his hay.

        Enter Cornwall, Regan, Gloucester, and servants

LEAR
Good morrow to you both.

CORNWALL   Hail to your grace.
        Kent is here set at liberty

REGAN
I am glad to see your highness.

LEAR
Regan, I think you are. I know what reason

I have to think so. If thou shouldst not be glad,
I would divorce me from thy mother's tomb,
Sepulchring an adult'ress. (*To Kent*) O, are you free?
Some other time for that. – Beloved Regan,
Thy sister's naught. O Regan, she hath tied
Sharp-toothed unkindness like a vulture here –   130
     (*laying his hand on his heart*)
I can scarce speak to thee – thou'lt not believe
With how depraved a quality – O Regan!

REGAN
     I pray you, sir, take patience. I have hope
     You less know how to value her desert
     Than she to scant her duty.

LEAR   Say? How is that?

REGAN
     I cannot think my sister in the least
     Would fail her obligation. If, sir, perchance,
     She have restrained the riots of your followers,
     'Tis on such ground and to such wholesome end
     As clears her from all blame.   140

LEAR
     My curses on her.

REGAN   O sir, you are old.
     Nature in you stands on the very verge
     Of his confine. You should be ruled and led
     By some discretion that discerns your state
     Better than you yourself. Therefore I pray you
     That to our sister you do make return.
     Say you have wronged her.

LEAR   Ask her forgiveness?
     Do you but mark how this becomes the house:
          (*he kneels*)
     'Dear daughter, I confess that I am old;
     Age is unnecessary; on my knees I beg   150

That you'll vouchsafe me raiment, bed, and food.'

REGAN

Good sir, no more! These are unsightly tricks.
Return you to my sister.

LEAR (*rising*)   Never, Regan.
She hath abated me of half my train,
Looked black upon me, struck me with her tongue,
Most serpent-like, upon the very heart.
All the stored vengeances of heaven fall
On her ingrateful top! Strike her young bones,
You taking airs, with lameness!

CORNWALL   Fie, sir, fie!

LEAR

160   You nimble lightnings, dart your blinding flames
Into her scornful eyes! Infect her beauty,
You fen-sucked fogs drawn by the powerful sun,
To fall and blister.

REGAN   O the blest gods!
So will you wish on me when the rash mood is on.

LEAR

No, Regan, thou shalt never have my curse.
Thy tender-hefted nature shall not give
Thee o'er to harshness. Her eyes are fierce; but thine
Do comfort, and not burn. 'Tis not in thee
To grudge my pleasures, to cut off my train,
170   To bandy hasty words, to scant my sizes,
And, in conclusion, to oppose the bolt
Against my coming in. Thou better knowest
The offices of nature, bond of childhood,
Effects of courtesy, dues of gratitude.
Thy half o'the kingdom hast thou not forgot,
Wherein I thee endowed.

REGAN   Good sir, to the purpose.

LEAR

    Who put my man i'the stocks?

     Tucket within

CORNWALL   What trumpet's that?

REGAN

    I know't – my sister's. This approves her letter

    That she would soon be here.

     Enter Oswald

                       Is your lady come?

LEAR

    This is a slave whose easy-borrowed pride   180

    Dwells in the fickle grace of her he follows.

    Out, varlet, from my sight!

CORNWALL   What means your grace?

LEAR

    Who stocked my servant? Regan, I have good hope

    Thou didst not know on't.

     Enter Gonerill

                Who comes here? O heavens!

    If you do love old men, if your sweet sway

    Allow obedience, if you yourselves are old,

    Make it your cause! Send down and take my part!

    (*To Gonerill*) Art not ashamed to look upon this beard?

    O Regan, will you take her by the hand?

GONERILL

    Why not by th'hand, sir? How have I offended?   190

    All's not offence that indiscretion finds

    And dotage terms so.

LEAR   O sides, you are too tough!

    Will you yet hold? – How came my man i'the stocks?

CORNWALL

    I set him there, sir; but his own disorders

    Deserved much less advancement.

LEAR   You? Did you?

REGAN

    I pray you, father, being weak, seem so.
    If till the expiration of your month
    You will return and sojourn with my sister,
    Dismissing half your train, come then to me.
200   I am now from home and out of that provision
    Which shall be needful for your entertainment.

LEAR

    Return to her, and fifty men dismissed!
    No, rather I abjure all roofs and choose
    To wage against the enmity o'th'air,
    To be a comrade with the wolf and owl –
    Necessity's sharp pinch! Return with her?
    Why, the hot-blooded France that dowerless took
    Our youngest born, I could as well be brought
    To knee his throne and, squire-like, pension beg
210   To keep base life afoot. Return with her!
    Persuade me rather to be slave and sumpter
    To this detested groom.

      He points to Oswald

GONERILL   At your choice, sir.

LEAR

    I prithee, daughter, do not make me mad.
    I will not trouble thee, my child. Farewell.
    We'll no more meet, no more see one another.
    But yet thou art my flesh, my blood, my daughter –
    Or rather a disease that's in my flesh,
    Which I must needs call mine. Thou art a boil,
    A plague-sore, or embossed carbuncle,
220   In my corrupted blood. But I'll not chide thee.
    Let shame come when it will, I do not call it.
    I do not bid the thunder-bearer shoot,
    Nor tell tales of thee to high-judging Jove.
    Mend when thou canst, be better at thy leisure;

I can be patient, I can stay with Regan,
I and my hundred knights.

REGAN   Not altogether so.
I looked not for you yet, nor am provided
For your fit welcome. Give ear, sir, to my sister;
For those that mingle reason with your passion
Must be content to think you old, and so —   230
But she knows what she does.

LEAR   Is this well spoken?

REGAN
I dare avouch it, sir. What, fifty followers?
Is it not well? What should you need of more?
Yea, or so many, sith that both charge and danger
Speak 'gainst so great a number? How in one house
Should many people under two commands
Hold amity? 'Tis hard, almost impossible.

GONERILL
Why might not you, my lord, receive attendance
From those that she calls servants, or from mine?

REGAN
Why not, my lord? If then they chanced to slack ye,   240
We could control them. If you will come to me,
For now I spy a danger, I entreat you
To bring but five-and-twenty; to no more
Will I give place or notice.

LEAR
I gave you all —

REGAN   And in good time you gave it.

LEAR
Made you my guardians, my depositaries;
But kept a reservation to be followed
With such a number. What, must I come to you
With five-and-twenty — Regan, said you so?

REGAN

250   And speak't again, my lord. No more with me.

LEAR

Those wicked creatures yet do look well-favoured
When others are more wicked. Not being the worst
Stands in some rank of praise. (*To Gonerill*) I'll go with
    thee.
Thy fifty yet doth double five-and-twenty,
And thou art twice her love.

GONERILL   Hear me, my lord;
What need you five-and-twenty, ten, or five
To follow, in a house where twice so many
Have a command to tend you?

REGAN   What need one?

LEAR

O, reason not the need! Our basest beggars
260   Are in the poorest thing superfluous.
Allow not nature more than nature needs –
Man's life is cheap as beast's. Thou art a lady;
If only to go warm were gorgeous,
Why, nature needs not what thou gorgeous wear'st,
Which scarcely keeps thee warm. But for true need –
You heavens, give me that patience, patience I need!
You see me here, you gods, a poor old man,
As full of grief as age, wretched in both;
If it be you that stirs these daughters' hearts
270   Against their father, fool me not so much
To bear it tamely; touch me with noble anger,
And let not women's weapons, water drops,
Stain my man's cheeks. No, you unnatural hags,
I will have such revenges on you both
That all the world shall – I will do such things –
What they are yet I know not; but they shall be
The terrors of the earth. You think I'll weep.

No, I'll not weep.
I have full cause of weeping;
  (*storm and tempest*)
                         but this heart
Shall break into a hundred thousand flaws   280
Or ere I'll weep. O Fool, I shall go mad!
  Exeunt Lear, Gloucester, Kent, the Fool, and Gentleman
CORNWALL Let us withdraw; 'twill be a storm.
REGAN
  This house is little; the old man and's people
  Cannot be well bestowed.
GONERILL
  'Tis his own blame; hath put himself from rest
  And must needs taste his folly.
REGAN
  For his particular, I'll receive him gladly,
  But not one follower.
GONERILL   So am I purposed.
  Where is my lord of Gloucester?
CORNWALL
  Followed the old man forth. He is returned.   290
  Enter Gloucester
GLOUCESTER
  The King is in high rage.
CORNWALL   Whither is he going?
GLOUCESTER
  He calls to horse; but will I know not whither.
CORNWALL
  'Tis best to give him way. He leads himself.
GONERILL
  My lord, entreat him by no means to stay.
GLOUCESTER
  Alack, the night comes on and the bleak winds
  Do sorely ruffle. For many miles about

There's scarce a bush.

REGAN   O sir, to wilful men
The injuries that they themselves procure
Must be their schoolmasters. Shut up your doors.
300   He is attended with a desperate train,
And what they may incense him to, being apt
To have his ear abused, wisdom bids fear.

CORNWALL
Shut up your doors, my lord; 'tis a wild night.
My Regan counsels well. Come out o'the storm.

                                                    Exeunt

                              *

III.1   *Storm still. Enter Kent and a Gentleman by*
               opposite doors

KENT Who's there besides foul weather?

GENTLEMAN
One minded like the weather, most unquietly.

KENT I know you. Where's the King?

GENTLEMAN
Contending with the fretful elements:
Bids the wind blow the earth into the sea,
Or swell the curlèd waters 'bove the main,
That things might change or cease; tears his white hair,
Which the impetuous blasts with eyeless rage
Catch in their fury and make nothing of;
10   Strives in his little world of man to out-storm
The to-and-fro conflicting wind and rain.
This night, wherein the cub-drawn bear would couch,
The lion and the belly-pinchèd wolf
Keep their fur dry, unbonneted he runs
And bids what will take all.

KENT   But who is with him?

GENTLEMAN

None but the Fool, who labours to out-jest
His heart-struck injuries.

KENT   Sir, I do know you,
And dare upon the warrant of my note
Commend a dear thing to you. There is division –
Although as yet the face of it is covered   20
With mutual cunning – 'twixt Albany and Cornwall;
Who have – as who have not that their great stars
Throned and set high – servants, who seem no less,
Which are to France the spies and speculations
Intelligent of our state. What hath been seen,
Either in snuffs and packings of the Dukes,
Or the hard rein which both of them hath borne
Against the old kind King, or something deeper,
Whereof, perchance, these are but furnishings –
But true it is, from France there comes a power   30
Into this scattered kingdom, who already,
Wise in our negligence, have secret feet
In some of our best ports and are at point
To show their open banner. Now to you:
If on my credit you dare build so far
To make your speed to Dover, you shall find
Some that will thank you making just report
Of how unnatural and bemadding sorrow
The King hath cause to plain.
I am a gentleman of blood and breeding,   40
And from some knowledge and assurance offer
This office to you.

GENTLEMAN

I will talk further with you.

KENT   No, do not.
For confirmation that I am much more

Than my out-wall, open this purse and take
What it contains. If you shall see Cordelia –
As fear not but you shall – show her this ring,
And she will tell you who that fellow is
That yet you do not know. Fie on this storm!
50   I will go seek the King.

GENTLEMAN

Give me your hand. Have you no more to say?

KENT

Few words, but to effect more than all yet:
That when we have found the King – in which your pain
That way, I'll this – he that first lights on him
Holla the other.   *Exeunt by opposite doors*

III.2   *Storm still. Enter Lear and the Fool*

LEAR

Blow, winds, and crack your cheeks! Rage! Blow!
You cataracts and hurricanoes, spout
Till you have drenched our steeples, drowned the cocks!
You sulphurous and thought-executing fires,
Vaunt-curriers of oak-cleaving thunderbolts,
Singe my white head! And thou all-shaking thunder,
Strike flat the thick rotundity o'the world,
Crack Nature's moulds, all germens spill at once
That makes ingrateful man!
10   FOOL O nuncle, court holy-water in a dry house is better
than this rain-water out o'door. Good nuncle, in; ask thy
daughters' blessing. Here's a night pities neither wise
men nor fools.

LEAR

Rumble thy bellyful! Spit, fire! Spout, rain!
Nor rain, wind, thunder, fire are my daughters.
I tax not you, you elements, with unkindness;

I never gave you kingdom, called you children.
You owe me no subscription; then let fall
Your horrible pleasure. Here I stand, your slave,
A poor, infirm, weak, and despised old man.   20
But yet I call you servile ministers,
That will with two pernicious daughters join
Your high-engendered battles 'gainst a head
So old and white as this. O, ho! 'Tis foul!

FOOL He that has a house to put's head in has a good head-
    piece:
        The cod-piece that will house
            Before the head has any,
        The head and he shall louse;
            So beggars marry many.   30
        The man that makes his toe
            What he his heart should make,
        Shall of a corn cry woe,
            And turn his sleep to wake.
    For there was never yet fair woman but she made mouths
    in a glass.
        Enter Kent

LEAR
    No, I will be the pattern of all patience.
    I will say nothing.

KENT Who's there?

FOOL Marry, here's grace and a cod-piece – that's a wise   40
    man and a fool.

KENT
    Alas, sir, are you here? Things that love night
    Love not such nights as these. The wrathful skies
    Gallow the very wanderers of the dark
    And make them keep their caves. Since I was man,
    Such sheets of fire, such bursts of horrid thunder,
    Such groans of roaring wind and rain I never

Remember to have heard. Man's nature cannot carry
Th'affliction nor the fear.

LEAR   Let the great gods
50   That keep this dreadful pudder o'er our heads
Find out their enemies now. Tremble, thou wretch
That hast within thee undivulgèd crimes
Unwhipped of justice. Hide thee, thou bloody hand,
Thou perjured, and thou simular of virtue
That art incestuous. Caitiff, to pieces shake,
That under covert and convenient seeming
Has practised on man's life. Close pent-up guilts,
Rive your concealing continents, and cry
These dreadful summoners grace. I am a man
60   More sinned against than sinning.

KENT   Alack, bare-headed?
Gracious my lord, hard by here is a hovel;
Some friendship will it lend you 'gainst the tempest.
Repose you there while I to this hard house –
More harder than the stones whereof 'tis raised;
Which even but now, demanding after you,
Denied me to come in – return and force
Their scanted courtesy.

LEAR   My wits begin to turn.
Come on, my boy. How dost my boy? Art cold?
I am cold myself. Where is this straw, my fellow?
70   The art of our necessities is strange
And can make vile things precious. Come, your hovel.
Poor fool and knave, I have one part in my heart
That's sorry yet for thee.

FOOL (*sings*)
                    He that has and a little tiny wit,
                    With heigh-ho, the wind and the rain,
                    Must make content with his fortunes fit,
                    Though the rain it raineth every day.

LEAR True, boy. Come, bring us to this hovel.

Exeunt Lear and Kent

FOOL This is a brave night to cool a courtesan. I'll speak
a prophecy ere I go: 80

    When priests are more in word than matter,
    When brewers mar their malt with water,
    When nobles are their tailors' tutors,
    No heretics burned but wenches' suitors –
    Then shall the realm of Albion
    Come to great confusion.

    When every case in law is right,
    No squire in debt nor no poor knight,
    When slanders do not live in tongues,
    Nor cutpurses come not to throngs,   90
    When usurers tell their gold i'the field,
    And bawds and whores do churches build –
    Then comes the time, who lives to see't,
    That going shall be used with feet.

This prophecy Merlin shall make; for I live before his
time.   *Exit*

Enter Gloucester and Edmund with lights   III.3

GLOUCESTER Alack, alack, Edmund, I like not this unnatural dealing. When I desired their leave that I might
pity him, they took from me the use of mine own house,
charged me on pain of perpetual displeasure neither to
speak of him, entreat for him, or any way sustain him.

EDMUND Most savage and unnatural!

GLOUCESTER Go to. Say you nothing. There is division
between the Dukes; and a worse matter than that. I
have received a letter this night; 'tis dangerous to be
spoken; I have locked the letter in my closet. These in-   10

juries the King now bears will be revenged home. There
is part of a power already footed. We must incline to the
King. I will look him and privily relieve him. Go you
and maintain talk with the Duke, that my charity be not
of him perceived. If he ask for me, I am ill and gone to
bed. If I die for it, as no less is threatened me, the King
my old master must be relieved. There is strange things
toward, Edmund. Pray you, be careful.   *Exit*

EDMUND

This courtesy forbid thee shall the Duke
20   Instantly know, and of that letter too.
This seems a fair deserving, and must draw me
That which my father loses – no less than all.
The younger rises when the old doth fall.   *Exit*

III.4   *Enter Lear, Kent, and the Fool*

KENT

Here is the place, my lord; good my lord, enter.
The tyranny of the open night's too rough
For nature to endure.
       Storm still

LEAR   Let me alone.

KENT

Good my lord, enter here.

LEAR   Wilt break my heart?

KENT

I had rather break mine own. Good my lord, enter.

LEAR

Thou think'st 'tis much that this contentious storm
Invades us to the skin; so 'tis to thee.
But where the greater malady is fixed
The lesser is scarce felt. Thou'dst shun a bear;
10   But if thy flight lay toward the roaring sea

Thou'dst meet the bear i'the mouth. When the mind's free
The body's delicate; this tempest in my mind
Doth from my senses take all feeling else
Save what beats there. – Filial ingratitude!
Is it not as this mouth should tear this hand
For lifting food to't? But I will punish home.
No, I will weep no more! In such a night
To shut me out! Pour on; I will endure.
In such a night as this! O Regan, Gonerill!
Your old kind father, whose frank heart gave all!   20
O, that way madness lies; let me shun that;
No more of that!

KENT   Good my lord, enter here.

LEAR

Prithee go in thyself; seek thine own ease.
This tempest will not give me leave to ponder
On things would hurt me more; but I'll go in.
(*To the Fool*) In, boy, go first. – You houseless poverty –
Nay, get thee in. I'll pray and then I'll sleep.

                                        Exit the Fool

Poor naked wretches, wheresoe'er you are,
That bide the pelting of this pitiless storm,
How shall your houseless heads and unfed sides,   30
Your looped and windowed raggedness, defend you
From seasons such as these? O, I have ta'en
Too little care of this! Take physic, pomp;
Expose thyself to feel what wretches feel,
That thou mayst shake the superflux to them
And show the heavens more just.

EDGAR (*within*)

Fathom and half, fathom and half! Poor Tom!

        Enter the Fool from the hovel

FOOL Come not in here, nuncle; here's a spirit. Help me,
    help me!

40 KENT Give me thy hand. Who's there?

FOOL A spirit, a spirit! He says his name's Poor Tom.

KENT What art thou that dost grumble there i'the straw?
Come forth.

Enter Edgar disguised as Poor Tom

EDGAR Away! The foul fiend follows me.

Through the sharp hawthorn blow the cold winds.
Humh! Go to thy bed and warm thee.

LEAR Didst thou give all to thy daughters? And art thou
come to this?

EDGAR Who gives anything to Poor Tom? whom the foul
50 fiend hath led through fire and through flame, through
ford and whirlpool, o'er bog and quagmire, that hath
laid knives under his pillow and halters in his pew, set
ratsbane by his porridge, made him proud of heart, to
ride on a bay trotting horse over four-inched bridges to
course his own shadow for a traitor. Bless thy five wits!
Tom's a-cold. O do, de, do, de, do, de. Bless thee from
whirlwinds, star-blasting, and taking! Do Poor Tom
some charity, whom the foul fiend vexes. There could I
have him now, and there, and there again, and there.

Storm still

LEAR
60 What, has his daughters brought him to this pass?
Couldst thou save nothing? Wouldst thou give 'em all?

FOOL Nay, he reserved a blanket; else we had been all
shamed.

LEAR
Now all the plagues that in the pendulous air
Hang fated o'er men's faults light on thy daughters!

KENT He hath no daughters, sir.

LEAR
Death, traitor! Nothing could have subdued nature
To such a lowness but his unkind daughters.

Is it the fashion that discarded fathers
Should have thus little mercy on their flesh?   70
Judicious punishment! 'Twas this flesh begot
Those pelican daughters.

EDGAR
     Pillicock sat on Pillicock Hill.
Alow, alow, loo, loo!

FOOL This cold night will turn us all to fools and madmen.

EDGAR Take heed o'the foul fiend, obey thy parents, keep
thy word's justice, swear not, commit not with man's
sworn spouse, set not thy sweet heart on proud array.
Tom's a-cold.   80

LEAR What hast thou been?

EDGAR A servingman, proud in heart and mind, that curled
my hair, wore gloves in my cap, served the lust of my
mistress' heart and did the act of darkness with her,
swore as many oaths as I spake words and broke them in
the sweet face of heaven; one that slept in the contriving
of lust and waked to do it. Wine loved I deeply, dice
dearly, and in woman out-paramoured the Turk – false
of heart, light of ear, bloody of hand; hog in sloth, fox in
stealth, wolf in greediness, dog in madness, lion in prey.   90
Let not the creaking of shoes nor the rustling of silks
betray thy poor heart to woman. Keep thy foot out of
brothels, thy hand out of plackets, thy pen from lenders'
books, and defy the foul fiend.
     Still through the hawthorn blows the cold wind,
     Says suum, mun, nonny.
Dolphin, my boy, boy, sesey! Let him trot by.
     Storm still

LEAR Thou wert better in a grave than to answer with thy
uncovered body this extremity of the skies. Is man no
more than this? Consider him well. Thou owest the   100

worm no silk, the beast no hide, the sheep no wool, the
cat no perfume. Ha! Here's three on's are sophisticated.
Thou art the thing itself! Unaccommodated man is no
more but such a poor, bare, forked animal as thou art.
Off, off, you lendings! Come, unbutton here.

He tears off his clothes

FOOL Prithee, nuncle, be contented; 'tis a naughty night
to swim in. Now a little fire in a wild field were like an
old lecher's heart – a small spark, all the rest on's body
cold. Look, here comes a walking fire.

Enter Gloucester with a torch

110 EDGAR This is the foul fiend Flibberdigibbet. He begins
at curfew and walks till the first cock. He gives the web
and the pin, squenies the eye and makes the harelip,
mildews the white wheat, and hurts the poor creature of
earth.

S'Withold footed thrice the 'old;
He met the nightmare and her nine-fold,
Bid her alight and her troth plight –
And aroint thee, witch, aroint thee!

KENT How fares your grace?

120 LEAR What's he?

KENT (*to Gloucester*) Who's there? What is't you seek?

GLOUCESTER What are you there? Your names?

EDGAR Poor Tom, that eats the swimming frog, the toad,
the todpole, the wall-newt and the water; that in the
fury of his heart, when the foul fiend rages, eats cow-
dung for sallets, swallows the old rat and the ditch-dog,
drinks the green mantle of the standing pool; who is
whipped from tithing to tithing and stock-punished and
imprisoned; who hath had three suits to his back, six
130 shirts to his body,

Horse to ride and weapon to wear –
But mice and rats and such small deer

Have been Tom's food for seven long year.
Beware my follower! Peace, Smulkin! Peace, thou fiend!
GLOUCESTER What, hath your grace no better company?
EDGAR The prince of darkness is a gentleman; Modo he's
    called and Mahu.
GLOUCESTER
Our flesh and blood, my lord, is grown so vile
That it doth hate what gets it.
EDGAR Poor Tom's a-cold.   140
GLOUCESTER
Go in with me. My duty cannot suffer
T'obey in all your daughters' hard commands;
Though their injunction be to bar my doors
And let this tyrannous night take hold upon you,
Yet have I ventured to come seek you out
And bring you where both fire and food is ready.
LEAR
First let me talk with this philosopher.
  (*To Edgar*) What is the cause of thunder?
KENT   Good my lord,
Take his offer, go into the house.
LEAR
I'll talk a word with this same learnèd Theban.   150
  (*To Edgar*) What is your study?
EDGAR How to prevent the fiend and to kill vermin.
LEAR Let me ask you one word in private.
    Lear and Edgar talk apart
KENT
Importune him once more to go, my lord.
His wits begin t'unsettle.
GLOUCESTER   Canst thou blame him? –
  (*storm still*)
His daughters seek his death. Ah, that good Kent,
He said it would be thus, poor banished man!

Thou sayest the King grows mad; I'll tell thee, friend,
I am almost mad myself. I had a son,
160 Now outlawed from my blood; he sought my life
But lately, very late. I loved him, friend,
No father his son dearer. True to tell thee,
The grief hath crazed my wits. What a night's this! –
I do beseech your grace –

LEAR   O, cry you mercy, sir.
    (*To Edgar*) Noble philosopher, your company.

EDGAR Tom's a-cold.

GLOUCESTER In, fellow, there, into th'hovel; keep thee
    warm.

LEAR
    Come, let's in all.

KENT   This way, my lord.

LEAR   With him!
170 I will keep still with my philosopher.

KENT Good my lord, soothe him: let him take the fellow.

GLOUCESTER Take him you on.

KENT Sirrah, come on. Go along with us.

LEAR Come, good Athenian.

GLOUCESTER No words, no words! Hush!

EDGAR
    Child Roland to the dark tower came;
    His word was still 'Fie, foh, and fum,
    I smell the blood of a British man.'   *Exeunt*

III.5   *Enter Cornwall and Edmund*

CORNWALL I will have my revenge ere I depart his house.

EDMUND How, my lord, I may be censured that nature
    thus gives way to loyalty, something fears me to think of.

CORNWALL I now perceive it was not altogether your
    brother's evil disposition made him seek his death; but

a provoking merit set a-work by a reprovable badness in himself.

EDMUND How malicious is my fortune that I must repent to be just! This is the letter he spoke of, which approves him an intelligent party to the advantages of France. O heavens! that this treason were not, or not I the detector.

CORNWALL Go with me to the Duchess.

EDMUND If the matter of this paper be certain, you have mighty business in hand.

CORNWALL True or false, it hath made thee Earl of Gloucester. Seek out where thy father is, that he may be ready for our apprehension.

EDMUND (*aside*) If I find him comforting the King it will stuff his suspicion more fully. (*Aloud*) I will persever in my course of loyalty, though the conflict be sore between that and my blood.

CORNWALL I will lay trust upon thee, and thou shalt find a dearer father in my love.   *Exeunt*

Enter Kent and Gloucester   III.6

GLOUCESTER Here is better than the open air. Take it thankfully; I will piece out the comfort with what addition I can. I will not be long from you.

KENT All the power of his wits have given way to his impatience. The gods reward your kindness!

Exit Gloucester

Enter Lear, Edgar, and the Fool

EDGAR Fraterretto calls me and tells me Nero is an angler in the lake of darkness. Pray, innocent, and beware the foul fiend.

FOOL Prithee, nuncle, tell me whether a madman be a gentleman or a yeoman.

LEAR A king, a king!

FOOL No! He's a yeoman that has a gentleman to his son;
for he's a mad yeoman that sees his son a gentleman
before him.

LEAR

To have a thousand with red burning spits
Come hissing in upon 'em!

EDGAR The foul fiend bites my back.

FOOL He's mad that trusts in the tameness of a wolf, a
horse's health, a boy's love, or a whore's oath.

LEAR

20   It shall be done; I will arraign them straight.
(*To Edgar*)
Come, sit thou here, most learnèd justicer.
(*To the Fool*)
Thou sapient sir, sit here. No, you she-foxes –

EDGAR Look where he stands and glares! Want'st thou
eyes at trial, madam?
      (*sings*)
                  Come o'er the burn, Bessy, to me.

FOOL (*sings*) Her boat hath a leak
                  And she must not speak
                  Why she dares not come over to thee.

EDGAR The foul fiend haunts Poor Tom in the voice of a
30   nightingale. Hoppedance cries in Tom's belly for two
white herring. Croak not, black angel! I have no food for
thee.

KENT

How do you, sir? Stand you not so amazed.
Will you lie down and rest upon the cushings?

LEAR

I'll see their trial first; bring in their evidence.
(*To Edgar*)
Thou robed man of justice, take thy place.

(*To the Fool*)
And thou, his yokefellow of equity,
Bench by his side. (*To Kent*) You are o'the commission;
Sit you too.

EDGAR Let us deal justly.   40
        Sleepest or wakest thou, jolly shepherd?
            Thy sheep be in the corn,
        And for one blast of thy minikin mouth
            Thy sheep shall take no harm.
    Pur, the cat is grey.

LEAR Arraign her first. 'Tis Gonerill! I here take my oath
    before this honourable assembly she kicked the poor
    King her father.

FOOL Come hither, mistress. Is your name Gonerill?

LEAR She cannot deny it.   50

FOOL Cry you mercy, I took you for a joint-stool.

LEAR
    And here's another whose warped looks proclaim
    What store her heart is made on. Stop her there!
    Arms, arms, sword, fire! Corruption in the place!
    False justicer, why hast thou let her 'scape?

EDGAR Bless thy five wits!

KENT
    O pity! Sir, where is the patience now
    That you so oft have boasted to retain?

EDGAR (*aside*)
    My tears begin to take his part so much
    They mar my counterfeiting.   60

LEAR
    The little dogs and all –
    Trey, Blanch, and Sweetheart – see, they bark at me.

EDGAR Tom will throw his head at them. Avaunt, you
    curs!

Be thy mouth or black or white,
Tooth that poisons if it bite,
Mastiff, greyhound, mongrel grim,
Hound or spaniel, brach or lym,
Or bobtail tike, or trundle-tail,
70   Tom will make him weep and wail;
For, with throwing thus my head,
Dogs leapt the hatch and all are fled.

Do, de, de, de. Sese! Come, march to wakes and fairs
and market-towns. Poor Tom, thy horn is dry.

LEAR Then let them anatomize Regan, see what breeds
about her heart. Is there any cause in nature that makes
these hard hearts? You, sir, I entertain for one of my hundred. Only I do not like the fashion of your garments.
You will say they are Persian; but let them be changed.

KENT
80   Now, good my lord, lie here and rest awhile.

LEAR Make no noise, make no noise; draw the curtains.
So, so. We'll go to supper i'the morning.

FOOL And I'll go to bed at noon.

Enter Gloucester

GLOUCESTER
Come hither, friend. Where is the King my master?

KENT
Here, sir; but trouble him not; his wits are gone.

GLOUCESTER
Good friend, I prithee take him in thy arms;
I have o'erheard a plot of death upon him.
There is a litter ready; lay him in't
And drive toward Dover, friend, where thou shalt meet
90   Both welcome and protection. Take up thy master;
If thou shouldst dally half an hour, his life,
With thine and all that offer to defend him,
Stand in assurèd loss. Take up, take up,

And follow me, that will to some provision
Give thee quick conduct.

KENT   Oppressèd nature sleeps.
This rest might yet have balmed thy broken sinews
Which, if convenience will not allow,
Stand in hard cure. (*To the Fool*) Come, help to bear
     thy master.
Thou must not stay behind.

GLOUCESTER   Come, come, away!
                    Exeunt Kent, Gloucester, and the Fool,
                                  bearing off the King

EDGAR
When we our betters see bearing our woes,   100
We scarcely think our miseries our foes.
Who alone suffers, suffers most i'the mind,
Leaving free things and happy shows behind;
But then the mind much sufferance doth o'erskip
When grief hath mates, and bearing fellowship.
How light and portable my pain seems now,
When that which makes me bend makes the King bow –
He childed as I fathered. Tom, away!
Mark the high noises, and thyself bewray
When false opinion, whose wrong thoughts defile thee,   110
In thy just proof repeals and reconciles thee.
What will hap more tonight, safe 'scape the King!
Lurk, lurk!   *Exit*

            Enter Cornwall, Regan, Gonerill, Edmund, and   III.7
            Servants
CORNWALL (*to Gonerill*) Post speedily to my lord your
husband, show him this letter. The army of France is
landed. – Seek out the traitor Gloucester.
                               Exeunt some Servants

REGAN Hang him instantly!

GONERILL Pluck out his eyes!

CORNWALL Leave him to my displeasure. Edmund, keep
you our sister company; the revenges we are bound to
take upon your traitorous father are not fit for your be-
holding. Advise the Duke where you are going to a most
festinate preparation; we are bound to the like. Our
posts shall be swift and intelligent betwixt us. Farewell,
dear sister. Farewell, my lord of Gloucester.

Enter Oswald

How now? Where's the King?

OSWALD

My lord of Gloucester hath conveyed him hence.
Some five- or six-and-thirty of his knights,
Hot questrists after him, met him at gate,
Who with some other of the lord's dependants
Are gone with him toward Dover, where they boast
To have well-armèd friends.

CORNWALL Get horses for your mistress.   *Exit Oswald*

GONERILL Farewell, sweet lord, and sister.

CORNWALL

Edmund, farewell.

Exeunt Gonerill and Edmund

Go seek the traitor Gloucester.
Pinion him like a thief; bring him before us.

Exeunt Servants

Though well we may not pass upon his life
Without the form of justice, yet our power
Shall do a curtsy to our wrath, which men
May blame but not control.

Enter Gloucester, brought in by two or three Servants

Who's there? The traitor?

REGAN Ingrateful fox, 'tis he!

CORNWALL Bind fast his corky arms.

GLOUCESTER

What means your graces? Good my friends, consider   30
You are my guests. Do me no foul play, friends.

CORNWALL

Bind him, I say.
  Servants tie his hands

REGAN   Hard, hard! O filthy traitor!

GLOUCESTER

Unmerciful lady as you are, I'm none.

CORNWALL

To this chair bind him. Villain, thou shalt find –
  Regan plucks his beard

GLOUCESTER

By the kind gods, 'tis most ignobly done
To pluck me by the beard.

REGAN

So white, and such a traitor!

GLOUCESTER   Naughty lady,
These hairs which thou dost ravish from my chin
Will quicken and accuse thee. I am your host;
With robbers' hands my hospitable favours   40
You should not ruffle thus. What will you do?

CORNWALL

Come, sir; what letters had you late from France?

REGAN

Be simple-answered, for we know the truth.

CORNWALL

And what confederacy have you with the traitors
Late footed in the kingdom –

REGAN

To whose hands you have sent the lunatic King? Speak!

GLOUCESTER

I have a letter guessingly set down
Which came from one that's of a neutral heart

And not from one opposed.

CORNWALL   Cunning.

REGAN   And false.

CORNWALL

50   Where hast thou sent the King?

GLOUCESTER   To Dover.

REGAN

Wherefore to Dover? Wast thou not charged at peril –

CORNWALL

Wherefore to Dover? Let him answer that.

GLOUCESTER

I am tied to the stake, and I must stand the course.

REGAN Wherefore to Dover?

GLOUCESTER

Because I would not see thy cruel nails
Pluck out his poor old eyes; nor thy fierce sister
In his anointed flesh rash boarish fangs.
The sea, with such a storm as his bare head
In hell-black night endured, would have buoyed up
60   And quenched the stellèd fires;
Yet, poor old heart, he holp the heavens to rain.
If wolves had at thy gate howled that dern time
Thou shouldst have said, 'Good porter, turn the key;
All cruels else subscribe.' But I shall see
The wingèd Vengeance overtake such children.

CORNWALL

See't shalt thou never. Fellows, hold the chair.
Upon these eyes of thine I'll set my foot.

GLOUCESTER

He that will think to live till he be old
Give me some help! – O, cruel! O, you gods!

REGAN

70   One side will mock another. Th'other too!

CORNWALL
  If you see Vengeance –
FIRST SERVANT   Hold your hand, my lord!
  I have served you ever since I was a child;
  But better service have I never done you
  Than now to bid you hold.
REGAN   How now, you dog!
FIRST SERVANT
  If you did wear a beard upon your chin
  I'd shake it on this quarrel.
    (*Cornwall draws his sword*)
                                What do you mean?
CORNWALL My villain!
    He lunges at him
FIRST SERVANT (*drawing his sword*)
  Nay then, come on, and take the chance of anger.
    He wounds Cornwall
REGAN
  Give me thy sword. A peasant stand up thus!
    She takes a sword and runs at him behind
FIRST SERVANT
  O, I am slain! My lord, you have one eye left   80
  To see some mischief on him. O!   *He dies*
CORNWALL
  Lest it see more, prevent it. Out, vile jelly!
  Where is thy lustre now?
GLOUCESTER
  All dark and comfortless. Where's my son Edmund?
  Edmund, enkindle all the sparks of nature
  To quit this horrid act.
REGAN   Out, treacherous villain!
  Thou call'st on him that hates thee. It was he
  That made the overture of thy treasons to us;
  Who is too good to pity thee.

GLOUCESTER

90   O my follies! Then Edgar was abused.

Kind gods, forgive me that and prosper him.

REGAN

Go thrust him out at gates and let him smell

His way to Dover.   *Exit a servant with Gloucester*

How is't, my lord? How look you?

CORNWALL

I have received a hurt. Follow me, lady.

Turn out that eyeless villain. Throw this slave

Upon the dunghill. Regan, I bleed apace.

Untimely comes this hurt. Give me your arm.

Exit Cornwall, supported by Regan

SECOND SERVANT

I'll never care what wickedness I do

If this man come to good.

THIRD SERVANT   If she live long,

100   And in the end meet the old course of death,

Women will all turn monsters.

SECOND SERVANT

Let's follow the old Earl, and get the Bedlam

To lead him where he would; his roguish madness

Allows itself to anything.

THIRD SERVANT

Go thou. I'll fetch some flax and whites of eggs

To apply to his bleeding face. Now heaven help him!

Exeunt by opposite doors

*

IV.1   *Enter Edgar*

EDGAR

Yet better thus, and known to be contemned,

Than still contemned and flattered. To be worst,
The lowest and most dejected thing of fortune,
Stands still in esperance, lives not in fear.
The lamentable change is from the best;
The worst returns to laughter. Welcome, then,
Thou unsubstantial air that I embrace!
The wretch that thou hast blown unto the worst
Owes nothing to thy blasts.

    Enter Gloucester, led by an Old Man

                    But who comes here?
My father, parti-eyed! World, world, O world!   10
But that thy strange mutations make us hate thee
Life would not yield to age.

OLD MAN   O my good lord,
I have been your tenant and your father's tenant
These fourscore years!

GLOUCESTER

Away! Get thee away! Good friend, be gone.
Thy comforts can do me no good at all;
Thee they may hurt.

OLD MAN   You cannot see your way.

GLOUCESTER

I have no way and therefore want no eyes;
I stumbled when I saw. Full oft 'tis seen
Our means secure us, and our mere defects   20
Prove our commodities. O dear son Edgar,
The food of thy abusèd father's wrath!
Might I but live to see thee in my touch
I'd say I had eyes again.

OLD MAN   How now? Who's there?

EDGAR (*aside*)

O gods! Who is't can say 'I am at the worst'?
I am worse than e'er I was.

OLD MAN   'Tis poor mad Tom.

EDGAR (*aside*)
> And worse I may be yet. The worst is not,
> So long as we can say 'This is the worst.'

OLD MAN
> Fellow, where goest?

GLOUCESTER   Is it a beggar-man?

30 OLD MAN Madman and beggar too.

GLOUCESTER
> He has some reason, else he could not beg.
> I'the last night's storm I such a fellow saw
> Which made me think a man a worm. My son
> Came then into my mind; and yet my mind
> Was then scarce friends with him. I have heard more since.
> As flies to wanton boys are we to the gods;
> They kill us for their sport.

EDGAR (*aside*)   How should this be?
> Bad is the trade that must play fool to sorrow,
> Angering itself and others. (*Aloud*) Bless thee, master!

GLOUCESTER
40 Is that the naked fellow?

OLD MAN   Ay, my lord.

GLOUCESTER
> Then prithee get thee away. If for my sake
> Thou wilt o'ertake us hence a mile or twain
> I'the way toward Dover, do it for ancient love,
> And bring some covering for this naked soul,
> Which I'll entreat to lead me.

OLD MAN   Alack, sir, he is mad.

GLOUCESTER
> 'Tis the time's plague when madmen lead the blind.
> Do as I bid thee, or rather do thy pleasure.
> Above the rest, begone.

OLD MAN
> I'll bring him the best 'parel that I have,

Come on't what will.   *Exit*

GLOUCESTER   Sirrah naked fellow!   50

EDGAR

Poor Tom's a-cold. (*Aside*) I cannot daub it further.

GLOUCESTER Come hither, fellow.

EDGAR (*aside*)

And yet I must. (*Aloud*) Bless thy sweet eyes, they bleed.

GLOUCESTER Knowest thou the way to Dover?

EDGAR Both stile and gate, horse-way and footpath, Poor
    Tom hath been scared out of his good wits. Bless thee,
    good man's son, from the foul fiend. Five fiends have
    been in Poor Tom at once: of lust, as Obidicut; Hob-
    bididence, prince of dumbness; Mahu, of stealing;
    Modo, of murder; Flibberdigibbet, of mopping and   60
    mowing, who since possesses chambermaids and
    waiting-women. So bless thee, master!

GLOUCESTER

Here, take this purse, thou whom the heavens' plagues
Have humbled to all strokes. That I am wretched
Makes thee the happier. Heavens deal so still!
Let the superfluous and lust-dieted man
That slaves your ordinance, that will not see
Because he does not feel, feel your power quickly!
So distribution should undo excess
And each man have enough. Dost thou know Dover?   70

EDGAR Ay, master.

GLOUCESTER

There is a cliff whose high and bending head
Looks fearfully in the confinèd deep;
Bring me but to the very brim of it
And I'll repair the misery thou dost bear
With something rich about me. From that place
I shall no leading need.

EDGAR   Give me thy arm;
　　Poor Tom shall lead thee.   *Exeunt*

IV.2   *Enter Gonerill and Edmund*
GONERILL
　　Welcome, my lord. I marvel our mild husband
　　Not met us on the way.
　　　　Enter Oswald
　　　　　　　　　　　　Now, where's your master?
OSWALD
　　Madam, within; but never man so changed.
　　I told him of the army that was landed.
　　He smiled at it. I told him you were coming.
　　His answer was 'The worse.' Of Gloucester's treachery
　　And of the loyal service of his son
　　When I informed him, then he called me sot
　　And told me I had turned the wrong side out.
10　What most he should dislike seems pleasant to him;
　　What like, offensive.
　　GONERILL (*to Edmund*) Then shall you go no further.
　　It is the cowish terror of his spirit
　　That dares not undertake. He'll not feel wrongs
　　Which tie him to an answer. Our wishes on the way
　　May prove effects. Back, Edmund, to my brother!
　　Hasten his musters and conduct his powers.
　　I must change arms at home and give the distaff
　　Into my husband's hands. This trusty servant
　　Shall pass between us; ere long you are like to hear,
20　If you dare venture in your own behalf,
　　A mistress's command. Wear this;
　　　　(*giving a favour*)   spare speech.
　　Decline your head; this kiss, if it durst speak,
　　Would stretch thy spirits up into the air.

Conceive; and fare thee well.

EDMUND
Yours in the ranks of death.

GONERILL   My most dear Gloucester!
                                        Exit Edmund

O, the difference of man and man!
To thee a woman's services are due;
A fool usurps my bed.

OSWALD   Madam, here comes my lord.
                                              Exit

        Enter Albany

GONERILL
I have been worth the whistling.

ALBANY   O Gonerill,
You are not worth the dust which the rude wind   30
Blows in your face. I fear your disposition:
That nature which contemns its origin
Cannot be bordered certain in itself.
She that herself will sliver and disbranch
From her material sap perforce must wither
And come to deadly use.

GONERILL No more; the text is foolish.

ALBANY
Wisdom and goodness to the vile seem vile;
Filths savour but themselves. What have you done,
Tigers not daughters, what have you performed?   40
A father, and a gracious agèd man,
Whose reverence even the head-lugged bear would lick,
Most barbarous, most degenerate, have you madded.
Could my good brother suffer you to do it?
A man, a prince, by him so benefited?
If that the heavens do not their visible spirits
Send quickly down to tame these vile offences,
It will come –

Humanity must perforce prey on itself
50 Like monsters of the deep.

GONERILL   Milk-livered man!
That bear'st a cheek for blows, a head for wrongs!
Who hast not in thy brows an eye discerning
Thine honour from thy suffering, that not knowest
Fools do those villains pity who are punished
Ere they have done their mischief. Where's thy drum?
France spreads his banners in our noiseless land,
With plumèd helm thy state begins to threat,
Whilst thou, a moral fool, sits still and cries
'Alack, why does he so?'

ALBANY   See thyself, devil!
60 Proper deformity shows not in the fiend
So horrid as in woman.

GONERILL   O vain fool!

ALBANY
Thou changèd and self-covered thing, for shame,
Be-monster not thy feature. Were't my fitness
To let these hands obey my blood,
They are apt enough to dislocate and tear
Thy flesh and bones. Howe'er thou art a fiend,
A woman's shape doth shield thee.

GONERILL Marry, your manhood! Mew!

        Enter a Messenger

ALBANY What news?

MESSENGER
70 O, my good lord, the Duke of Cornwall's dead,
Slain by his servant, going to put out
The other eye of Gloucester.

ALBANY   Gloucester's eyes?

MESSENGER
A servant that he bred, thrilled with remorse,
Opposed against the act, bending his sword

To his great master; who, thereat enraged,
Flew on him and amongst them felled him dead,
But not without that harmful stroke which since
Hath plucked him after.

ALBANY   This shows you are above,
You justicers, that these our nether crimes
So speedily can venge! But, O, poor Gloucester!   80
Lost he his other eye?

MESSENGER   Both, both, my lord.
This letter, madam, craves a speedy answer.
'Tis from your sister.

GONERILL (*aside*)   One way I like this well.
But being widow, and my Gloucester with her,
May all the building in my fancy pluck
Upon my hateful life. Another way
The news is not so tart. – (*Aloud*) I'll read and answer.

                                             Exit

ALBANY
Where was his son when they did take his eyes?

MESSENGER
Come with my lady hither.

ALBANY   He is not here.

MESSENGER
No, my good lord; I met him back again.   90

ALBANY Knows he the wickedness?

MESSENGER
Ay, my good lord. 'Twas he informed against him,
And quit the house on purpose that their punishment
Might have the freer course.

ALBANY   Gloucester, I live
To thank thee for the love thou show'dst the King
And to revenge thine eyes. Come hither, friend;
Tell me what more thou knowest.   *Exeunt*

IV.3   *Enter Kent and a Gentleman*

KENT Why the King of France is so suddenly gone back
    know you no reason?

GENTLEMAN Something he left imperfect in the state,
    which since his coming forth is thought of, which im-
    ports to the kingdom so much fear and danger that his
    personal return was most required and necessary.

KENT Who hath he left behind him general?

GENTLEMAN The Marshal of France, Monsieur La Far.

KENT Did your letters pierce the Queen to any demon-
10   stration of grief?

GENTLEMAN

    Ay, sir; she took them, read them in my presence,
    And now and then an ample tear trilled down
    Her delicate cheek. It seemed she was a queen
    Over her passion who, most rebel-like,
    Sought to be king o'er her.

KENT   O, then it moved her?

GENTLEMAN

    Not to a rage; patience and sorrow strove
    Who should express her goodliest. You have seen
    Sunshine and rain at once; her smiles and tears
    Were like a better way; those happy smilets
20   That played on her ripe lip seem not to know
    What guests were in her eyes, which parted thence
    As pearls from diamonds dropped. In brief,
    Sorrow would be a rarity most beloved
    If all could so become it.

KENT   Made she no verbal question?

GENTLEMAN

    Faith, once or twice she heaved the name of father
    Pantingly forth, as if it pressed her heart,
    Cried 'Sisters! Sisters! Shame of ladies! Sisters!
    Kent! Father! Sisters! – What, i'the storm? i'the night?

Let pity not be believed!' There she shook
The holy water from her heavenly eyes,   30
And clamour moistened; then away she started
To deal with grief alone.

KENT   It is the stars,
The stars above us govern our conditions.
Else one self mate and make could not beget
Such different issues. You spoke not with her since?

GENTLEMAN No.

KENT
Was this before the King returned?

GENTLEMAN   No, since.

KENT
Well, sir, the poor distressèd Lear's i'the town,
Who sometime in his better tune remembers
What we are come about, and by no means   40
Will yield to see his daughter.

GENTLEMAN   Why, good sir?

KENT
A sovereign shame so elbows him: his own unkindness
That stripped her from his benediction, turned her
To foreign casualties, gave her dear rights
To his dog-hearted daughters – these things sting
His mind so venomously that burning shame
Detains him from Cordelia.

GENTLEMAN   Alack, poor gentleman!

KENT
Of Albany's and Cornwall's powers you heard not?

GENTLEMAN 'Tis so. They are afoot.

KENT
Well, sir, I'll bring you to our master Lear   50
And leave you to attend him. Some dear cause
Will in concealment wrap me up awhile.
When I am known aright you shall not grieve

Lending me this acquaintance. I pray you
Go along with me.   *Exeunt*

IV.4   *Enter, with drum and colours, Cordelia, Doctor,*
              and soldiers

CORDELIA
    Alack, 'tis he! Why, he was met even now
    As mad as the vexed sea, singing aloud,
    Crowned with rank fumiter and furrow-weeds,
    With hardokes, hemlock, nettles, cuckoo-flowers,
    Darnel, and all the idle weeds that grow
    In our sustaining corn. (*To soldiers*) A century send forth;
    Search every acre in the high-grown field
    And bring him to our eye.   *Exeunt soldiers*
                    (*To Doctor*) What can man's wisdom
    In the restoring his bereavèd sense?
10 He that helps him, take all my outward worth.
DOCTOR
    There is means, madam.
    Our foster-nurse of nature is repose,
    The which he lacks; that to provoke in him
    Are many simples operative, whose power
    Will close the eye of anguish.
CORDELIA   All blest secrets,
    All you unpublished virtues of the earth,
    Spring with my tears! Be aidant and remediate
    In the good man's distress. Seek, seek for him,
    Lest his ungoverned rage dissolve the life
20 That wants the means to lead it.
                    Enter a Messenger
MESSENGER   News, madam:
    The British powers are marching hitherward.

CORDELIA
    'Tis known before. Our preparation stands
    In expectation of them. O dear father,
    It is thy business that I go about.
    Therefore great France
    My mourning and importuned tears hath pitied.
    No blown ambition doth our arms incite
    But love, dear love, and our aged father's right.
    Soon may I hear and see him!   *Exeunt*

    Enter Regan and Oswald   IV.5

REGAN
    But are my brother's powers set forth?
OSWALD   Ay, madam.
REGAN
    Himself in person there?
OSWALD   Madam, with much ado.
    Your sister is the better soldier.
REGAN
    Lord Edmund spake not with your lord at home?
OSWALD No, madam.
REGAN
    What might import my sister's letter to him?
OSWALD I know not, lady.
REGAN
    Faith, he is posted hence on serious matter.
    It was great ignorance, Gloucester's eyes being out,
    To let him live. Where he arrives he moves   10
    All hearts against us. Edmund, I think, is gone,
    In pity of his misery, to dispatch
    His nighted life — moreover to descry
    The strength o'th'enemy.

OSWALD

    I must needs after him, madam, with my letter.

REGAN

    Our troops set forth tomorrow; stay with us.
    The ways are dangerous.

OSWALD   I may not, madam.

    My lady charged my duty in this business.

REGAN

    Why should she write to Edmund? Might not you
20   Transport her purposes by word? Belike –
    Some things – I know not what – I'll love thee much –
    Let me unseal the letter.

OSWALD   Madam, I had rather –

REGAN

    I know your lady does not love her husband –
    I am sure of that – and at her late being here
    She gave strange œillades and most speaking looks
    To noble Edmund. I know you are of her bosom.

OSWALD I, madam?

REGAN

    I speak in understanding. Y'are; I know't.
    Therefore I do advise you take this note:
30   My lord is dead; Edmund and I have talked,
    And more convenient is he for my hand
    Than for your lady's. You may gather more.
    If you do find him, pray you give him this;
    And when your mistress hears thus much from you,
    I pray desire her call her wisdom to her.
    So fare you well.
    If you do chance to hear of that blind traitor,
    Preferment falls on him that cuts him off.

OSWALD

    Would I could meet him, madam! I should show

What party I do follow.

REGAN   Fare thee well.   *Exeunt*   40

Enter Gloucester and Edgar in peasant's clothes   IV.6

GLOUCESTER
  When shall I come to the top of that same hill?

EDGAR
  You do climb up it now. Look how we labour.

GLOUCESTER
  Methinks the ground is even.

EDGAR   Horrible steep.
  Hark, do you hear the sea?

GLOUCESTER   No, truly.

EDGAR
  Why then your other senses grow imperfect
  By your eyes' anguish.

GLOUCESTER   So may it be indeed.
  Methinks thy voice is altered, and thou speak'st
  In better phrase and matter than thou didst.

EDGAR
  Y'are much deceived. In nothing am I changed
  But in my garments.

GLOUCESTER   Methinks y'are better spoken.   10

EDGAR
  Come on, sir; here's the place. Stand still! How fearful
  And dizzy 'tis to cast one's eyes so low!
  The crows and choughs that wing the midway air
  Show scarce so gross as beetles. Halfway down
  Hangs one that gathers sampire – dreadful trade!
  Methinks he seems no bigger than his head.
  The fishermen that walk upon the beach
  Appear like mice, and yon tall anchoring bark
  Diminished to her cock; her cock, a buoy

20   Almost too small for sight. The murmuring surge
That on th'unnumbered idle pebble chafes
Cannot be heard so high. I'll look no more,
Lest my brain turn, and the deficient sight
Topple down headlong.

GLOUCESTER   Set me where you stand.

EDGAR

Give me your hand. You are now within a foot
Of th'extreme verge. For all beneath the moon
Would I not leap upright.

GLOUCESTER   Let go my hand.

Here, friend, 's another purse; in it a jewel
Well worth a poor man's taking. Fairies and gods
30   Prosper it with thee! Go thou further off.
Bid me farewell; and let me hear thee going.

EDGAR

Now fare ye well, good sir.

GLOUCESTER   With all my heart.

EDGAR (*aside*)

Why I do trifle thus with his despair
Is done to cure it.

GLOUCESTER (*kneeling*) O you mighty gods!
This world I do renounce, and in your sights
Shake patiently my great affliction off.
If I could bear it longer and not fall
To quarrel with your great opposeless wills,
My snuff and loathèd part of nature should
40   Burn itself out. If Edgar live, O bless him!
Now, fellow, fare thee well.

EDGAR   Gone, sir. Farewell.

    Gloucester throws himself forward

And yet I know not how conceit may rob
The treasury of life, when life itself
Yields to the theft. Had he been where he thought,

By this had thought been past. – Alive or dead?
Ho, you, sir! Friend! Hear you, sir? Speak! –
Thus might he pass indeed. Yet he revives –
What are you, sir?

GLOUCESTER   Away, and let me die.

EDGAR

Hadst thou been aught but gossamer, feathers, air,
So many fathom down precipitating,   50
Thou'dst shivered like an egg; but thou dost breathe,
Hast heavy substance, bleed'st not, speak'st, art sound.
Ten masts at each make not the altitude
Which thou hast perpendicularly fell.
Thy life's a miracle. Speak yet again.

GLOUCESTER But have I fallen or no?

EDGAR

From the dread summit of this chalky bourn.
Look up a-height. The shrill-gorged lark so far
Cannot be seen or heard. Do but look up.

GLOUCESTER

Alack, I have no eyes.   60
Is wretchedness deprived that benefit
To end itself by death? 'Twas yet some comfort
When misery could beguile the tyrant's rage
And frustrate his proud will.

EDGAR   Give me your arm.
Up – so. How is't? Feel you your legs? You stand.

GLOUCESTER

Too well, too well.

EDGAR   This is above all strangeness.
Upon the crown o'the cliff what thing was that
Which parted from you?

GLOUCESTER   A poor unfortunate beggar.

EDGAR

As I stood here below methought his eyes

70 Were two full moons; he had a thousand noses,
    Horns welked and waved like the enridgèd sea.
    It was some fiend. Therefore, thou happy father,
    Think that the clearest gods, who make them honours
    Of men's impossibilities, have preserved thee.

GLOUCESTER

    I do remember now. Henceforth I'll bear
    Affliction till it do cry out itself
    'Enough, enough', and die. That thing you speak of,
    I took it for a man; often 'twould say
    'The fiend, the fiend'; he led me to that place.

EDGAR

80 Bear free and patient thoughts.

    Enter Lear fantastically dressed with wild flowers
                                    But who comes here?
    The safer sense will ne'er accommodate
    His master thus.

LEAR No, they cannot touch me for coining. I am the
    King himself.

EDGAR O thou side-piercing sight!

LEAR Nature's above art in that respect. There's your
    press-money. — That fellow handles his bow like a crow-
    keeper. — Draw me a clothier's yard. — Look, look, a
    mouse! — Peace, peace! this piece of toasted cheese will
90 do't. — There's my gauntlet; I'll prove it on a giant. —
    Bring up the brown bills. — O, well flown, bird! I'the
    clout, i'the clout! Hewgh! — Give the word.

EDGAR Sweet marjoram.

LEAR Pass.

GLOUCESTER I know that voice.

    He falls to his knees

LEAR Ha! Gonerill with a white beard! They flattered me
    like a dog and told me I had the white hairs in my beard
    ere the black ones were there. To say 'ay' and 'no' to

everything that I said! 'Ay' and 'no' too was no good
divinity. When the rain came to wet me once and the   100
wind to make me chatter; when the thunder would not
peace at my bidding; there I found 'em, there I smelt
'em out. Go to, they are not men o'their words. They
told me I was everything. 'Tis a lie: I am not ague-
proof.

GLOUCESTER
    The trick of that voice I do well remember.
    Is't not the King?

LEAR   Ay, every inch a king.
    When I do stare see how the subject quakes.
    I pardon that man's life. What was thy cause?
    Adultery?   110
    Thou shalt not die. Die for adultery? No.
    The wren goes to't, and the small gilded fly
    Does lecher in my sight.
    Let copulation thrive; for Gloucester's bastard son
    Was kinder to his father than my daughters
    Got 'tween the lawful sheets.
    To't, luxury, pell-mell, for I lack soldiers.
    Behold yon simpering dame
    Whose face between her forks presages snow,
    That minces virtue and does shake the head   120
    To hear of pleasure's name –
    The fitchew nor the soilèd horse goes to't
    With a more riotous appetite.
    Down from the waist they are centaurs,
    Though women all above;
    But to the girdle do the gods inherit,
    Beneath is all the fiends' –
    There's hell, there's darkness, there is the sulphurous
    pit – burning, scalding, stench, consumption! Fie, fie,
    fie! Pah, pah! Give me an ounce of civet; good apothe-   130

cary, sweeten my imagination. There's money for
thee.

He gives flowers

GLOUCESTER O, let me kiss that hand!

LEAR Let me wipe it first; it smells of mortality.

GLOUCESTER

O ruined piece of nature! This great world
Shall so wear out to naught. Dost thou know me?

LEAR I remember thine eyes well enough. Dost thou
squiny at me? No, do thy worst, blind Cupid; I'll not
love. Read thou this challenge; mark but the penning

140 of it.

GLOUCESTER

Were all thy letters suns, I could not see.

EDGAR (*aside*)

I would not take this from report. It is;
And my heart breaks at it.

LEAR Read.

GLOUCESTER What, with the case of eyes?

LEAR O, ho, are you there with me? No eyes in your head,
nor no money in your purse? Your eyes are in a heavy
case, your purse in a light; yet you see how this world
goes.

150 GLOUCESTER I see it feelingly.

LEAR What, art mad? A man may see how this world goes
with no eyes. Look with thine ears. See how you justice
rails upon yon simple thief. Hark in thine ear – change
places and, handy-dandy, which is the justice, which is
the thief? Thou hast seen a farmer's dog bark at a
beggar?

GLOUCESTER Ay, sir.

LEAR And the creature run from the cur? There thou
mightst behold the great image of authority: a dog's

160 obeyed in office.

Thou rascal beadle, hold thy bloody hand.
Why dost thou lash that whore? Strip thy own back.
Thou hotly lusts to use her in that kind
For which thou whipp'st her. The usurer hangs the cozener.
Thorough tattered clothes great vices do appear;
Robes and furred gowns hide all. Plate sins with gold,
And the strong lance of justice hurtless breaks;
Arm it in rags, a pygmy's straw does pierce it.
None does offend, none, I say none; I'll able 'em.
Take that of me, my friend, (*giving flowers*) who have
    the power   170
To seal th'accusers' lips. Get thee glass eyes,
And like a scurvy politician seem
To see the things thou dost not. Now, now, now, now!
Pull off my boots. Harder, harder – so.

EDGAR

O matter and impertinency mixed,
Reason in madness!

LEAR

If thou wilt weep my fortunes, take my eyes.
I know thee well enough; thy name is Gloucester.
Thou must be patient; we came crying hither.
Thou knowest the first time that we smell the air   180
We wawl and cry. I will preach to thee – Mark!
   He takes off his coronet of flowers

GLOUCESTER Alack, alack the day!

LEAR

When we are born we cry that we are come
To this great stage of fools. – This's a good block.
It were a delicate stratagem to shoe
A troop of horse with felt. I'll put't in proof;
And when I have stolen upon these son-in-laws,
Then kill, kill, kill, kill, kill, kill!
   He throws down his flowers and stamps on them

Enter a Gentleman and two attendants. Gloucester
and Edgar draw back

GENTLEMAN

    O, here he is. Lay hand upon him. – Sir,

190   Your most dear daughter –

LEAR

    No rescue? What, a prisoner? I am even

    The natural fool of fortune. Use me well;

    You shall have ransom. Let me have surgeons;

    I am cut to the brains.

GENTLEMAN   You shall have anything.

LEAR

    No seconds? All myself?

    Why, this would make a man a man of salt,

    To use his eyes for garden water-pots,

    Ay, and laying autumn's dust. I will die bravely,

    Like a smug bridegroom. What! I will be jovial.

200   Come, come, I am a king; masters, know you that?

GENTLEMAN

    You are a royal one, and we obey you.

LEAR Then there's life in't. Come, and you get it you shall
get it by running. Sa, sa, sa, sa.

                   Exit running, followed by attendants

GENTLEMAN

    A sight most pitiful in the meanest wretch,

    Past speaking of in a king. – Thou hast one daughter

    Who redeems nature from the general curse

    Which twain have brought her to.

EDGAR (*coming forward*)

    Hail, gentle sir.

GENTLEMAN   Sir, speed you; what's your will?

EDGAR

    Do you hear aught, sir, of a battle toward?

GENTLEMAN

Most sure and vulgar. Everyone hears that   210
Which can distinguish sound.

EDGAR   But, by your favour,
How near's the other army?

GENTLEMAN

Near, and on speedy foot. The main descry
Stands on the hourly thought.

EDGAR   I thank you, sir; that's all.

GENTLEMAN

Though that the Queen on special cause is here,
Her army is moved on.

EDGAR   I thank you, sir.

Exit Gentleman

GLOUCESTER (*coming forward*)

You ever-gentle gods, take my breath from me.
Let not my worser spirit tempt me again
To die before you please.

EDGAR   Well pray you, father.

GLOUCESTER Now, good sir, what are you?   220

EDGAR

A most poor man made tame to fortune's blows,
Who, by the art of known and feeling sorrows,
Am pregnant to good pity. Give me your hand,
I'll lead you to some biding.

GLOUCESTER   Hearty thanks;
The bounty and the benison of heaven
To boot, and boot!

Enter Oswald

OSWALD   A proclaimed prize! Most happy!
That eyeless head of thine was first framed flesh
To raise my fortunes. Thou old unhappy traitor,
Briefly thyself remember; the sword is out
That must destroy thee.

230 GLOUCESTER   Now let thy friendly hand
   Put strength enough to't.
        Edgar intervenes

OSWALD   Wherefore, bold peasant,
   Darest thou support a published traitor? Hence,
   Lest that th'infection of his fortune take
   Like hold on thee. Let go his arm!

EDGAR
   'Chill not let go, zir, without vurther 'cagion.

OSWALD Let go, slave, or thou diest!

EDGAR Good gentleman, go your gate and let poor volk
   pass. And 'choud ha' bin zwaggered out of my life,
   'twould not ha' bin zo long as 'tis by a vortnight. Nay,
240 come not near th'old man; keep out, che vor' ye, or I'ce
   try whether your costard or my ballow be the harder.
   'Chill be plain with you.

OSWALD Out, dunghill!

EDGAR 'Chill pick your teeth, zir. Come; no matter vor
   your foins.
        They fight

OSWALD
   Slave, thou hast slain me. Villain, take my purse.
   If ever thou wilt thrive, bury my body
   And give the letters which thou find'st about me
   To Edmund, Earl of Gloucester. Seek him out
250 Upon the English party. O, untimely
   Death! – Death –   *He dies*

EDGAR
   I know thee well: a serviceable villain,
   As duteous to the vices of thy mistress
   As badness would desire.

GLOUCESTER   What, is he dead?

EDGAR
   Sit you down, father; rest you. –

Let's see these pockets. The letters that he speaks of
May be my friends. He's dead. I am only sorry
He had no other deathsman. Let us see.
Leave, gentle wax; and manners blame us not;
To know our enemies' minds we rip their hearts;   260
Their papers is more lawful.
　　(*He reads the letter*)
Let our reciprocal vows be remembered. You have many
opportunities to cut him off; if your will want not, time and
place will be fruitfully offered. There is nothing done if he
return the conqueror. Then am I the prisoner, and his bed
my gaol; from the loathed warmth whereof deliver me and
supply the place for your labour.
　　Your — wife, so I would say — affectionate servant,
　　　　　　　　　　　　　　　　　　　　Gonerill.

O indistinguished space of woman's will!   270
A plot upon her virtuous husband's life,
And the exchange, my brother! Here in the sands
Thee I'll rake up, the post unsanctified
Of murderous lechers; and in the mature time
With this ungracious paper strike the sight
Of the death-practised Duke. For him 'tis well
That of thy death and business I can tell.

GLOUCESTER
　　The King is mad; how stiff is my vile sense,
　　That I stand up and have ingenious feeling
　　Of my huge sorrows! Better I were distract;   280
　　So should my thoughts be severed from my griefs,
　　And woes by wrong imaginations lose
　　The knowledge of themselves.
　　　　Drum afar off
EDGAR　　　　　　　　　　　　Give me your hand.
　　Far off methinks I hear the beaten drum.
　　Come, father, I'll bestow you with a friend.   *Exeunt*

IV.7   *Enter Cordelia, Kent, and Doctor*

CORDELIA
    O thou good Kent, how shall I live and work
    To match thy goodness? My life will be too short
    And every measure fail me.

KENT
    To be acknowledged, madam, is o'er-paid.
    All my reports go with the modest truth,
    Nor more, nor clipped, but so.

CORDELIA   Be better suited.
    These weeds are memories of those worser hours.
    I prithee put them off.

KENT   Pardon, dear madam,
    Yet to be known shortens my made intent.
10 My boon I make it that you know me not
    Till time and I think meet.

CORDELIA
    Then be't so, my good lord.
                    (*To Doctor*) How does the King?

DOCTOR Madam, sleeps still.

CORDELIA
    O you kind gods,
    Cure this great breach in his abusèd nature!
    Th'untuned and jarring senses O wind up
    Of this child-changèd father.

DOCTOR   So please your majesty,
    That we may wake the King. He hath slept long.

CORDELIA
    Be governed by your knowledge and proceed
20 I'the sway of your own will. Is he arrayed?

DOCTOR
    Ay, madam; in the heaviness of sleep
    We put fresh garments on him.

        Enter Gentleman ushering Lear in a chair carried by
        servants. All fall to their knees

GENTLEMAN

   Be by, good madam, when we do awake him;

   I doubt not of his temperance.

CORDELIA   Very well.

   Music sounds offstage

DOCTOR

   Please you draw near. – Louder the music there!

CORDELIA (*kneeling by the chair and kissing his hand*)

   O my dear father! Restoration hang

   Thy medicine on my lips; and let this kiss

   Repair those violent harms that my two sisters

   Have in thy reverence made.

KENT   Kind and dear princess!

CORDELIA

   Had you not been their father, these white flakes   30

   Did challenge pity of them. Was this a face

   To be opposed against the jarring winds?

   To stand against the deep dread-bolted thunder,

   In the most terrible and nimble stroke

   Of quick cross lightning? To watch, poor perdu,

   With this thin helm? Mine enemy's dog,

   Though he had bit me, should have stood that night

   Against my fire; and wast thou fain, poor father,

   To hovel thee with swine and rogues forlorn

   In short and musty straw? Alack, alack!   40

   'Tis wonder that thy life and wits at once

   Had not concluded all. – He wakes! Speak to him.

DOCTOR Madam, do you; 'tis fittest.

CORDELIA

   How does my royal lord? How fares your majesty?

LEAR

   You do me wrong to take me out o'the grave.

   Thou art a soul in bliss; but I am bound

   Upon a wheel of fire, that mine own tears

    Do scald like molten lead.

CORDELIA   Sir, do you know me?

LEAR

    You are a spirit, I know. Where did you die?

50 CORDELIA Still, still far wide!

DOCTOR

    He's scarce awake. Let him alone awhile.

LEAR

    Where have I been? Where am I? Fair daylight?

    I am mightily abused. I should even die with pity

    To see another thus. I know not what to say.

    I will not swear these are my hands. Let's see.

    I feel this pin-prick. Would I were assured

    Of my condition.

CORDELIA   O look upon me, sir,

    And hold your hand in benediction o'er me.

     Lear falls to his knees

    No, sir, you must not kneel.

LEAR   Pray do not mock me.

60 I am a very foolish fond old man,

    Four score and upward, not an hour more nor less,

    And, to deal plainly,

    I fear I am not in my perfect mind.

    Methinks I should know you, and know this man;

    Yet I am doubtful; for I am mainly ignorant

    What place this is; and all the skill I have

    Remembers not these garments; nor I know not

    Where I did lodge last night. Do not laugh at me,

    For, as I am a man, I think this lady

70 To be my child Cordelia.

CORDELIA (*weeping*)   And so I am, I am.

LEAR

    Be your tears wet? Yes, faith! I pray, weep not.

    If you have poison for me I will drink it.

I know you do not love me, for your sisters
Have, as I do remember, done me wrong.
You have some cause; they have not.

CORDELIA   No cause, no cause.

LEAR
Am I in France?

KENT   In your own kingdom, sir.

LEAR Do not abuse me.

DOCTOR
Be comforted, good madam. The great rage,
You see, is killed in him; and yet it is danger
To make him even o'er the time he has lost.   80
Desire him to go in; trouble him no more
Till further settling.

CORDELIA   Will't please your highness walk?

LEAR You must bear with me. Pray you now, forget and
forgive. I am old and foolish.

Exeunt all but Kent and Gentleman

GENTLEMAN Holds it true, sir, that the Duke of Cornwall
was so slain?

KENT Most certain, sir.

GENTLEMAN Who is conductor of his people?

KENT As 'tis said, the bastard son of Gloucester.

GENTLEMAN They say Edgar, his banished son, is with   90
the Earl of Kent in Germany.

KENT Report is changeable. 'Tis time to look about. The
powers of the kingdom approach apace.

GENTLEMAN The arbitrament is like to be bloody. Fare
you well, sir.   *Exit*

KENT
My point and period will be throughly wrought,
Or well or ill, as this day's battle's fought.   *Exit*

*

V.I   *Enter, with drum and colours, Edmund, Regan,*
             gentlemen, and soldiers

EDMUND (*to a gentleman*)
    Know of the Duke if his last purpose hold
    Or whether since he is advised by aught
    To change the course. (*To Regan*) He's full of alteration
    And self-reproving. (*To gentleman*) Bring his constant
        pleasure.   *Exit gentleman*

REGAN
    Our sister's man is certainly miscarried.

EDMUND
    'Tis to be doubted, madam.

REGAN   Now, sweet lord,
    You know the goodness I intend upon you.
    Tell me but truly – but then speak the truth –
    Do you not love my sister?

EDMUND   In honoured love.

REGAN
10 But have you never found my brother's way
    To the forfended place?

EDMUND   That thought abuses you.

REGAN
    I am doubtful that you have been conjunct
    And bosomed with her, as far as we call hers.

EDMUND No, by mine honour, madam.

REGAN
    I never shall endure her; dear my lord,
    Be not familiar with her.

EDMUND   Fear not.
    She and the Duke her husband!

             Enter, with drum and colours, Albany, Gonerill, and
             soldiers

GONERILL (*aside*)
    I had rather lose the battle than that sister

Should loosen him and me.

ALBANY

Our very loving sister, well be-met.   20
Sir, this I heard; the King is come to his daughter,
With others whom the rigour of our state
Forced to cry out. Where I could not be honest,
I never yet was valiant. For this business,
It touches us as France invades our land,
Not bolds the King, with others – whom, I fear,
Most just and heavy causes make oppose.

EDMUND

Sir, you speak nobly.

REGAN   Why is this reasoned?

GONERILL

Combine together 'gainst the enemy.
For these domestic and particular broils   30
Are not the question here.

ALBANY   Let's then determine
With th'ancient of war on our proceeding.

EDMUND

I shall attend you presently at your tent.

REGAN Sister, you'll go with us?

GONERILL No.

REGAN

'Tis most convenient. Pray go with us.

GONERILL (aside)

O, ho, I know the riddle. (Aloud) I will go.

                                Exeunt both the armies

     As Albany is going out, enter Edgar

EDGAR

If e'er your grace had speech with man so poor,
Hear me one word.

ALBANY (to his captains) I'll overtake you.

                                (To Edgar) Speak.

EDGAR

40   Before you fight the battle, ope this letter.
    If you have victory, let the trumpet sound
    For him that brought it. Wretched though I seem,
    I can produce a champion that will prove
    What is avouchèd there. If you miscarry,
    Your business of the world hath so an end,
    And machination ceases. Fortune love you.

ALBANY

    Stay till I have read the letter.

EDGAR   I was forbid it.
    When time shall serve, let but the herald cry
    And I'll appear again.   *Exit*

ALBANY

50   Why, fare thee well. I will o'erlook thy paper.
        Enter Edmund

EDMUND

    The enemy's in view; draw up your powers.
    Here is the guess of their true strength and forces
    By diligent discovery; but your haste
    Is now urged on you.

ALBANY   We will greet the time.   *Exit*

EDMUND

    To both these sisters have I sworn my love;
    Each jealous of the other as the stung
    Are of the adder. Which of them shall I take?
    Both? One? Or neither? Neither can be enjoyed
    If both remain alive. To take the widow
60   Exasperates, makes mad, her sister Gonerill,
    And hardly shall I carry out my side,
    Her husband being alive. Now then, we'll use
    His countenance for the battle, which being done,
    Let her who would be rid of him devise
    His speedy taking off. As for the mercy

Which he intends to Lear and to Cordelia,
The battle done and they within our power,
Shall never see his pardon; for my state
Stands on me to defend, not to debate. *Exit*

Alarum within. Enter, with drum and colours, Lear,   V.2
Cordelia holding his hand, and soldiers, over the
stage, and exeunt
Enter Edgar and Gloucester

EDGAR

Here, father, take the shadow of this tree
For your good host. Pray that the right may thrive.
If ever I return to you again
I'll bring you comfort.

GLOUCESTER   Grace go with you, sir!

Exit Edgar

Alarum and retreat within. Enter Edgar

EDGAR

Away, old man! Give me thy hand; away!
King Lear hath lost; he and his daughter ta'en.
Give me thy hand; come on.

GLOUCESTER

No further, sir; a man may rot even here.

EDGAR

What, in ill thoughts again? Men must endure
Their going hence even as their coming hither;   10
Ripeness is all. Come on.

GLOUCESTER   And that's true too. *Exeunt*

V.3   *Enter in conquest with drum and colours Edmund;*
             Lear and Cordelia as prisoners; soldiers, Captain

EDMUND

      Some officers take them away. Good guard,
      Until their greater pleasures first be known
      That are to censure them.

CORDELIA   We are not the first
      Who with best meaning have incurred the worst.
      For thee, oppressèd King, I am cast down;
      Myself could else out-frown false Fortune's frown.
      (*To Edmund*)
      Shall we not see these daughters and these sisters?

LEAR

      No, no, no, no! Come, let's away to prison.
      We two alone will sing like birds i'the cage;
10   When thou dost ask me blessing I'll kneel down
      And ask of thee forgiveness; so we'll live,
      And pray, and sing, and tell old tales, and laugh
      At gilded butterflies, and hear poor rogues
      Talk of court news; and we'll talk with them too –
      Who loses and who wins, who's in, who's out –
      And take upon's the mystery of things
      As if we were God's spies; and we'll wear out,
      In a walled prison, packs and sects of great ones
      That ebb and flow by the moon.

EDMUND   Take them away.

LEAR

20   Upon such sacrifices, my Cordelia,
      The gods themselves throw incense. Have I caught thee?
          (*He embraces her*)
      He that parts us shall bring a brand from heaven
      And fire us hence like foxes. Wipe thine eyes;
      The good-years shall devour them, flesh and fell,

Ere they shall make us weep. We'll see 'em starved first.
Come.   *Exeunt Lear and Cordelia, guarded*

EDMUND

Come hither, captain. Hark.
Take thou this note; go follow them to prison.
One step I have advanced thee; if thou dost
As this instructs thee, thou dost make thy way   30
To noble fortunes. Know thou this, that men
Are as the time is; to be tender-minded
Does not become a sword; thy great employment
Will not bear question; either say thou'lt do't
Or thrive by other means.

CAPTAIN   I'll do't, my lord.

EDMUND

About it; and write happy when th' hast done.
Mark, I say 'instantly'; and carry it so
As I have set it down.

CAPTAIN

I cannot draw a cart nor eat dried oats;
If it be man's work, I'll do't.   *Exit*   40
    *Flourish. Enter Albany, Gonerill, Regan, and
    Officers*

ALBANY

Sir, you have showed today your valiant strain,
And Fortune led you well. You have the captives
Who were the opposites of this day's strife;
I do require them of you, so to use them
As we shall find their merits and our safety
May equally determine.

EDMUND   Sir, I thought it fit
To send the old and miserable King
To some retention and appointed guard;
Whose age had charms in it, whose title more,
To pluck the common bosom on his side   50

And turn our impressed lances in our eyes
Which do command them. With him I sent the Queen,
My reason all the same; and they are ready
Tomorrow or at further space t'appear
Where you shall hold your session. At this time
We sweat and bleed; the friend hath lost his friend,
And the best quarrels in the heat are cursed
By those that feel their sharpness.
The question of Cordelia and her father
60   Requires a fitter place.

ALBANY   Sir, by your patience,
I hold you but a subject of this war,
Not as a brother.

REGAN   That's as we list to grace him.
Methinks our pleasure might have been demanded
Ere you had spoke so far. He led our powers,
Bore the commission of my place and person,
The which immediacy may well stand up
And call itself your brother.

GONERILL   Not so hot!
In his own grace he doth exalt himself
More than in your addition.

REGAN   In my rights,
70   By me invested, he compeers the best.

ALBANY
That were the most if he should husband you.

REGAN
Jesters do oft prove prophets.

GONERILL   Holla, holla!
That eye that told you so looked but asquint.

REGAN
Lady, I am not well; else I should answer
From a full-flowing stomach. (*To Edmund*) General,
Take thou my soldiers, prisoners, patrimony,

Dispose of them, of me; the walls is thine.
Witness the world that I create thee here
My lord and master.

GONERILL   Mean you to enjoy him?

ALBANY

The let-alone lies not in your good will.   80

EDMUND

Nor in thine, lord.

ALBANY   Half-blooded fellow, yes.

REGAN (*to Edmund*)

Let the drum strike and prove my title thine.

ALBANY

Stay yet; hear reason. Edmund, I arrest thee
On capital treason, and, in thy attaint,
    (*he points to Gonerill*)
This gilded serpent. For your claim, fair sister,
I bar it in the interest of my wife.
'Tis she is sub-contracted to this lord,
And I her husband contradict your banns.
If you will marry, make your loves to me;
My lady is bespoke.

GONERILL   An interlude!   90

ALBANY

Thou art armed, Gloucester; let the trumpet sound.
If none appear to prove upon thy person
Thy heinous, manifest, and many treasons,
There is my pledge.
    He throws down his glove
                        I'll make it on thy heart,
Ere I taste bread, thou art in nothing less
Than I have here proclaimed thee.

REGAN   Sick, O sick!

GONERILL (*aside*)

If not, I'll ne'er trust medicine.

EDMUND (*throwing down his glove*)
> There's my exchange. What in the world he is
> That names me traitor, villain-like he lies.
> Call by the trumpet. He that dares approach,
> On him, on you – who not? – I will maintain
> My truth and honour firmly.

ALBANY   A herald, ho!

> *Enter a Herald*
>
> Trust to thy single virtue; for thy soldiers,
> All levied in my name, have in my name
> Took their discharge.

REGAN   My sickness grows upon me.

ALBANY
> She is not well. Convey her to my tent.

>   *Exit Regan, supported*
>
> Come hither, herald; let the trumpet sound,
> And read out this.

> *A trumpet sounds*

HERALD (*reading*) *If any man of quality or degree within the*
lists of the army will maintain upon Edmund, supposed
Earl of Gloucester, that he is a manifold traitor, let him
appear by the third sound of the trumpet. He is bold in his
defence.

> (*First trumpet*)
>
> Again!
>
> (*Second trumpet*)
>
> Again!
>
> *Third trumpet*
> *Trumpet answers within. Enter Edgar armed, a*
> *trumpet before him*

ALBANY
> Ask him his purposes, why he appears
> Upon this call o'the trumpet.

HERALD   What are you?

Your name, your quality, and why you answer
This present summons?

EDGAR   Know, my name is lost,
By treason's tooth bare-gnawn and canker-bit;   120
Yet am I noble as the adversary
I come to cope.

ALBANY   Which is that adversary?

EDGAR
What's he that speaks for Edmund, Earl of Gloucester?

EDMUND
Himself. What sayest thou to him?

EDGAR   Draw thy sword,
That if my speech offend a noble heart
Thy arm may do thee justice. Here is mine.
    He draws his sword
Behold; it is the privilege of mine honours,
My oath, and my profession. I protest,
Maugre thy strength, place, youth, and eminence,
Despite thy victor sword and fire-new fortune,   130
Thy valour and thy heart, thou art a traitor,
False to thy gods, thy brother, and thy father,
Conspirant 'gainst this high illustrious prince,
And, from th'extremest upward of thy head
To the descent and dust below thy foot,
A most toad-spotted traitor. Say thou 'no',
This sword, this arm, and my best spirits are bent
To prove upon thy heart, whereto I speak,
Thou liest.

EDMUND   In wisdom I should ask thy name;
But since thy outside looks so fair and warlike   140
And that thy tongue some 'say of breeding breathes,
What safe and nicely I might well delay
By rule of knighthood, I disdain and spurn.
Back do I toss these treasons to thy head,

With the hell-hated lie o'erwhelm thy heart,
Which, for they yet glance by and scarcely bruise,
This sword of mine shall give them instant way
Where they shall rest for ever. Trumpets, speak!

Alarums. Fights. Edmund falls

ALBANY (*to Edgar, about to kill Edmund*)
Save him, save him!

GONERILL   This is practice, Gloucester.
150   By the law of war thou wast not bound to answer
An unknown opposite. Thou art not vanquished,
But cozened and beguiled.

ALBANY   Shut your mouth, dame,
Or with this paper shall I stop it. – Hold, sir!
(*To Gonerill*)
Thou worse than any name, read thine own evil.
No tearing, lady! I perceive you know it.

GONERILL
Say if I do; the laws are mine, not thine.
Who can arraign me for't?

ALBANY   Most monstrous! O!
(*To Edmund*)
Knowest thou this paper?

EDMUND   Ask me not what I know.

Exit Gonerill

ALBANY
Go after her. She's desperate. Govern her.

Exit First Officer

EDMUND
160   What you have charged me with, that have I done,
And more, much more; the time will bring it out.
'Tis past; and so am I. But what art thou
That hast this fortune on me? If thou'rt noble,
I do forgive thee.

EDGAR   Let's exchange charity.

I am no less in blood than thou art, Edmund;
If more, the more th' hast wronged me.
My name is Edgar, and thy father's son.
The gods are just, and of our pleasant vices
Make instruments to plague us:
The dark and vicious place where thee he got   170
Cost him his eyes.

EDMUND   Th' hast spoken right. 'Tis true.
The wheel is come full circle; I am here.

ALBANY
Methought thy very gait did prophesy
A royal nobleness. I must embrace thee.
Let sorrow split my heart if ever I
Did hate thee or thy father.

EDGAR   Worthy prince,
I know't.

ALBANY   Where have you hid yourself?
How have you known the miseries of your father?

EDGAR
By nursing them, my lord. List a brief tale;
And when 'tis told, O that my heart would burst!   180
The bloody proclamation to escape
That followed me so near – O, our life's sweetness,
That we the pain of death would hourly die
Rather than die at once – taught me to shift
Into a madman's rags, t'assume a semblance
That very dogs disdained; and in this habit
Met I my father with his bleeding rings,
Their precious stones new lost; became his guide,
Led him, begged for him, saved him from despair,
Never – O fault! – revealed myself unto him   190
Until some half hour past, when I was armed,
Not sure, though hoping, of this good success,
I asked his blessing, and from first to last

Told him my pilgrimage; but his flawed heart —
Alack, too weak the conflict to support —
'Twixt two extremes of passion, joy and grief,
Burst smilingly.

EDMUND   This speech of yours hath moved me,
And shall perchance do good. But speak you on;
You look as you had something more to say.

ALBANY

200   If there be more, more woeful, hold it in;
For I am almost ready to dissolve,
Hearing of this.

EDGAR   This would have seemed a period
To such as love not sorrow; but another
To amplify too much would make much more
And top extremity.
Whilst I was big in clamour, came there in a man,
Who, having seen me in my worst estate,
Shunned my abhorred society; but then finding
Who 'twas that so endured, with his strong arms

210   He fastened on my neck and bellowed out
As he'd burst heaven, threw him on my father,
Told the most piteous tale of Lear and him
That ever ear received; which in recounting
His grief grew puissant, and the strings of life
Began to crack. Twice then the trumpets sounded,
And there I left him tranced.

ALBANY   But who was this?

EDGAR

Kent, sir, the banished Kent, who, in disguise,
Followed his enemy king and did him service
Improper for a slave.

          Enter a Gentleman with a bloody knife

GENTLEMAN

220   Help, help! O, help!

EDGAR   What kind of help?

ALBANY   Speak, man.

EDGAR

What means this bloody knife?

GENTLEMAN   'Tis hot; it smokes!

It came even from the heart of – O, she's dead!

ALBANY Who dead? Speak, man.

GENTLEMAN

Your lady, sir; your lady! And her sister

By her is poisoned; she confesses it.

EDMUND

I was contracted to them both. All three

Now marry in an instant.

EDGAR   Here comes Kent.

   Enter Kent

ALBANY

Produce the bodies, be they alive or dead.

                    Exit Gentleman

This judgement of the heavens that makes us tremble

Touches us not with pity. (*To Kent*) O, is this he?   230

The time will not allow the compliment

Which very manners urges.

KENT   I am come

To bid my King and master aye good night.

Is he not here?

ALBANY   Great thing of us forgot.

Speak, Edmund, where's the King? and where's Cordelia?

   Gonerill's and Regan's bodies are brought out

See'st thou this object, Kent?

KENT

Alack, why thus?

EDMUND   Yet Edmund was beloved.

The one the other poisoned for my sake

And after slew herself.

240   ALBANY Even so. Cover their faces.

EDMUND

     I pant for life; some good I mean to do
     Despite of mine own nature. Quickly send –
     Be brief in it – to the castle, for my writ
     Is on the life of Lear and on Cordelia.
     Nay, send in time!

ALBANY   Run, run, O run!

EDGAR

     To who, my lord? Who has the office? Send
     Thy token of reprieve.

EDMUND

     Well thought on. (*To Second Officer*) Take my sword,
     Give it the captain.

EDGAR   Haste thee for thy life.

                           Exit Second Officer

EDMUND

250   He hath commission from thy wife and me
     To hang Cordelia in the prison, and
     To lay the blame upon her own despair,
     That she fordid herself.

ALBANY

     The gods defend her. Bear him hence awhile.

                       Edmund is borne off
     Enter Lear with Cordelia in his arms, followed by
     Second Officer and others

LEAR

     Howl, howl, howl! O, you are men of stones!
     Had I your tongues and eyes I'd use them so
     That heaven's vault should crack. She's gone for ever.
     I know when one is dead and when one lives;
     She's dead as earth. Lend me a looking-glass;
260   If that her breath will mist or stain the stone,
     Why then she lives.

KENT   Is this the promised end?

EDGAR

Or image of that horror?

ALBANY   Fall and cease!

LEAR

This feather stirs – she lives! If it be so,
It is a chance which does redeem all sorrows
That ever I have felt.

KENT   O my good master!

LEAR

Prithee away.

EDGAR   'Tis noble Kent, your friend.

LEAR

A plague upon you, murderers, traitors all!
I might have saved her; now she's gone for ever.
Cordelia, Cordelia, stay a little. Ha!
What is't thou sayest? Her voice was ever soft,   270
Gentle and low – an excellent thing in woman.
I killed the slave that was a-hanging thee.

SECOND OFFICER

'Tis true, my lords; he did.

LEAR   Did I not, fellow?

I have seen the day, with my good biting falchion
I would have made him skip. I am old now
And these same crosses spoil me. – Who are you?
Mine eyes are not o'the best, I'll tell you straight.

KENT

If Fortune brag of two she loved and hated
One of them we behold.

LEAR

This is a dull sight. Are you not Kent?

KENT   The same –   280

Your servant Kent. Where is your servant Caius?

LEAR

    He's a good fellow, I can tell you that;

    He'll strike, and quickly too. He's dead and rotten.

KENT

    No, my good lord; I am the very man –

LEAR I'll see that straight.

KENT

    That from your first of difference and decay

    Have followed your sad steps –

LEAR   You are welcome hither.

KENT

    Nor no man else. All's cheerless, dark, and deadly.

    Your eldest daughters have fordone themselves,

290   And desperately are dead.

LEAR   Ay, so I think.

ALBANY

    He knows not what he sees, and vain is it

    That we present us to him.

EDGAR   Very bootless.

    Enter a Messenger

MESSENGER

    Edmund is dead, my lord.

ALBANY   That's but a trifle here.

    You lords and noble friends, know our intent:

    What comfort to this great decay may come

    Shall be applied. For us, we will resign

    During the life of this old majesty

    To him our absolute power.

    (*To Edgar and Kent*)   You to your rights

    With boot, and such addition as your honours

300   Have more than merited. All friends shall taste

    The wages of their virtue, and all foes

    The cup of their deservings. – O, see, see!

LEAR

    And my poor fool is hanged! No, no, no life!

    Why should a dog, a horse, a rat have life,

    And thou no breath at all? Thou'lt come no more;

    Never, never, never, never, never.

    Pray you undo this button. Thank you, sir.

    Do you see this? Look on her! Look, her lips!

    Look there! Look there!   *He dies*

EDGAR   He faints. My lord, my lord!

KENT

    Break, heart; I prithee break.

EDGAR   Look up, my lord.   310

KENT

    Vex not his ghost. O, let him pass. He hates him

    That would upon the rack of this tough world

    Stretch him out longer.

EDGAR   He is gone indeed.

KENT

    The wonder is he hath endured so long.

    He but usurped his life.

ALBANY

    Bear them from hence. Our present business

    Is general woe.

    (*To Kent and Edgar*)

                Friends of my soul, you twain,

    Rule in this realm, and the gored state sustain.

KENT

    I have a journey, sir, shortly to go.

    My master calls me, I must not say no.   320

EDGAR

    The weight of this sad time we must obey;

    Speak what we feel, not what we ought to say.

    The oldest hath borne most; we that are young

    Shall never see so much nor live so long.

                    Exeunt with a dead march

An Account of the Text

The great difficulty in establishing an acceptable text for *King Lear* arises from the duplication of evidence, an embarrassment of witnesses whose credentials can be investigated but not finally tested. The text appears in two separate definitive editions, in the first Folio (1623; referred to here and in the Commentary as F) of Shakespeare's plays and in a quarto (small format) text of 1608 (referred to as Q): *M. William Shakespeare his True Chronicle History of the life and death of King Lear and his three daughters. With the unfortunate life of Edgar, son and heir to the Earl of Gloucester, and his sullen and assumed humour of Tom of Bedlam.* The title page goes on to tell us that it is printed 'as it was played before the King's Majesty at Whitehall upon S. Stephen's night in Christmas holidays' – that is, on 26 December. The year must have been 1606, for the text was entered in the Register of the Stationers' Company on 26 November 1607, with the same title as above, and naming the same occasion of performance.

The entry may have been official but the consensus view among textual critics has been, for most of the twentieth century, that the 1608 Quarto is in some sense a 'bad' quarto – one of those texts not supplied to the publisher by the acting company but obtained for publication by some more oblique method. In this sense it can be counted as one of the 'divers stolen and surreptitious copies' against which the editors of the first Folio warned their readers '. . . where before you were abused with divers stolen and surreptitious copies, maimed and deformed by the frauds and stealths of injurious imposters that exposed them, even those are now offered to your view cured and perfect of their limbs, and all the rest absolute in their numbers [that is, versification] as he conceived them'. This is, of course, advertising copy rather than fact, but (as in the best advertising copy) there is a grain of truth in it. The theatrical companies were always anxious to avoid premature publication of works whose value was enhanced by the theatres' monopoly. After about 1600 Shakespeare's company seems to have been very effective in preventing good copies of his plays from reaching print. The printers, however, retained their appetite for Shakespearian texts, and a small number of these (five in total) reached print. In all these cases it looks as if the route to the printing-house was an illicit one. But that is not in itself a reason to suppose that a text so printed lacks authenticity.

Certainly, at a first glance, the 1608 *King Lear* seems to show signs of the deterioration one would associate with underhand procurement: lines cobbled together clumsily, verse collapsed into prose, prose turned into verse, sharp phrasings rendered as commonplace ones. An extreme example of the difference between Quarto and Folio can be seen in the last lines that Lear speaks in the play. These are printed in the Folio as

> Do you see this? Looke on her? Looke her lips
> Looke there, looke there

The same moment is represented in the Quarto more simply, as

> O,o,o,o.

Yet it would be easy to exaggerate the badness of this Quarto. It cannot be regarded simply as a botched version of the F text: it contains some 300 lines not in the Folio (and the Folio in turn contains some 100 lines not in the Quarto). The explanatory hypothesis that is needed is one that will account for both its 'badness' and its 'goodness', both its importance as a source of apparently genuine Shakespearian readings and the presence of the film of corruption that so obviously distorts what it presents. The first serious attempt to deal with this issue in terms of Elizabethan theatrical practice derived from work by W. W. Greg and other members of 'The New Bibliography' movement (see

F. P. Wilson, *Shakespeare and the New Bibliography* (1970)). These
men found theatrical manuscripts subject to degeneration when
the actors (for one reason or another) sought to supply the text
of a play whose prompt book was not available; among the
corruptions were some that seemed to derive from mishearings
rather than misreadings, as if based on the memories of actors
rather than a sight of the script. Since this characteristic appears
also in Q *King Lear* – 'in sight' for 'insight', 'have' for 'of',
'dogge so bade' for 'dog's obeyed' – there is an initial presump-
tion that this also is a text in which hearing has played a part in
the transmission. If it was the actors who supplied the publishers
with a text reconstructed in this way, it could hardly have been
the main actors, the patented shareholders, for they were the very
people with the greatest interest in retaining copyright. It has
been pointed out that the errors that seem to derive from memory
rather than misreading in the 1608 *King Lear* are concentrated
on a small number of scenes; other scenes (for example, III.4, 5,
6) are too accurate to be the result of mere memory. Dr Alice
Walker suggests that the two boy actors who played Gonerill and
Regan were (appropriately enough) the agents who betrayed the
text to the mutilations of the printer. They did this, it is suggested,
by reciting the scenes in which they appeared, and by copying
the rest from the author's rough draft or 'foul papers' at such
times as they could catch a glimpse of them. There is evidence
that these 'foul papers' were preserved, probably as second copies,
in case the prompt book should be lost. The disadvantage of this
view is that it requires the invention of two unprovable
hypotheses, thus squaring the difficulty.

The version of the play produced by this or some other method
seems to have created grave problems for the printer who set it
up in type. The manuscript must have been difficult to read,
imposing a continuous struggle to get the readings right, or even
plausible, and eventually there had to be wholesale resettings.
The first sheet (eight pages) is, in the twelve surviving copies,
without corrections (though not without errors). But thereafter
the Quarto shows a scattering of about 146 substantive variant
readings. Most of these were corrections made, it should be noted,
while the press continued in operation, so that corrected pages
on one side of the sheet are (in about half of the cases) matched

with uncorrected pages on the other side. This leaves modern scholarship with the task of discriminating those words that reflect a rereading of the manuscript from those that reflect the common sense of the printer, his desire to do no more than turn out a neat and intelligible piece of work. Of the 146 substantive 'corrections' that Greg discusses in his account of the variants, some certainly show the printer returning to the manuscript. The uncorrected version of II.4.126 reads

I would deuose me from thy mothers fruit

The corrector turns this into

I would diuorse me from thy mothers tombe,

which obviously derives from something more than a clever guess.

On the other hand, the corrector often indulged in mere guesswork, as when he changed 'deptoued' (II.4.132) to 'depriued' instead of the obviously authentic reading, 'deprau'd', found in the Folio, or when he curtailed the meaningless 'battero' to 'bat' instead of going to the manuscript and discovering the strange word 'ballow' (as printed in F). It should be noted that the practice of the time makes it very improbable that Shakespeare himself had anything to do with the printing process.

However depraved the 1608 Quarto might be from a company point of view, the company-backed printers of the first Folio still found it convenient to use the Quarto as the basis for the new version they were offering to the public as 'cured and perfect of [its] limbs'. (In fact it now seems probable that the basic copy was a second quarto, reprinted from the first, and also dated 1608 but actually printed in 1619, as part of an effort to make an unauthorized collection of Shakespeare's plays). Before it got to the printer's shop this copy must have been annotated with corrections, taken, no doubt, from the playhouse originals. The company thus fulfilled their duty to 'our Shakespeare', without losing control of the official prompt copy, bearing the licence to perform.

There can be no argument that the new material incorporated in the Folio text greatly improved its intelligibility: prose was reassembled as verse and nonsense as sense. One's pleasure in the restoration is, however, limited by a number of factors. The text which supplied the corrections was presumably that in current theatrical use in 1622. That may have been the same one as was used in 1605, or it may have been affected by theatrical modifications. We know that plays were revised to keep up with shifts in theatrical fashion, but it is hard to align the changes between Q and F with any such movement. One whole scene (IV.3) is missing in F. There is recurrent evidence of a desire to simplify the staging. In IV.7 both the music and the doctor are gone, the latter replaced (as in IV.4) by an easier-to-use 'Gentleman'. The invasion of Britain by France is largely concealed, though this may reflect censorship rather than theatrical cutting. Censorship may be suspected on two other occasions, in the removal of I.2.143–9 – the account of prophecies to be fulfilled (including maledictions against king and nobles) – and of I.4.138–53, in which the king is called a 'fool' and reference is made to the greed of 'great men' for monopolies. Many cuts seem designed only to make the play shorter. Passages like II.6.100–113 and V.3.202–19, may seem indispensable to the modern reader, but the play as a theatrical structure will hang together perfectly well without them.

Another reason for reserve about the F text derives from the fact that it was set up by two of the more incompetent compositors in the printing-house, one an apprentice and the other a careless journeyman. There is evidence of their eyes and their minds wandering from the line in hand. Thus 'pregnant and potential spurs' (II.1.75) is misprinted in the Folio 'pregnant and potentiall spirits', probably because the compositor's eye caught the '-its' ending of 'profits' in the line before.

Lastly, in *King Lear* as throughout its length, the Folio is concerned to express its material in up-to-date and 'correct' English, or even in that kind of English that the individual compositor preferred. A number of the new readings in F may be attributed to this rather than to the recovery of truly Shakespearian readings. The substitution of 'squints' (III.4.112) for 'squenies' (printed as 'squemes' in the Quarto) may well be of this kind, like 'sticke' for 'rash' at III.7.57 or 'sterne' for 'dern' at III.7.62. In smaller things modernization is probably

commoner and more difficult to detect, but examples I assume
are 'yond' for 'yon' (IV.6.18, 118, and 152) and 'if' for 'and'
(II.2.42).

The Quarto is quite without indications of act and scene divisions. In this it follows the common form of early play publication. The Folio, on the other hand, sets out the enumeration of
acts and scenes with great clarity and exactitude. It need not be
supposed that the enumeration reflects Shakespeare's precise
intention; it is rather part of the later literary and even classical
polish applied to the plays. But it is a rational convenience, and
like all modern editors I follow F except in three instances. In
Act II *'Actus Secundus, Scena Prima'* is marked, and then *'Scena
Secunda'*, but the third and fourth scenes of Act II in the modern
division are not marked. It could be argued that Kent is present
on the stage (in the stocks) continuously from II.2 to II.4 and
that the Folio recognizes this in its scene division – it does not
give Kent an exit at II.2.171. This is possible, but it does
not correspond with normal Elizabethan dramaturgy. Act II,
scene 3 is delocalized and separate, whether Kent is on the stage
or not. The other place where the Folio misleads is in Act IV,
where the F text omits IV.3. It follows that scenes 4, 5 and 6 of
this act are misnumbered as 3, 4 and 5. Act IV, scene 7 is, however,
correctly described (*'Scena Septima'*); this suggests that someone
discovered the error during the printing of the Folio, avoided a
continuation of it, but did not correct the instances already
perpetrated.

The present text is based on the Folio; but all the variants to
be discovered in the Quarto (corrected and uncorrected) have
been considered, and have been admitted if a good enough argument for their superiority could be discovered. Where the Folio
has been printed from the uncorrected state of the Quarto, I have
treated the corrected readings (where these are not duplicated by
the Folio corrector) as primary authority. A list of the places
where the Quarto has been preferred to the Folio is given below
(list 1). I also give a list of places where neither Q nor F is accepted
(stage directions excluded). The third list is of stage directions.
It should be noted that I have assumed a higher degree of
authority for the Quarto in stage directions than in text. If Q
represents memories of a theatrical performance, then it is likely

to be more accurate in describing what happened on the stage than in giving the detail of what was spoken. The two texts often differ in the kind of directions they give. F, as a company text, is not interested in stage directions except where props (the stocks, the thunder machine, trumpets) are concerned, or where persons are to be got on and off the stage. Q on the other hand is more concerned with description and less with business, but only at two points – the fall at 'Dover Cliff', and the fight between Edgar and Oswald – is substantive stage action described which is wholly omitted by the Folio. Both texts leave many important and significant stage actions undescribed, and so I have been fairly free with additional directions, as collation list 3 will show. I assume that this is a play in which the physical relationship of person to person and the range of significant gesture are very important, and often (especially in the scenes of folly and madness) far from obvious. In the elaborately scored scenes in the middle of the play it is sometimes difficult to discover which person is being addressed, and I have sought to clarify this in the stage directions.

The last collation lists 'rejected readings' and will enable the reader to see some ways in which the present text differs from others. It will be seen that it follows the Folio in more places than its contemporaries. The history of modern texts of *King Lear* is (with some exceptions) a history of drift from Quarto to Folio. The old 'Cambridge' text of Clark and Wright (1891), the foundation of modern textual scholarship, differs from the present text in over 260 substantive readings (not including lineation and stage directions). Most of these variants derive from the substitution of Folio for Quarto readings; the greater obviousness of the former's vocabulary often makes it seem 'safer' or 'more probable', especially in the absence of a general theory of the relationship of the texts. Readings that appear to be unusual if not unique among modern texts appear at I.1.5 and 70, I.5.46, II.1.8 and 119, III.6.22, IV.1.10, IV.3.20, IV.7.21, 23 and 53, V.1.16, V.3.158 and 275.

In the text I have normalized the speech-prefixes, preferring 'Edmund' to 'Bastard' (the commoner form in Q and F) and 'Oswald' to 'Steward' (the standard form in Q and F). I have kept the F form 'Gonerill' (Q has 'Gonorill') since I know of no relevant authority by which to correct it. I have also preferred F's 'Albany' and 'Corn[e]wall' to Q's 'Duke', and F's 'Gloucester' to Q's 'Gloster', though I accept that 'Gloucester' may reflect only Folio modernization.

COLLATIONS

Quotations from Q and F are given in the original spelling, except that 'long s' (ſ) has been replaced by 's'.

ι

Readings accepted from Q, with substantive alternatives from F which have been rejected (given as the final element in each entry).

I.1

   35 liege] Lord
   74 possesses] professes
 104 To love my father all] *omitted*
 149 stoops] falls
 155 a pawn] pawne
 156 nor fear] nere feare
 168 vow] vowes
 188 GLOUCESTER] (*Glost.*); *Cor.*
 214 best object] obiect
 225 well] will
 241 Lear] King
 289 not been] beene
 302 hit] sit

I.2

 41–2 *prose*] *verse* (. . . it: | . . . them, | . . . blame)
  55 waked] wake
 95–7 EDMUND Nor is . . . earth] *omitted*
 127 disposition to] disposition on
 130 Fut] *omitted*
 132 Edgar] *omitted*
 143–9 as of . . . astronomical] *omitted*

I.3

17–21 Not to . . . abused] (*prose in* Q); *omitted*

25–6 I would . . . speak] (*prose in* Q); *omitted*

27 very] *omitted*

I.4

98 KENT Why, Fool] *Lear.* Why my Boy

138–53 That lord . . . snatching] *omitted*

158 thy crown] thy Crownes

174 fools] Foole

193 crust nor] crust, not

228–31 LEAR I would . . . father] *omitted*

254 O . . . come] *omitted*

301 Yea . . . this] *omitted*

II.1

2–4 *prose*] *verse* (. . . bin | . . . notice | . . . Duchesse | . . . night)

2 you] your

10–11 *prose*] *verse* (. . . toward, | . . . Albany)

52 But] And

69 I should] should I

70 ay, though] though

75 spurs] spirits

77 I never got him] *omitted*

78 why] wher

86 strange news] strangenesse

119 price] (*uncorrected*: prise; *corrected*: poyse); prize

II.2

42 and] if

76 Renege] Reuenge

128 respect] respects

139–43 His fault . . . with] *omitted*

143 The King] The King his Master, needs

148 For . . . legs] *omitted*

149 Come] *Corn.* Come

II.3

15 mortified bare arms] mortified Armes

II.4

18–19 LEAR No, no . . . have] *omitted*

30 panting] painting

     33 whose] those
   181 fickle] fickly
   295 bleak] high

III.1

   7–15 tears . . . take all] *omitted*
  30–42 But true . . . to you] *omitted*

III.2

    3 drowned] drown

III.4

   12 this] (*corrected*; *uncorrected*: the); the
   51 ford] Sword
   87 I deeply] I deerely
  110 foul fiend] foule
  111 till the first] at first
  128 stock-punished] stockt, punish'd
  129 hath had] hath

III.5

   9 letter he] Letter which hee
  24 dearer] deere

III.6

 17–55 EDGAR The foul . . . 'scape] *omitted*
  69 tike] tight
  76 makes] make
 95–9 KENT Oppressèd . . . behind. GLOUCESTER] *omitted*
100–113 EDGAR When we . . . lurk] *omitted*

III.7

  57 rash] sticke
  62 dern] sterne
98–106 SECOND SERVANT I'll never . . . help him] *omitted*

IV.1

  10 parti-eyed] (*corrected*; *uncorrected*: poorlie, leed);
      poorely led
  41 Then prithee] *omitted*
 57–62 Five fiends . . . master] *omitted*

IV.2

  17 arms] names
  28 A fool] (*corrected*; *uncorrected*: My foote); My Foole
     bed] (*corrected*; *uncorrected*: body); body
  29 whistling] (*corrected*; *uncorrected*: whistle); whistle

31–50 I fear . . . deep] *omitted*
53–9 that not . . . he so] *omitted*
60 shows] (*corrected; uncorrected:* seemes); seemes
62–9 ALBANY Thou . . . news] *omitted*
75 threat] threat
79 justicers] (*corrected; uncorrected:* Iustices); Iustices

IV.3
1–55 KENT Why . . . me] *omitted*

IV.4
11 DOCTOR] *Gent.*
18 distress] desires

IV.5
39 meet him] meet

IV.6
18, 118, 152 yon] yond
71 enridgèd] enraged
83 coining] crying
134 *prose*] *two lines* (. . . first, | . . . Mortality)
198 Ay . . . dust] *omitted*
205 one] a

IV.7
13, 17, 21, 43, 51, 78 DOCTOR] *Gent.* (or *Gen.*)
23 GENTLEMAN] *omitted*
24 doubt not] doubt
24–5 Very . . . there] *omitted*
33–6 To stand . . . helm] *omitted*
59 No, sir,] *omitted*
79–80 and yet . . . lost] (*prose in* Q); *omitted*
85–97 GENTLEMAN Holds . . . fought] *omitted*

V.1
11–13 EDMUND That . . . hers] *omitted*
18–19 GONERILL I had . . . me] (*prose in* Q); *omitted*
23–8 Where . . . nobly] *omitted*
33 EDMUND I shall . . . tent] *omitted*
46 love] loues

V.3
39–40 CAPTAIN I cannot . . . do't] *omitted*
48 and appointed guard] (*corrected; uncorrected omits*); *omitted*

55–60 At this time . . . place] *omitted*
    84 attaint] arrest
   127 it is the priviledge] it is my priuiledge, | The
        priuiledge
   194 my] our
202–19 EDGAR This would . . . slave] *omitted*
   291 sees] saies

2

Emendations incorporated in the present text (not including stage
directions, or variants judged to derive from spelling rather than
meaning, or from the obvious correction of obvious error).

The Characters in the Play] *not in* Q, F
I.1
   110 mysteries] mistresse Q; miseries F
283–5 *verse in* Q, F (. . . say, | . . . both, | . . . to night)
I.2
    21 top the] tooth' Q; to'th' F
I.3
 23–7 *prose in* Q, F
I.4
211–13 *prose in* Q, F
252–3 *prose in* Q, F
   302 Let] Ha? Let F; *not in* Q
   340 a-taxed for] alapt Q *uncorrected*; attaskt for Q
        corrected; at task for F
I.5
 44–5 *prose in* Q, F
    46 KNIGHT] *Gent.* F; *Seruant.* Q
II.2
 45–6 *prose in* Q, F
   141 contemned'st] contaned Q *uncorrected*; temnest Q
        corrected; *not in* F
II.4
    55 Hysterica] *Historica* Q, F
    73 ha' . . . use] haue . . . follow Q; hause . . . follow F

III.1

> 10 out-storm] outscorne Q; *not in* F

III.2

> 85–6 Then shall . . . confusion] *placed after* build (*line* 92)
> *in* F; *not in* Q

III.4

> 45 *prose in* Q, F
>   blow the cold winds] blowes the cold wind Q;
>   blow the windes F
> 60 What, has his] What, his Q; Ha's his F
> 73 *prose in* Q, F
> 95–6 *prose in* Q, F
> 112 squenies] queues Q *uncorrected*; squemes Q *corrected*;
>   squints F
> 138–9 *prose in* Q, F

III.6

> 21 justicer] Iustice Q; *not in* F
> 24–5 madam? | Come . . . me] madam come . . . mee Q;
>   *not in* F
> 25 burn] broome Q; *not in* F
> 33–4 *prose in* Q; *not in* F
> 47 she kicked] kickt Q; *not in* F
> 68 lym] him Q; Hym F
> 99–101 *prose in* Q; *not in* F

III.7

> 44–5 *prose in* Q, F
> 99–101 *prose in* Q; *not in* F
> 105–6 *prose in* Q; *not in* F

IV.1

> 60 Flibberdigibbet] *Stiberdigebit* Q; *not in* F

IV.2

> 32 its origin] it origin Q *uncorrected*; ith origin Q
>   *corrected*; *not in* F
> 47 these] the Q *uncorrected*; this Q *corrected*; *not in* F
> 57 begins to threat] begin threats Q *uncorrected*; begins
>   thereat Q *corrected*; *not in* F

IV.3

> 11 Ay, sir] I say Q; *not in* F

16 strove] streme Q; *not in* F
31 moistened] moystened her Q; *not in* F

IV.6

118–27 *prose in* Q, F
161–74 *prose in* Q, F
166 Plate] Place F; *not in* Q
184 This's a] This a Q, F

V.1

12–13 *prose in* Q; *not in* F

V.3

211 him] me Q; *not in* F
221–2 *prose in* Q, F
273 SECOND OFFICER] *Cap.* Q; *Gent.* F

3

The following list of stage directions concerns itself only with those added to, or considerably adapted from, the substantive texts, Q and F, where the editor's interpretation of requirements has been involved. Provision of exits, where these are clearly demanded by the context, is not recorded; nor is the common slight adjustment of the point at which entries and exits are mentioned; these are often a line or two early in F. Asides and other indicators of the mode of utterance ('*aloud*', '*sings*', etc.) are always editorial, as are indicators of the person addressed, and these are not collated.

I.1

35 *Exeunt Gloucester and Edmund*] *Exit* F
161 *He makes to strike him*] *not in* Q, F
266 *Flourish. Exeunt Lear, Burgundy, Cornwall, Albany, Gloucester, and attendants*] *Flourish. Exeunt* F; *Exit Lear and Burgundie* Q

I.4

0 *Enter Kent in disguise*] *Enter Kent* Q, F
7 *Enter Lear and Knights*] *Enter Lear and Attendants* F
8 *Exit First Knight*] *not in* Q, F
43 *Exit Second Knight*] *not in* Q, F
46 *Exit Third Knight*] *not in* Q, F

47 *Enter Third Knight*] *not in* Q, F
75 *Exit Third Knight*] *not in* Q, F
76 *Exit another Knight*] *not in* Q, F
83 *He strikes him*] *not in* Q, F
85 *He trips him*] *not in* Q, F
91 *He pushes Oswald out*] *not in* Q, F
94 *He gives him money*] *not in* Q, F
194 *He points to Lear*] *not in* Q, F
268 *(he strikes his head)*]*not in* Q, F
269 *Exeunt Kent and Knights*] *not in* Q, F
271 *He kneels*] *not in* Q, F

I.5

o *Enter Lear, Kent, Knight, and the Fool*] *Enter Lear,
    Kent, Gentleman, and Foole* F

II.1

o *. . . by opposite doors*] *Enter . . . seuerally* F
35 *He wounds himself in the arm*] *not in* Q, F
42 *Exeunt some servants*] *not in* Q, F

II.2

o *Enter Kent and Oswald by opposite doors*] *Enter Kent,
    and Steward seuerally* F
30 *He brandishes his sword*] *not in* Q, F
38 *Oswald tries to escape*] *not in* Q, F
39 *He beats him*] *not in* Q, F
148 *Kent is put in the stocks*] *not in* Q, F

II.4

o *Kent still in the stocks*] *not in* Q, F
130 *(laying his hand on his heart)*] *not in* Q, F
148 *(he kneels)*] *not in* Q, F
153 *(rising)*] *not in* Q, F
212 *He points to Oswald*] *not in* Q, F
281 *Exeunt Lear, Gloucester, Kent, the Fool, and
    Gentleman*] *Exeunt Lear, Leister, Kent, and Foole* Q;
    Exeunt F

III.1

o *. . . by opposite doors*] *. . ., seuerally* F
55 *Exeunt by opposite doors*] *Exeunt* Q, F

III.4

37, 43 *Enter the Fool from the hovel . . . Enter Edgar*

disguised as Poor Tom] Enter Edgar, and Foole F
(after line 36)

105 *He tears off his clothes*] not in Q, F

153 *Lear and Edgar talk apart*] not in Q, F

III.6

99 *Exeunt Kent, Gloucester, and the Fool, bearing off the
King*] Exeunt F

III.7

20 *Exit Oswald*] not in Q, F

23 *Exeunt Servants*] not in Q, F

32 *Servants tie his hands*] not in Q, F

34 *Regan plucks his beard*] not in Q, F

76, 77, *(Cornwall draws his sword) . . . He lunges at him*

78 *. . . (drawing his sword) . . . He wounds Cornwall*]
draw and fight Q (after line 77)

81 *He dies*] not in Q, F

97 *Exit Cornwall, supported by Regan*] Exeunt F

106 *Exeunt by opposite doors*] Exit Q

IV.2

21 *(giving a favour)*] not in Q, F

IV.4

0 *Enter, with drum and colours, Cordelia, Doctor, and
soldiers*] Enter with Drum and Colours, Cordelia,
Gentlemen, and Souldiours F; Enter Cordelia, Docter
and others Q

IV.6

0 *Enter Gloucester and Edgar in peasant's clothes*] Enter
Gloucester, and Edgar F

41 *Gloucester throws himself forward*] He fals Q

80 *Enter Lear fantastically dressed with wild flowers*]
Enter Lear mad Q

95 *He falls to his knees*] not in Q, F

132 *He gives flowers*] not in Q, F

170 *(giving flowers)*] not in Q, F

181 *He takes off his coronet of flowers*] not in Q, F

188 *He throws down his flowers and stamps on them*]
not in Q, F

*Enter a Gentleman and two attendants. Gloucester and
Edgar draw back*] Enter three Gentlemen Q

203 *Exit running, followed by attendants*] *Exit King
    running* Q

208 (*coming forward*)] *not in* Q, F

217 (*coming forward*)] *not in* Q, F

231 *Edgar intervenes*] *not in* Q, F

IV.7

22 *Enter Gentleman ushering Lear in a chair carried by
   servants. All fall to their knees*] *Enter Lear in a chaire
   carried by Servants* F

24 *Music sounds offstage*] *not in* Q, F

26 (*kneeling by the chair and kissing his hand*)] *not in* Q, F

58 *Lear falls to his knees*] *not in* Q, F

70 (*weeping*)] *not in* Q, F

95 *Exit*] *not in* Q, F

V.1

37 *As Albany is going out, enter Edgar*] *Enter Edgar* Q,
   F

V.3

21 (*He embraces her*)] *not in* Q, F

26 *Exeunt Lear and Cordelia, guarded*] *Exit* F

84 (*he points to Gonerill*)] *not in* Q, F

94 *He throws down his glove*] *not in* Q, F

98 (*throwing down his glove*)] *not in* Q, F

106 *Exit Regan, supported*] *not in* Q, F

115 *Trumpet answers within. Enter Edgar armed, a trumpet
    before him*] *Trumpet answers within. Enter Edgar
    armed* F; *Enter Edgar at the third sound, a trumpet
    before him* Q

126 *He draws his sword*] *not in* Q, F

148 *Alarums. Fights. Edmund falls*] *Alarums. Fights* F
    (*after* save him!)

149 *to Edgar, about to kill Edmund*] *not in* Q, F

159 *Exit First Officer*] *not in* Q, F

219 *Enter a Gentleman with a bloody knife*] *Enter a
    Gentleman* F; *Enter one with a bloudie knife* Q

228 *Exit Gentleman*] *not in* Q, F

249 *Exit Second Officer*] *not in* Q, F

254 *Edmund is borne off*] *not in* Q, F
    followed by Second Officer and others] *not in* Q, F

4

This list sets against the readings of the present text (printed to the left of the square bracket) substantive readings of other modern editions – in particular those of Peter Alexander (1951), Kenneth Muir (1952), Dover Wilson and Duthie (1960) – which have been considered and rejected. Similar readings can, of course, be found in many other editions. The reading cited from the present text can be understood to derive from F except where an asterisk directs attention to list 1 above (in which case the reading derives from Q) or where it is an emendation recorded above in list 2. In most cases the rejected readings derive from editors' preference for the Quarto, and in such cases '(Q)' indicates the source. In the same way '(F)' is used to indicate derivation from the Folio. Sometimes the rejected reading is an emendation – often to be traced back to the eighteenth-century editors – and in such cases the Q reading (if variant) is supplied before the rejected reading.

I.1

    5 qualities] equalities (Q)
   74 square] spirit (Q)
  128 the third] this third (Q)
  163 Kill] Do. | Kill (Q)
      thy fee] the fee (Q)
*168 vow] vows (F)
  206 up in] up on (Q)
  237 intends to do] intends (Q)
  239 stands] stand (Q)
  248 and fortunes] of fortune (Q)
  281 covers] (F, Q); covert

I.2

  133 pat] and pat (Q)

I.4

   21 he's] he is (Q)
40–41 me if . . . dinner. I] me. If . . . dinner. I
  111 the Lady Brach] (Ladie oth'e brach Q); Lady the
       Brach; the Lady's brach
  199 Sir] (F, Q); *omitted*

212 it's] it (Q)

*254 sir] *omitted*

*301 Yea] Ha (F)

302 Let] Ha! Let (F). *See Commentary*

I.5

1 Gloucester] (F, Q); Cornwall

44 *most editors add the direction 'Enter a Gentleman'*

46 KNIGHT] (*Seruant*. Q); GENTLEMAN (F)

II.1

8 kissing] bussing (Q)

39 stand] stand's (Q)

45 the thunder] their thunder (Q)

51 latched] lanch'd (Q)

*52 But] And (F)

76 O strange] strong (Q)

77 letter, said he] letter (Q)

119 price] poise (Q); prize. *See Commentary*

II.2

55 A tailor] Ay, a tailor (Q)

75 Being] Bring (Q)

   the] their (Q)

80 Smile] Smoile (F, Q)

149 my lord] my good lord (Q)

II.3

19 Sometimes . . . sometime] Sometimes . . . sometimes
   (Q)

II.4

2 messengers] messenger (Q)

*19 Yes] Yes, yes

52 for thy] (*not in* Q); from thy

73 ha' . . . use] have . . . follow (Q). *See Commentary*

97 commands, tends, service] commands her service
   (Q); commands their service

143 his] her (Q)

163 blister] blast her pride (Q); blister her

164 rash mood is on] rash mood (Q)

*181 fickle] sickly (F)

261 needs –] (needs: F); needs, (Q)

266 that patience] (F, Q); patience

III.1

    10 out-storm] out-scorn (Q)

    20 is] be (Q)

    48 that] your (Q)

III.2

    9 makes] make (Q)

    54 simular] simular man (Q)

    57 Has] Hast (Q)

    71 And] That (Q)

    78 boy] my good boy (Q)

  85–6 Then shall . . . confusion] *placed after line* 92 (F)

III.4

    45 cold winds] cold wind (Q); winds (F)

    46 thy bed] thy cold bed (Q)

    78 word's justice] words justly (Q); word justly

    96 mun, nonny] (hay no on ny Q); mun, hey no

       nonny; mun, hey, nonny, nonny

III.6

    *22 No] Now

    *53 store] stone

III.7

    52 answer] first answer (Q)

    58 bare] loved (Q)

    76 What] (F, Q); REGAN What

IV.1

    *10 parti-eyed] poorly led (F); poorly eyed

    38 fool] the fool (Q)

    *60 mopping] mocking

IV.2

    *28 A fool usurps my bed] My Fool usurps my body (F)

    *29 whistling] whistle (F)

    *32 its] (ith Q *corrected*); it (Q *uncorrected*)

IV.3

    *20 seem] seemed

    *29 be believed] believe it

    *31 And clamour] That clamour

IV.6

    15 sampire] (F, Q); samphire

 *18, 118, 152 yon] yond (F)

97 the white] white (Q)

128–32 (*prose*)] (F, Q); *verse*

130–31 civet; good apothecary, sweeten] civet, good apothecary, to sweeten (Q)

158–60 (*prose*)] (F, Q); *verse*

165 great] small (Q)

184 This's] This (F, Q); This'

202 Come] Nay (Q)

250 English] British (Q)

260 we] we'ld (Q)

IV.7

*21 DOCTOR] GENTLEMAN (F)

*23 GENTLEMAN] DOCTOR

32 jarring] warring (Q)

49 Where] when (Q)

53 even] (eu'n F); e'en (Q)

58 hand] hands (Q)

V.1

16 Fear not] Fear me not (Q)

21 heard] hear (Q)

36 Pray] pray you (Q)

V.3

5 I am] am I (Q)

77 is] (*not in* Q); are

100 the] thy (Q)

102 ho!] ho! | EDMUND A herald, ho, a herald (Q) *Enter a Herald*] (F (*after* firmly.)); *most editors place after line* 106

108 this.] this. | OFFICER Sound, trumpet! (Q)

113 *defence.*] defence. | EDMUND Sound (Q); defence. | EDMUND Sound trumpet

129 place, youth] youth, place (Q)

153 stop] stople (Q)

158 EDMUND] GONERIL (Q)

273 SECOND OFFICER] CAPTAIN (Q); OFFICER

275 him] them (Q)

*291 sees] says (F)

ADDITIONAL NOTE (1996)

The account of the relation between the Quarto and Folio texts of *King Lear* given above has been challenged in the last fifteen years or so by an alternative explanation of the evidence. The classic statement of the new theory is to be found in Michael Warren's 'Quarto and Folio *King Lear*' published in *Shakespeare, Pattern of Excelling Nature*, ed. Bevington and Halio (1978), but the textual impulse can be traced back to E. A. J. Honigmann's *The Stability of Shakespeare's Text* (1965). The members of this movement (whose contiguous points of view are conveniently set out in *The Division of the Kingdoms: Shakespeare's Two Versions of 'King Lear'*, ed. Michael Warren and Gary Taylor (1983)) argue that Q and F are not complementarily imperfect versions of one play (as suggested above) but two distinct Shakespearian plays – a first version of 1605–6 and a revised version of 1610. The arguments advanced to make this point are partly bibliographical and partly literary-critical.

The new theory derives its main impulse from dissatisfaction with those that preceded it, which clearly failed to solve all the contradictions that lie between Q and F, and which often showed an improper lack of tentativeness in expression. The idea of revision (even if not authorial revision) is well attested in Elizabethan playhouse practice; and F has often been thought to reflect a tidying-up of the (complete) play, so that it would be easier to handle on the stage. The new argument has certainly opened up what could be seen as a bibliographical closed shop; but we should notice that mere textual evidence is seldom susceptible of only one explanation: and clearly it cannot *require* us to believe either that F is a revision or that Q and F are both derived from a single original. The scholar, if he is to convince, is obliged to venture beyond facts into speculations why the variants occur, and these speculations have a tendency to derive from the merely personal taste which calls some readings misprints and others defensible Shakespearian locutions, or from undiscussed a priori positions – see Marion Trousdale, 'A Trip Through the Divided Kingdom', *Shakespeare Quarterly* 37 (1986), pp. 218–23.

The basic given of the literary defence is the fact that the final speech in the play is assigned to Edgar in F and to Albany in Q. Any number of printing-house accidents could have produced this variation, or it may reflect an uncoordinated piece of play-house revision. Michael Warren argues that it points us to a whole pattern of changes – and in this he is followed by all other members of the movement – changes designed to make Albany look like the 'stronger' character in Q, and the 'weaker' one in F. To sustain this argument many individual passages in both texts have to be read from the angle of a presumed authorial *intention*. And such angles are easily available to an accomplished literary critic (or director) reading through the poetically open and evasive words; and it would not be difficult for a method actor to discover in these any number of secret biographies which he could draw on to depict either 'weakness' or 'strength'. The basic problem lies indeed in the very easiness of this kind of interpretation.

The text presented in this present volume is a unified 'conflated' text – one drawing on readings from both Q and F, and so, as is said, a modern fabrication perhaps never performed on any Elizabethan stage, and never seen in print before the eighteenth century. For this reason both current 'Oxford' and 'Cambridge' series print separate texts of Q and F *King Lear*. But that solution of the problem is not acceptable here. The rigidity (and indeed old-fashionedness) of the conceptions used (two artefacts, each having the status of a literary classic, each to be protected from addition or subtraction) bears little relation to the status of unprinted theatrical texts, present in the playhouse as open resources from which different performances could be drawn for different occasions (such as performances at court, or in the country). When neither variant text can be given a clear claim to total truth it seems only proper to replicate that open resource-fulness. Moreover, when theoretical clarity fails it seems right to give weight to practical matters. If the additions found in both Q and F are entirely or mostly by Shakespeare (and there is little argument about this), then it is right to allow readers (and these, not textual scholars, are the audience aimed at) to enjoy all the poetry Shakespeare wrote; and to enjoy it in a form whose general coherence (within the limits common to Elizabethan drama) has stirred only occasional and uncoordinated objections among the generations who have been moved and inspired by its existence.

Words for Music in King Lear

The traditional expressions of socially accepted madness in the snatches of court Fool and Bedlam beggar in *King Lear* involve the idea of music, and probably were given, in Elizabethan performance, the reality of music. We may take it that the roles of Edgar and the Fool were played by two of the singing actors in the company. Neither the Quarto nor the Folio, however, has any stage directions indicating singing. It has been left to editors to imagine what music was used. Dr F. W. Sternfeld, to whose work I am indebted, has listed eighteen places in the play where one might expect singing (*Music in Shakespearean Tragedy* (1963)). His list is valuable; but it cannot be accepted just as it stands. It includes one item which does not seem to be a lyric – the Fool's 'prophecy' at the end of III.2: fourteen lines which can be rearranged as two stanzas, but still lack the regularity of strophic composition. There are also four passages (items 7, 13, 14 and 15 below) which might have been sung but are not included by Dr Sternfeld. My list therefore contains twenty-one items.

It will be seen that these passages all occur in five scenes in the first three acts of the play; and that the singing role of the Fool is abandoned in III.4 when Poor Tom joins the group on stage – except that 'Come o'er the burn, Bessy' is shared between the two singing actors.

Three of the passages (items 4, 12 and 19) seem to be from ballads with a wide currency; for two of these (4 and 19) music of the early seventeenth century survives, and is transcribed on p. 160. Item 12 ('He that has and a little tiny wit') is related, of course, to the last song of *Twelfth Night*, but no music earlier than the eighteenth century has survived. A transcription is printed in the Penguin Shakespeare edition of *Twelfth Night*.

For the rest, no tunes with any likelihood of authenticity survive. One can only guess from the subject-matter and the metrical form whether these are traditional words using traditional music; brief comments on these probabilities are given in the list. At least ten of the passages seem unlikely to have been associated with traditional tunes.

Below I indicate the metrical form of each passage, listing the number of stresses in each line aligned above the rhyme scheme (represented by letters); the line division and possible stanzaic structure are indicated by commas and semi-colons.

1. I.4.117–26 (FOOL Have more than thou showest)

        2   2   2   2   2   2   2   2   2   2
        a, a, a, a, a, a, b, b, b, b

The repetition of the (anapaestic) rhythmic structure and of the same rhyme suggests an attempt to create an effect of incantation through words alone, making music superfluous.

2. I.4.138–45 (FOOL That lord that counselled thee)

        3   3   3   3   3   3   3   3
        a, b, a, b;   c, d, d, d

The form is strophically accurate. But the subject matter is so germane to *King Lear* that if the passage does have a ballad origin the words must have been much modified. There is an obvious parallel with traditional 'counting-out' songs.

3. I.4.163–6 (FOOL Fools had ne'er less grace in a year)

        4   3   4   3
        a, b, a, b

The form is apt for music, but these words cannot be traditional.

4. I.4.171–4 (FOOL Then they for sudden joy did weep)

4   3   4   3
a, b, a, b

Lines three and four are obviously Shakespeare's invention, but the first two lines appear (with variations) in several ballad scraps and adaptations of the period. One of these supplies the music cited on p. 160; it was written in manuscript in a printed book of 1609 (Thomas Ravencroft's *Pammelia*) now in the British Museum, with the following words:

> Late as I waked out of sleep
>   I heard a pretty thing:
> Some men for sudden joy do weep,
>   And some for sorrow sing.

In the transcription below, Shakespeare's words are fitted to the same tune. The words may be sung as a round, the second and third voices entering at the eighth and fifteenth bars; but of course no such effect was sought in *King Lear*.

5. I.4.192–4 (FOOL Mum, mum! | He that keeps nor crust nor crumb)

2   4   4
a, a, a

On the repeated rhyme see under item 1. The tone is more that of a proverb than a song.

6. I.4.211–12 (FOOL The hedge-sparrow fed the cuckoo so long)

4   4
a, a

Again, more a proverb than a song.

7. I.4.221 (FOOL Whoop, Jug, I love thee!)

$$3$$
$$a$$

Sounds like a ballad-refrain, but not otherwise known.

8. I.4.314–18 (FOOL A fox, when one has caught her)

$$3 \quad 2 \quad 2 \quad 3 \quad 2$$
$$a, \quad a, \quad a, \quad a, \quad a$$

Sounds like a comic exercise in rhyming words notoriously difficult to pronounce.

9. II.4.46–51 (FOOL Fathers that wear rags)

$$3 \quad 3 \quad 3 \quad 3 \quad 3 \quad 3$$
$$a, \quad b, \quad a, \quad b, \quad c, \quad c$$

Does not sound like traditional ballad material.

10. II.4.74–81 (FOOL That sir which serves and seeks for gain)

$$4 \quad 3 \quad 4 \quad 3 \quad 4 \quad 3 \quad 4 \quad 3$$
$$a, \quad b, \quad a, \quad b; \quad c, \quad d, \quad c, \quad d$$

There is no reason why this should not be a ballad; but there is no evidence to connect it with one.

11. III.2.27–34 (FOOL The cod-piece that will house)

$$3 \quad 3 \quad 3 \quad 3 \quad 3 \quad 3 \quad 3 \quad 3$$
$$a, \quad b, \quad a, \quad b; \quad c, \quad d, \quad c, \quad d$$

The compression and obliquity of language makes this unsuitable for music.

12. III.2.74–7 (FOOL He that has and a little tiny wit)

4 4 4 4
a, b, a, c

The stage direction in the Folio printing of *Twelfth Night* ('*Clowne sings*') tells us that this was a song in Shakespeare's day; but no music of that period has survived.

13. III.4.45 (POOR TOM Through the sharp hawthorn blow the cold winds)

4
a

The phrase is obviously related to Edgar's nakedness; but it would have most effect if derived from traditional material.

14. III.4.73 (POOR TOM Pillicock sat on Pillicock Hill)

4
a

Sounds like a ballad-refrain, but not otherwise known. I have assumed that 'Alow, alow, loo, loo!' – the line following – is an imitation of the huntsman's cry and is not part of a traditional song.

15. III.4.95–6 (POOR TOM Still through the hawthorn blows the cold wind)

4 3
a, b

See under item 13. Line 96 *may* be connected with line 95, and I have so printed it; but it may be a quite disparate remark.

16. III.4.115–18 (POOR TOM S'Withold footed thrice the 'old)

4 4 4 4
a, a, bb, c

Form and content suggest incantation rather than song.

17. III.4.131–3 (POOR TOM Horse to ride and weapon to wear)

4   4   4
a,   a,   a

The source in *Bevis of Hampton* makes music unlikely.

18. III.4.176–8 (POOR TOM Child Roland to the dark tower came)

4   4   4
a,   a,   a

The material is, in part at least, traditional. But these do not sound like words for music.

19. III.6.25–8 (POOR TOM *and* FOOL Come o'er the burn, Bessy, to me)

3   2   2   3
a,   b,   b,   a

Various pieces of music with this title have survived. They raise the question whether Tom should sing the full three lines of the original –

> Come o'er the burn, Bessy,
> Thou little pretty Bessy,
> Come o'er the burn, Bessy, to me –

or merely the shortened version. For the transcription on p. 160 I have assumed the latter. The first line is, I take it, merely a cue, used to suggest the song to the audience, to provide a basis on which the Fool can embroider his parody.

The transcription gives the refrain sections of the tune with this heading found in a Cambridge lute manuscript (MS. Dd. 2. 11, fol. 80ᵛ). This seems more appropriate than any tune extracted from the elaborate contrapuntal setting in a British Museum manuscript (Additional MS. 5665, fols. 143–4). I have placed inside square brackets the part of the refrain which is not printed in Shakespeare's text.

20. III.6.41–4 (POOR TOM Sleepest or wakest thou, jolly shepherd?)

$$4 \quad 3 \quad 4 \quad 3$$
$$a, \quad b, \quad c, \quad b$$

Form and content would make a ballad source quite plausible.

21. III.6.65–72 (POOR TOM Be thy mouth or black or white)

$$4 \quad 4 \quad 4 \quad 4 \quad 4 \quad 4 \quad 4 \quad 4$$
$$a, \quad a, \quad b, \quad b, \quad c, \quad c, \quad d, \quad d$$

These trochaic octosyllabics suggest incantation rather than song. They are strongly reminiscent of the witches' incantations in *Macbeth*.

4. I.4.171–4 (Then they for sudden joy did weep)

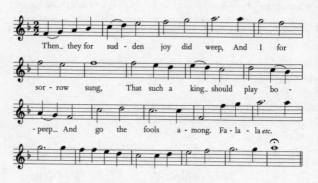

Then they for sud - den joy did weep, And I for sor - row sung, That such a king should play bo - -peep And go the fools a - mong. Fa - la - la *etc.*

19. III.6.25–8 (Come o'er the burn, Bessy, to me)

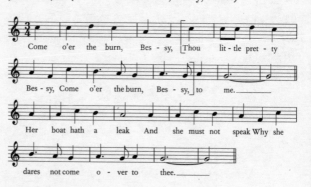

Come o'er the burn, Bes - sy, Thou lit - tle pret - ty Bes - sy, Come o'er the burn, Bes - sy, to me. Her boat hath a leak And she must not speak Why she dares not come o - ver to thee.

Commentary

Biblical quotations are taken from the Bishops' Bible (1568, etc.), the version that was probably best known to Shakespeare.

The Characters in the Play: GENTLEMEN: *Gentleman* appears in several scenes of the play – II.4, III.1, IV.3, IV.6 (after 188), IV.7 (after 22), and V.3 (after 219). There is no clear carry-over from one scene to another, and all these may be different characters. It is clear that the Folio text has a strong tendency to call all supporting actors *Gentlemen*. Sometimes the Quarto is more discriminating, sometimes not. If he is a single person the *Gentleman* (like the *Knight* in I.5) attends Lear; he leaves Gloucester's castle with him (II.4), is sent by Kent to meet Cordelia (III.1), reports her reactions and is taken to meet Lear (IV.3), comes to find him (IV.6), and attends him in IV.7.

I.1

The scene which generates all the subsequent action. A short prelude introducing the names and natures of Gloucester and Edmund leads into a headlong ritual of abdication and 'auction' of the country. Loyalty and sense are exiled from Britain in the persons of Cordelia and Kent, but taken up by the King of France. Hypocrisy and opportunism are left in charge of self-ignorant greatness.

o *Edmund*: Normally the name used for this character in speech-prefixes and stage directions throughout the play, in both Q and F, is *Bastard*.

1 *had . . . affected*: Was fond of.

3 *to us*: To our people (perhaps an attempt to include Edmund in the conversation).

6 *curiosity in neither can make choice of either's moiety*: Not even the most scrupulous weighing of advantages can make either prefer the share given to the other. *moiety*: Share.

8 *His breeding . . . hath been at my charge*: I have been financially responsible for his upbringing (or 'I might be held responsible for his birth').

10 *braȝed to it*: Brazen about it.

11 *conceive*: Understand (with secondary reference to 'become pregnant').

15 *smell a fault*: A *fault* is both (1) a sin; (2) a loss of scent by the hounds.

17 *proper*: Handsome (but with, perhaps, an ironic undertone of *proper* meaning 'appropriate' (to the *fault*)).

18 *by order of law*: Legitimate.

19 *dearer in my account*: The first of the many financial puns in this scene, unless *charge* above (8) be so considered.

20 *knave*: Boy. The sense of 'villain' was available to Shakespeare and may be present by irony. *something*: Somewhat.

29 *sue*: Beg.

30 *I shall study deserving*: I shall make every effort to deserve your esteem.

31 *out*: Out of the country. This helps to explain the ignorance of Edmund's nature shown both by his brother and by his father.

32 *a sennet*: A trumpet call (announcing a movement of important characters). *a coronet*: This seems to be designed to be part of a ritual of 'parting' the kingdom, expressed in a no doubt abbreviated form in 139.

33 *Attend*: Usher into our presence.

36 *darker*: Hitherto undivulged.

37 *the map*: Marshall McLuhan says 'the map was also a novelty . . . and was key to the new vision of peripheries of power and wealth . . . the map brings forward

at once a principal theme of *King Lear*, namely the isolation of the visual sense as a kind of blindness' (*The Gutenberg Galaxy* (1962), p. 11).

37–8 *we have divided* | *. . . our kingdom*: The text 'Every kingdom divided against itself shall be brought to naught' (Matthew 12:25) would occur to many Elizabethan minds.

38 *'tis our fast intent*: *fast* means 'firm', and sorts oddly with *shake* in the following line. Notice the similar contradiction in 41, where *unburdened* leads to *crawl*. The impression is given of the abdication as a charade rather than a necessity.

43 *constant will to publish*: Settled intention to promulgate.

44 *several*: Separate.

45 *prevented*: Forestalled.

46 *Great*: Noble, powerful.

49 *both*: Shakespeare sets *both* before three (instead of the usual two) cognate nouns in several other places.

50 *Interest of territory*: Right or title to the territory.

52 *largest*: Most generous.

53 *Where nature doth with merit challenge*: To the person in whom natural filial affection can be rewarded as if it were objective *merit* (since the merit and the filial love challenge one another as equals).

55 *I love you more than word can wield the matter*: The matter of my love is too weighty to be lifted or expressed by language.

56 *space, and liberty*: Freedom from confinement, and the enjoyment of that freedom.

59 *As much as . . . father found*: As much as any father ever found himself to be loved.

60 *breath*: 'Speech' rather than 'life' – repeating the idea of 55.
unable: Incompetent.

61 *Beyond all manner of 'so much'*: Beyond all manner of ways of saying 'so much'.

62 *Love, and be silent*: Gonerill has *spoken* of love. Cordelia therefore finds speech devalued; she cannot speak, but only love in fact, and so be silent.

63 *bounds*: Boundaries.

64 *champains*: Flat open country.

65 *wide-skirted meads*: Widely spread-out meadows.

67 *Be this perpetual*: This is no temporary division of the kingdom. From now on, Britain will cease to exist as an entity.

69 *self*: Same.

    mettle: Spirit. But the pun on 'metal' is given strength by *price* and *worth* in the following line (and by their opposition to *true heart*) – with the implication: 'My price can be measured in metal.'

70 *price me*: Evaluate myself. F reads *priʒe*, but the two words were not clearly differentiated, and *price* seems the more appropriate modern form.

71 *names my very deed*: Gives the very particulars of my deed.

    deed: (1) Action; (2) legal instrument. Regan finds in her heart a document containing the very words that Gonerill has been using.

72 *that*: In that.

74 *Which the most precious square of sense possesses*: Which the senses, not 'out of square' (unbalanced) but in their proper constitution – the constitution that is so precious to us – possess.

75 *felicitate*: Joyful.

76 *poor*: Because (1) she feels the lack of gifts within her; (2) she cannot join in the exchange of these high-flown 'golden' sentiments, and must be *poor* as a result.

77–8 *my love's | More ponderous than my tongue*: Cf. 55 and 91–2, where we find the same sense of the glib tongue as the lever of the heart's weighty affections. This supports F's *ponderous* against Q's *richer*.

79 *hereditary ever*: See the note on 67.

81 *validity*: Shakespeare frequently uses the word in the sense of 'value'.

83 *least*: Littlest (or perhaps, as youngest, 'last in precedence'). Cordelia's low stature may be implied elsewhere (for example, 198 of this scene). The Q reading, *last, not least*, is easier, but the text may have been

remembered in this form because of the very triteness
of the phrase.

84 *milk of Burgundy*: Burgundy was notable for the
fertility of its land, though not particularly devoted to
milk production.

85 *interessed*: Admitted (as to a privilege).

87 *Nothing*: I can say nothing designed *to draw | A third
more opulent*. I refuse to enter this charade.

93 *According to my bond*: According to my bounden duty,
the bond of natural affection and respect between child
and parent.

97 *those duties back as are right fit*: The duties that are
fitting to be returned, in answer to your kindnesses,
and *According to my bond*.

98 *Obey you, love you, and most honour you*: Shakespeare
seems to be remembering the marriage service in the
Prayer Book ('Wilt thou obey him, love, honour, and
keep him . . .'), in preparation for the comparison with
the duties owed to a husband.

100 *all*: With the whole of themselves.
Haply: Perhaps.

101 *take my plight*: Accept my troth-plight (vow of
marriage).

106 *untender*: Inflexible, stiff in opinions.

107 *true*: Growing straight; stiff, perhaps, but accurate and
unerring.

110 *mysteries*: F reads *miseries*, Q, *mistresse*. This provides
a good example of the way in which both texts can
contribute to the true reading.
Hecat and the night: Following the *radiance of the sun*,
and preceding *the orbs*, this may refer to Hecat – more
properly 'Hecatè' – as the moon; but *mysteries* suggests
the Hecat who presides over witchcraft.

111–12 *the operation of the orbs | From whom we do exist, and
cease to be*: The influence of the stars on the lives of
men, controlling life and death.

116 *Scythian*: An inhabitant of the region now occupied
by Russia, remarked by the Roman poets as savage and
barbarous.

117–18 *he that makes his generation messes | To gorge his appetite*:
A barbarian, who chops up his parents (or his chil-
dren) for food, just out of gluttony. The sense of
generation as 'parents' gives a slightly better parallel
with the actual parent–child situation that Lear sees.

118–19 *shall to my bosom | Be as well neighboured, pitied, and
relieved*: Shall be as close to my bosom, and as within
the kindnesses of intimate kinship. The forecast of his
own situation in the heath scenes should be noticed.

120 *sometime*: Former.

122 *dragon*: Appropriate to the British (as against English)
monarchy, imagined as carrying the Welsh red dragon
emblem on their coats-of-arms.

123 *set my rest*: (1) Stake all I have on the bet (a term in
the card game of primero); (2) repose in retirement.

124 *nursery*: Nursing, loving care.
Hence and avoid my sight: Addressed, presumably, to
Cordelia; but it appears that she does not obey, and
that Lear accepts this, since he calls for France and
Burgundy.

126 *Who stirs*: Get moving, somebody! Don't stand staring!

128 *digest*: Assimilate, incorporate.

129 *Let pride, which she calls plainness, marry her*: Instead
of a dowry to win a husband, she will have to buy one
with the pride which she thinks of as plain-speaking.

131–2 *all the large effects | That troop with majesty*: All the
splendid panoply that accompanies the condition of
being a king; and also all that *results* from being a king.
Lear is to be a king outside the world of cause and
effect.

132 *by monthly course*: Moving round, one month with
Regan, one month with Gonerill, and so on.

133 *With reservation*: The privilege (of having the knights)
being reserved or exempted from the agreement.

135 *Only*: As a sole exception

136 *th'addition*: The external honours.

137 *Revenue*: Accented on the second syllable.

139 *This coronet part between you*: They are to divide royal
authority (symbolized by the coronet) between them.

Perhaps one should imagine an appropriate stage action in which Gonerill and Regan touch or grasp the coronet.

143 *The bow is bent and drawn; make from the shaft*: You have wound up your speech in order to make some important point. Now let the point (barbed, no doubt) fly forward like an arrow. *make from* is unknown to dictionaries, but must give some sense like 'let go'.

144-5 *Let it fall rather, though the fork invade | The region of my heart*: I should prefer that my argumentative point should not hit you, even if the mis-shot arrow should kill me instead.

145-6 *Be Kent unmannerly | When Lear is mad*: My lack of manners could be justified only if you were mad.

146 *thou*: The second-person singular, normally used to inferiors and intimates, is very extraordinary when applied to a king; Kent seems to be trying shock therapy in an attempt to bring Lear to his senses.

147-9 *duty ... power ... flattery ... honour ... majesty*: Kent presents an allegorical diagram of the relationships. *duty* (Kent) must speak when *power* (Lear) bows to *flattery* (Gonerill and Regan); *honour* (Kent) must be plain-spoken when *majesty* (Lear) is foolish.

149 *stoops to folly*: The F reading, *falls to folly*, is easily explained by the conflation in the compositor's memory of the sound of *folly* and the idea of *stoops*.

Reserve thy state: Both this (the F reading) and Q's *Reuerse thy doome* make reasonable sense. Q is not only, however, the weaker text in general; here it gives a more obvious sense, more likely to be the product of a vulgarizing and simplifying memory than the F reading, which has the sense 'Don't give away your power' (repeated in *Revoke thy gift* below – 164). There would be little point in linking 'Reverse thy doom' ('Cancel your sentence on Cordelia') to *best consideration*; but *Reserve thy state* links well: 'Do not give your power away; hold back your decision and consider it carefully.'

150–51 *in thy best consideration check | This hideous rashness*:
Restrain this terrible speed of abdication by pausing
and considering it well.

151 *Answer my life my judgement*: I will stake my life on
my opinion.

153–4 *whose low sounds | Reverb no hollowness*: 'Empty vessels
sound most'; so, by inversion, those who make little
noise may be thought to do so because they lack the
hollow hearts of hypocrites. *Reverb* seems to be a
Shakespearian coinage for 'reverberate'.

157 *motive*: That which promotes (my action).

158–9 *let me still remain | The true blank of thine eye*: Instead
of ordering me out of your sight, make me always the
means of point-blank true aim from your eyes; looking
through me you will see things accurately. *blank* has
usually been taken to mean 'the bull's-eye of a target';
but the evidence suggests rather that *true blank* means
'the direct line of sight', as of an arrow or gun directed
'truly', that is point-blank, at its target.

158 *still*: Always.

160 *Apollo*: An appropriate god to invoke at this point,
as he was both the archer god (the god of straight
aiming at targets) and the sun god (the god of clear
seeing).

161 *miscreant*: Unbeliever. Kent has denied the gods.

163–4 *thy fee bestow | Upon the foul disease*: Give the reward
you should lavish on healthful advisers to those against
whom they advise you, those who will be your death.

168 *That*: Seeing that.

169 *strained pride*: Pride that leads you to excess.

170 *betwixt our sentence and our power*: Between my words
and my deeds, my legal enactment and the fulfilment
of it.

171 *nor . . . nor*: Neither . . . nor.

172 *Our potency made good*: The potential of my power
being fulfilled in execution. Lear says that since Kent
has interposed himself between *sentence* and *power* he
will find no gap between these two in his case: the
sentence and power will appear together.

177 *trunk*: Body.

179 *This shall not be revoked*: The emphasis is on *This*, with reference to 164.

180–87 *Fare thee well . . . country new*: Kent's couplets, divided formally between the King, Cordelia, Gonerill and Regan, 'princes', mark the recession of the verse-level from immediate passion to sententious generality.

180–81 *sith thus thou wilt appear, | Freedom lives hence and banishment is here*: Since you are determined to act the tyrant, there can be no freedom in Britain.

184 *approve*: Confirm.

185 *effects*: Results, realizations. The antithesis in 184 and 185 is, once again, that between *words* and *deeds*.

187 *shape his old course*: 'Continue to act upon the same principles' (Dr Johnson) – of faithfulness, truth, and plain-speaking.
      Flourish: A fanfare (used on the stage to mark the ceremonial entry (or exit) of important persons).

191 *in the least*: At the lowest.

196 *so*: Dear, expensive, worth a large dowry.

198 *little-seeming substance*: The phrase is difficult to disentangle (the hyphen is, of course, a modern addition). The charge can hardly be that Cordelia is *little*; but it is likely to involve *seeming* (hypocrisy) – a Shakespearian obsession. Perhaps the best interpretation is an ironic one, 'that girl so devoted to *substance* and fact, so *little* concerned with *seeming*'.

199 *pieced*: Augmented (here used ironically).

200 *fitly like*: Please by its fitness.

202 *those infirmities she owes*: The disabilities she possesses. He proceeds to enumerate them.
      owes: Owns.

204 *strangered with our oath*: Made a stranger (to me) by my swearing to sever our relationship (above, 113 ff.).

206 *Election makes not up in such conditions*: It is impossible to settle a choice (*Take her or leave her*) when the condition of the lady is of the kind you describe. This explains the *I know no answer* at 201.

208 *tell*: (1) Report to; (2) count.

208 *For you*: As for you.

209 *make such a stray*: Stray so far.

211 *T'avert your liking a more worthier way*: To turn your love in the direction of some person more worth it.

212–13 *Nature is ashamed | Almost t'acknowledge hers*: Lear seems to be denying Cordelia not only kinship to him, but kinship to the human species.

214 *your best object*: The thing you best liked to gaze upon.

215 *The argument of your praise*: The theme you chose for praise.

217 *to*: As to.

217–18 *dismantle | So many folds of favour*: Strip away the protective clothing of your favour (the first appearance of the idea of stripping clothes, later so important in the play).

219–20 *Must be of such unnatural degree | That monsters it*: Must be so far beyond ordinary human offences as to be monstrous.

220–21 *or your fore-vouched affection | Fall into taint*: If her offence is not monstrous then the alternative is for the affection for her you used to affirm to become suspect.

221 *which to believe*: To believe that her offence is so monstrous.

221–3 *to believe . . . Must be a faith that reason without miracle | Should never plant*: To believe (in so impossible a thing) requires *faith*, and faith cannot be implanted by rational means, unaccompanied by the miraculous.

224 *If for I want*: If it is because I lack.

225 *and purpose not*: Without intending to fulfil what I have spoken.

227 *murder*: Critics have made the point that *murder* is a crime Cordelia need not clear herself of, for no one has accused her of it; but she is rehearsing here not her own real crimes, but the extremes that might be assumed of *a wretch whom Nature is ashamed | Almost t'acknowledge hers*.

228 *dishonoured*: Dishonourable.

230 *for which*: For want of which.

231 *still-soliciting*: Always ogling for favours.

235 *tardiness in nature*: Natural reticence.

236–7 *leaves the history unspoke | That it intends to do*: Does not speak out the inner thoughts which, none the less, it purposes to enact.

239 *regards that stands*: The coupling of a plural subject with a singular verb was not a clear breach of grammar in Elizabethan English.

239–40 *regards that stands | Aloof from th'entire point*: Considerations (of dowry etc.) that stand quite apart from the single unqualified issue (love).

242 *portion*: Dowry.

248 *Since that*: Since. Elizabethan English adds 'that' to several conjunctions and relative adverbs ('if that', 'when that', etc.) without altering sense, but giving added emphasis.

respect and fortunes are his love: What he's in love with is worldly status and wealth.

250–51 *art most rich, being poor, | Most choice, forsaken, and most loved, despised*: Some of the resonance of these lines no doubt comes from the reminiscence of 2 Corinthians 6:10, where Paul speaks of the ministry of Christ as 'poor, yet making many rich . . . having nothing, and yet possessing all things'.

254–65 *Gods, gods! . . . our benison*: The couplets indicate (as usual) a formalization of the attitudes involved.

254–5 *from their cold'st neglect | My love should kindle*: He loves her because the gods seem to have abandoned her – the opposite process to that appearing in Burgundy.

258 *waterish Burgundy*: Burgundy is full of streams and rivers; but the principal implication of *water* here is of weakness, dilution (as against *wine*).

259 *unprized-precious*: Offered at no price at all by her father, but regarded as precious by me.

260 *though unkind*: Though they have not acted like a family to you (yet you should preserve family decencies to them).

261 *Thou losest here, a better where to find*: *here* and *where* are nouns: 'You are losing this place, in order to find

a better place elsewhere.'

265 *benison*: Blessing

268 *washed*: (1) Washed with tears; (2) cleared, able to see you as you really are.

271 *as they are named*: By their true (unpleasant) names.

272 *To your professèd bosoms*: To the tender care you have alleged you felt.

276 *study*: Effort, endeavour.

278 *At Fortune's alms*: As a charity give-away
    scanted: Stinted.

279 *are worth the want that you have wanted*: Deserve the want of that (affection) which you have shown you lack (towards your father).

280 *plighted cunning*: The cunning that (1) is pleated, plaited, folded under, concealed; (2) involves 'plighting', or swearing as the truth, things that are false.

281 *Who covers faults, at last with shame derides*: Time begins by concealing faults, but at last reveals them, to the shame and derision of the malefactors.

295 *look*: Expect.

296 *imperfections of long-ingraffed condition*: Faults firmly implanted (grafted) in his character.

297 *unruly waywardness*: Unpredictable petulance.

299 *unconstant starts*: Sudden jerks (as of a frightened horse).

301 *compliment of leave-taking*: Ceremonious farewell.

302 *hit together*: This probably means 'agree with one another', 'fit in with one another', but 'aim together' is also possible. In any case the sense of physical violence cannot be wholly discounted.

303–4 *If our father carry authority with such disposition as he bears, this last surrender of his will but offend us*: If our father persists in acting over our heads, as he just has, this power that he has just surrendered to us will only do us harm.

306 *We must do something*: The emphasis is on *do* as against *think* in the line before.
    and i'th'heat: And strike while the iron is hot.

I.2

Edmund reveals that he is as evilly calculating as Gonerill and Regan (though more self-analytical). Gloucester parallels Lear in folly, but on a lower level of energy. Superstition makes him a prey to ruthless intellectual exploitation – as does the relaxed guile-lessness of Edgar.

1 *Nature*: A key-word in the play. What seems to be meant here is a sanction that precedes civilized law, the law of nations, and lays stress on those endowments that promote life in its most primitive conditions, nature red in tooth and claw.

goddess: Edmund must be thinking of a mother-Nature goddess, a goddess of fertility, whose rights precede those of civilization.

law: The 'law', that is, of the jungle.

2 *services are bound*: Edmund sees his relation to his *goddess* as a parody of the feudal 'service' owed to a liege lord.

3 *Stand in the plague of custom*: Be subject to the disabilities that customary law imposes on younger sons. Edmund might seem to be referring here to his bastardy – the audience already knows about this (I.1.12–15) – but it emerges in 5 that he is talking about his status as a younger son.

4 *The curiosity of nations*: The fine discriminations established by mere national laws.

deprive me: (1) Reduce my powers; (2) disinherit me (younger sons did not, bastards could not, inherit).

5 *For that*: Because.

moonshines: Months.

6 *Lag of*: Lagging behind.

bastard . . . base: Edmund plays on *base*: (1) ('base-born') bastard; (2) low, vile, despicable. He proceeds to prove *bastard* untrue as a description, because he is not *base* in the second sense.

7 *my dimensions are as well-compact*: I am as well formed.

8 *generous*: Gentleman-like.

as true: As truly stamped in my father's image.

9 *honest madam*: The legitimate's married mother.

10–21 *base . . . legitimate*: 'Any word, if repeated over and over in a monotone, seems to lose its significance. Edmund plays this trick with *base* and *legitimate*, in order to prove that they are meaningless terms' (G. L. Kittredge).

11–12 *Who . . . take | More composition and fierce quality*: Whose making requires more vigorous effort and energy.

11 *lusty stealth of nature*: *lusty* involves both vigour and lust: 'natural' love (or lust) has to be vigorously taken, or stolen.

14 *fops*: Fools.

17–18 *Our father's love . . . legitimate*: Recalling Gloucester's words at I.1.19.

19 *speed*: Prosper.

20 *invention*: Power of inventing (lies).

21 *top the*: This is an emendation from Q's *tooth'* and F's *to'th'*. *top* gives excellent and Edmund-like extension to the meanings of *base* in the preceding line: the *base* (low) will *top* (surpass, be higher than) the legitimate Edgar.

23 *France in choler parted*: We have not seen this; but the phrase serves as convenient and dramatic shorthand for the mode of relationship between Cordelia and the rest of her family.

24 *prescribed his power*: Instructed about what power he may possess. The Q reading, *subscribd his power*, is possible, but need not be preferred.

25 *Confined to exhibition*: Restricted to a small allowance.

26 *Upon the gad*: Suddenly (as a horse is caused to bolt by a goad or *gad*).

28 *put up*: Pocket, conceal.

33–4 *dispatch*: (1) Haste; (2) removal.

34–5 *The quality of nothing hath not such need to hide itself*: If there was nothing there, you wouldn't need to hide it; it is not the nature of nothing to require concealment.

35–6 *If it be nothing I shall not need spectacles*: Note the anticipated irony: here Gloucester is confident of the power of his eyesight to distinguish *something* from *nothing*; later he learns, without eyes, the potentialities that stem from deprivation, or *nothing*.

38–9 *for so much as I have perused*: As far as I have read it.

39 *o'erlooking*: Perusal.

42 *to blame*: Objectionable.

45 *essay*: The same word as 'assay', a first trial or sip – used technically of the official 'tasting' of a great person's food.

46 *policy and reverence*: Politic trick of making us reverence (hendiadys for 'policy of reverence').

47 *to the best of our times*: In the heyday of our life.

48 *our oldness cannot relish them*: We are too old to enjoy them.

49–51 *an idle and fond bondage . . . suffered*: The tyrannical oppression of one's elders (in withholding patrimonies etc.) is a kind of slavery that it is needless and foolish to submit to, for it operates through our passivity, not because of its strength.

51–2 *If our father would sleep till I waked him*: If our father were put into my power to decide his sleeping or waking (that is, death or life).

53, 56 *revenue*: Accented on the second syllable.

61 *closet*: Study.

62 *character*: Handwriting.

65 *in respect of that*: Considering what the subject matter really is.

70 *sounded you*: Taken soundings or measurements of your depths.

73 *fit*: Appropriate.
at perfect age: Being fully mature and adult.

74 *ward*: A minor, under protection of a guardian who managed his affairs.

77 *detested*: Detestable.

83 *run a certain course*: Proceed through certainties.
where: Whereas.

86 *pawn down*: Stake.

87 *feel*: Test.

88 *pretence of danger*: Dangerous intention.

90 *meet*: Proper.

91–2 *by an auricular assurance have your satisfaction*: Satisfy yourself with certainties based on what you yourself hear.

98 *Wind me into him*: Screw yourself into his inmost thoughts. *me* is the so-called 'ethic dative' and need not be construed in a modern paraphrase.
Frame: Organize.

98–9 *after your own wisdom*: As you think best.

99 *unstate myself*: Give up my rank and fortune.

99–100 *a due resolution*: A state where my doubts were duly resolved.

101 *presently*: At once.
convey: Manage.

102 *withal*: Therewith.

103 *late*: Recent (possibly remembering the eclipses of September and October 1605).

104–6 *Though the wisdom of nature can reason it thus and thus, yet nature finds itself scourged by the sequent effects*: Though science can explain natural events in rational terms, the results hurt us none the less for that.

109, 114 *villain*: Edgar, who by the very breath of treachery has become ignoble, a *villain* (villein) in the sense of 'peasant').

109–10 *the prediction*: (1) The prediction implied by the eclipses; (2) the prediction of the end of the world in the New Testament, and especially the signs of this described in Mark 13.

111 *bias of nature*: Natural tendency (to love one's children, etc.).

112–13 *hollowness*: Lack of inner substance to support external appearance.

115 *it shall lose thee nothing*: 'A backhanded promise to reward his detective work' (G. L. Kittredge).

118 *excellent*: (1) Extreme; (2) splendid (from Edmund's anti-human point of view).
foppery: Folly.

119–20 *sick in fortune – often the surfeits of our own behaviour*: Reduced in fortune as a result of our excesses (as overeating produces vomiting).

120 *guilty of*: Responsible for.

123 *treachers*: Traitors.

by spherical predominance: Because certain planets (in their spheres) were ascendant at the time of our birth.

126–8 *An admirable evasion of whoremaster man, to lay his goatish disposition to the charge of a star*: It is strange that lecherous man should evade responsibility for his lechery by saying that a star made him like that.

126 *admirable*: Truly strange and wonder-worthy. Cf. *excellent* (118).

129 *Dragon's tail*: A name given to the intersection of the orbit of the descending moon with the line of the sun's orbit. Chaucer (*A Treatise on the Astrolabe*, II.4) names 'the Tail of the Dragon' among the 'wicked planets'.

Ursa Major: The Great Bear. In astrological terms the horoscope is governed by Mars and Venus, producing a temperament not only daring and impetuous (*rough*) but also lascivious and adulterous (*lecherous*); but it may be that the Dragon and the Bear are mentioned only because of the associations with violence that these animals suggest.

130 *Fut*: Probably the same as ''sfoot': by Christ's foot).

131 *that I am*: What I am (that is, rough and lecherous).

132 *bastardizing*: Being conceived as a bastard.

133 *pat*: In the nick of time.

like the catastrophe of the old comedy: Old-fashioned comedy, he implies, contrived the catastrophe (or ending) too mechanically, so that the required coincidence always turned up just when convenient.

134 *cue*: A theatrical word, fitting to *comedy* and *catastrophe*. Edmund tells us he is about to play a new role.

134–5 *a sigh like Tom o'Bedlam*: It is not clear why Tom o'Bedlam – the madman-beggar from the Bethlehem (*Bedlam*) or any other madhouse – should have a characteristic *sigh* – though he may well have *whined*.

136 *divisions*: (1) Conflicts – of father against son etc. as in 110–11; (2) musical 'divisions' – counterpoint against plainsong.

Fa, sol, la, mi: Edmund sings (I assume) the notes F,

G, A, B natural (using the names given to these notes
in the C and G hexachords of the musical system
pertaining in Shakespeare's day). He thus moves across
the interval of the augmented fourth, called '*diabolus
in musica*' (the devil in music) in the current musical
mnemonic: '*Mi contra Fa est diabolus in musica*'. The
phrase reflects the enmity between the tritone and the
normal system of harmony. Shakespeare seems to be
creating something like a musical emblem or 'motto
theme' for the character of his discordant Bastard.

142 *the effects . . . succeed*: The results follow.

146 *diffidences*: Mistrustings.

147 *dissipation of cohorts*: Break-up of military companies.

149 *sectary astronomical*: Devotee of astrology.

158 *forbear his presence*: Avoid meeting him.

159 *qualified*: Reduced.

160–61 *with the mischief of your person it would scarcely allay*:
Even if he did physical violence to you it would hardly
diminish.

163–4 *have a continent forbearance*: Contain your feelings (and
keep away from him).

166 *fitly*: At the appropriate time.

171 *told . . . but faintly*: Given only a faint impression of.

172 *the image and horror*: The horrible picture that is true.

173 *anon*: Soon.

178 *practices*: Machinations.

   I see the business: I understand how my plot should
   advance.

179 *if not by birth, have lands by wit*: Because he is a bastard
he cannot inherit lands by *birth*, but he may be clever
enough to achieve them.

180 *All with me's meet that I can fashion fit*: Whatever I can
turn to my purposes I will regard as justified.

I.3

Time has elapsed since I.1, and Lear is now staying
with Gonerill. This scene prepares us for what we see
in I.4, and allows us to understand the calculation that
lies behind the violences exposed there.

   0 *Oswald*: Q and F directions and speech-prefixes call

him *Steward*. The use of the personal name in the speech-prefixes and stage directions of modern editions derives from its authentic use as a speech-prefix in a passage of the Q text which gives two alternative perversions of I.4.332 (given to *Stew.* in F). The name *Oswald* also appears in the text, at I.4.310, 324, and 330. It is probable that Shakespeare used this name because he read that it was an Anglo-Saxon name for a steward. The Steward's costume should be an important facet of his character.

4 *By day and night*: This is sometimes taken to be an oath; but it is more likely, in the context of *every hour*, to mean 'at all times'.

5 *flashes*: Breaks out suddenly.

7 *upbraids us*: Note the transfer of the royal plural from Lear to Gonerill.

10 *come slack of former services*: Are less attentive in serving him than previously.

14 *come to question*: Be made an issue.

15 *distaste it*: Find it offensive.

21 *With checks, as flatteries, when they are seen abused*: This has been interpreted as 'with punishment instead of flattery when flattery becomes excessive' and as 'with punishments as well as flatteries when they (the old) are misled'.

25 *occasions*: Opportunities, excuses.

26 *speak*: Rebuke him.
   straight: At once.

I.4

The conflict implicit in I.1 and prepared for in I.3 breaks out in action. Bluntness in the disguised Kent and the nagging truth of the Fool lead up to Lear's violent repudiation of Gonerill and her calculated insults. Varieties of loyalty and respect for the past are opposed to icy and well-prepared control of the present situation.

1 *as well*: In addition to the disguise he is wearing.

2 *my speech*: My normal way of speaking.
   diffuse: Confuse, obscure.

3 *carry through itself to that full issue*: Achieve my aim completely.

3–4 *that full issue | For which I razed my likeness*: Kent is
the first of several in this play (Edgar, Lear, Gloucester)
who 'die into life', become effective morally by losing
their old social personality.

4 *razed my likeness*: Altered my appearance. If he did
this by shaving off his beard the word *raze* would be
particularly appropriate.

banished Kent: In case the audience have not recog-
nized his voice, he announces his identity.

5 *where thou dost stand condemned*: In the presence of
Lear.

6 *come*: Come to pass that.

7 *full of labours*: Hard-working.

Horns within: To indicate the hunt that Lear returns
from.

Knights: F reads *Enter Lear and Attendants* (Q: *Enter
Lear*) but the speech-prefixes below refer only to *Knight*
(Q: *Seruant*). Some knights must be present if
Gonerill's image of Lear's household is to make sense.
The advice to the King in 63–5 suggests a rank above
that of a common servant. On the other hand the
imperiousness of Lear's commands would suggest that
he is dealing with servants – though the orders given
to the man who speaks in 63–5 are as imperious as any
others in the scene. The usual modern stage direction
gives *Knights and Attendants*, but I assume that knights
are adequate to all the needs of the scene. Q keeps a
Knight in II.4 (F: *Gentleman*); but thereafter neither
text mentions Knights.

10 *A man*: An ordinary human being (see 34–5; with a
secondary sense of 'a servant').

11 *What dost thou profess*: Kent's point in *A man* – that
he can offer only his basic humanity – is not understood by Lear. He asks, 'What arts distinguish this
man?', presuming that those who come to the King
come because they have some special talent. Kent takes
another sense of *profess*, and replies in his own terms:
'My art is to be myself – ordinary, decent, honest.'

13 *I do profess to be no less than I seem*: Kent's phrase has

a second sense, aimed to remind the audience that he is, in fact, much *more* than he seems.

16 *judgement*: The most plausible sense is 'the Last Judgement', giving moral meaning to the rest of life.

16–17 *eat no fish*: It is not clear what this means; but certainly it is a joke of the brusque kind that comes to characterize Kent in his Caius persona.

25 *You*: Notice the distinction between *thou* and *you* in this passage.

30 *Authority*: This, like *Service* (23), suggests the tendency of this exchange to turn the characters into personifications of abstract qualities such as were characteristic of morality plays. Cf. I.1.147–9.

32 *curious*: Finely wrought. Kent implies that he is too blunt to be good at fine-spun rhetoric.

46 *clotpoll*: One with a 'clod' for his *poll* (head), a fool.

53 *roundest*: Most downright and uncompromising.

58 *ceremonious affection*: Combination of the affection due to a father and the ceremony appropriate to a king.

60 *the general dependants*: The mass of servants.
   the Duke himself: If one were to examine dramatic evidence as if in a court of law this would be found unreliable. Albany later (270) is *ignorant* of the situation, and the rest of his conduct in the play confirms the truth of this ignorance. The speech of the Knight here marks Shakespeare's anxiety to emphasize the isolation of Lear.

66 *rememberest*: Remind.

66–7 *mine own conception*: What I have thought.

67 *faint*: Not 'imperceptible', but 'languid'.

68–9 *jealous curiosity*: Tendency to suspect trifles as injuries to my dignity.

69 *a very pretence*: An actual intention.

73 *the Fool hath much pined away*: The first description of the Fool characterizes him as delicate and sensitive. Coleridge remarked that he 'is no comic buffoon . . . Accordingly, he is prepared for – brought into living connexion with the pathos of the play, with the sufferings' (*Coleridge on Shakespeare*, ed. Terence Hawkes (1969), p. 204).

83 *bandy*: The technical term for a stroke in tennis. The
dialogue following picks up the tennis metaphor; from
'bandying' looks, Lear turns to blows. Oswald objects
to being made a tennis-ball; Kent trips him and says
that football, a plebeian game, is more suitable for him
than tennis, a royal and noble game.

89 *differences*: The species or classes of men, dividing a
servant from a king, and, incidentally, football from
tennis.

90 *lubber*: Clumsy fellow.

90–92 *Have you wisdom? So*: The Steward hesitates before
accepting the push through the door. Kent's phrase
means 'Surely you have more sense than to resist'. The
So marks the Steward's 'wise' acceptance of the situation, and his exit.

94 *earnest*: Lear hires Kent as his servant with the usual
initial token-payment, a pledge of further payment to
come.

96 *pretty knave*: Dainty lad.

97 *take my coxcomb*: Have my fool's cap (for your *earnest*,
for you show yourself apt to act as a fool if you bind
yourself to one who's out of favour).

100 *and*: If.

smile as the wind sits: Adapt your behaviour to the
currents of power.

100–101 *thou'lt catch cold*: (1) The *wind* of power will make you
suffer; (2) you'll be turned out of doors (ironic anticipation).

102–3 *banished two on's daughters, and did the third a blessing*:
A paradoxical inversion of the apparent situation. But
(the Fool implies) the values of I.1 *were* inverted.

102 *on's*: Of his.

104 *nuncle*: 'Mine uncle' in childish talk becomes transformed into 'my nuncle'. Hence *nuncle* becomes the
word of a fool for his guardian or superior.

107–8 *If I gave them . . . thy daughters*: Even if (like you) I
had given away all my possessions I should have something left, good evidence of my folly (in giving things
away). I will give you one coxcomb as a first sign of

folly; beg from your daughters if you want a second
sign.

109 *the whip*: Domestic fools were (like madmen) whipped
into submission.

110 *must to kennel*: Must go out of doors to the dog-house.

110–12 *he must be whipped out when the Lady Brach may stand
by the fire and stink*: Truth is whipped out of doors like
a dog, but the falsely fawning bitch-hound (*Brach*) is
allowed to remain comfortably indoors, however
unpleasant the result.

113 *A pestilent gall to me*: This may refer to the Fool and
his speeches – 'How this fellow makes me wince!' –
but is more likely to pick up some inner train of
passion deriving from memory of Gonerill's household – 'How intolerably bitter is the situation I'm in!'
gall is both 'the bitter secretion of the liver' and 'a
sore place'.

117–26 *Have more than thou showest . . . two tens to a score*: If
you can be entirely prudent and self-concealing you
will accumulate possessions.

119 *thou owest*: You own.

120 *Ride more than thou goest*: That is, use your horse's
legs rather than your own.
goest: Walk.

121 *Learn more than thou trowest*: Listen to much and believe
little.

122 *Set less than thou throwest*: Not clear; possibly 'gamble
small stakes for large winnings'.

125–6 *more | Than two tens to a score*: This has been thought
to refer to usurious increase; but it is probably only a
riddling way of saying 'more than you would expect'.

127 *nothing*: Nonsense.

128 *like the breath of an unfee'd lawyer*: Following up the
proverb: 'A lawyer will not plead but for a fee' – no
fee, no breath, nothing.

129 *use*: Usury. Lear's reply recurs to the arithmetical point
that nothing cannot be multiplied into something.

132–3 *so much the rent of his land comes to*: Dover Wilson
suggests that the point being made is that all rent is

'something for nothing', a return without work done
to earn it. More simply, Lear has now no land.

138 *That lord*: An oblique way of pointing to Lear himself,
as is implied by the following piece of play-acting.

141 *for him stand*: Impersonate him.

143 *presently*: Immediately.

145 *found out*: Discovered (in spite of his 'disguise' as a
sane man).

there: He points to where Lear is standing.

147–8 *that thou wast born with*: Probably Shakespeare does
not intend the Fool to call Lear 'a born fool', but rather
to make the point that we are all born with folly as a
characteristic.

150 *No . . . will not let me*: Kent's *altogether fool* is taken by
the Fool to mean 'having all the folly there is'.

151 *a monopoly out*: A right to sole possession granted by
the sovereign. This reference to a great abuse of the
time has been thought to account for the omission of
the whole passage (138–53) from F.

151–2 *and ladies too*: Presumably these words should be illustrated by some indecency with the Fool's bauble.

157 *the meat*: The edible part.

159 *borest thine ass on thy back o'er the dirt*: Like the old man
in the fable who did not wish to overload his ass, and
carried him to market (Poggio's *Facetiae* (1470), §24).

161–2 *If I speak like myself in this, let him be whipped that
first finds it so*: Let the man who says that this is folly
be whipped, for he is the real fool.

163 *grace*: Favour.

164 *foppish*: Foolish: The wise men now take the places of
the fools, who in consequence lose their popularity.

165 *know not how their wits to wear*: The *wise men*, slavishly
imitative of the manners of the time, don't know how
to show their wisdom; in attempting to follow fashion
they become fools.

166 *apish*: Foolishly imitative.

168–9 *madest thy daughters thy mothers*: Gave your daughters
the right to chastise you.

173 *play bo-peep*: Behave with childish folly.

177 *And*: If.

185 *What makes that frontlet on*: What are you doing, wearing that headband of frowns?

188-9 *an O without a figure*: A zero with no other figure before it to give it value.

193-4 *He that keeps nor crust nor crumb, | Weary of all, shall want some*: He who (like Lear) in his weariness of the world gives away everything will come to want some of the things he has given away.

195 *a shelled peascod*: Since a peascod is the 'shell', one that is *shelled* is nothing.

196-209 *Not only, sir . . . proceeding*: The rhetoric of Gonerill's speech seems designed to convey an impression of cold venom. Notice the length of sentence (199-209 form one sentence), the elaboration of the subordinate clauses, the lack of concrete imagery, the sharpness of the alliteration (*found . . . safe . . . fearful; protect . . . put; 'scape censure . . . redresses sleep;* etc.), the balance of abstractions, the deviousness of the rhythm.

196 *all-licensed*: Allowed to say and do what he pleases.

197 *insolent*: Contemptuous of rightful authority.

198 *carp*: Find fault, reprehend.

199 *rank*: Gross.

201 *safe redress*: Sure remedy.

202 *too late*: Only too recently.

203-4 *put it on | By your allowance*: Encourage it by your sanction.

205 *nor the redresses sleep*: And the remedies will not be slow.

206-9 *Which in the tender of a wholesome weal . . . call discreet proceeding*: The process of remedy, resulting from care (*tender*) for the health of the state (*weal*), might well harm you in a way that under normal circumstances would be called shameful; but the necessities of the state will then allow that it is *discreet proceeding* to prefer your harm to the state's.

211 *The hedge-sparrow fed the cuckoo*: The *cuckoo* is (like Gonerill) an admirable example of 'necessities of state'; laid in the hedge-sparrow's nest, it grows so big from the hedge-sparrow's (Lear's) nourishing that it

becomes *discreet proceeding* for it to make room for itself by biting off its foster-parent's head.

212 *it's had*: It has had. (Shakespeare is often careless of the sequence of tenses, as from the past (*fed*) above to the perfect tense here.)

    it head . . . it young: The usual possessive of 'it' is 'his'; 'it' for 'its' seems especially common in 'baby talk'.

213 *So out went the candle*: Lear is presumably the candle of the state, whose extinction plunges the people into darkness.

216 *fraught*: Stored, loaded.

217 *dispositions*: States of mind.

219–20 *May not an ass know when the cart draws the horse*: Even a fool like me can see that things are the wrong way round here (a daughter giving instructions to the King her father).

221 *Whoop, Jug, I love thee*: Perhaps the refrain from a lost song. Obviously it repudiates the involvement with others which appears in the preceding line.

    Jug: Joan.

224 *notion*: Power to understand.

225 *Waking? 'Tis not so*: Lear assumes he must be dreaming (as later, with Cordelia, in IV.7).

228 *I would learn that*: I seek an answer to the question 'Who am I?'

228–30 *for by the marks of sovereignty, knowledge, and reason, I should be false persuaded I had daughters*: An expanded paraphrase of this might read: 'When I look I see on myself the insignia of a king; and am not aware that in terms of knowledge and reason I have lost the right to rely on my assumptions; on these accounts I should suppose I was right in thinking I was King Lear, who had *daughters* (that is, children owing reverence and obedience). But no such "daughter" can be seen, so I cannot be King Lear.'

231 *Which*: This may (1) stand for 'whom', relating back to the *I* of Lear's speech, or (2) refer back to *Lear's shadow* in 227. In the latter case we must suppose that the Fool is following his own uninterrupted train of thought, just as Lear is in 226 and 228.

233 *admiration*: Perhaps 'astonishing behaviour'. G. L.
Kittredge says 'pretending to wonder who you are'.
is much o'the savour: Has the same taste or character-
istics.

234 *pranks*: Childish or malicious games.

234–45 *beseech . . . desired . . . A little . . .*: In this speech words
of humility alternate with words of insolent censure,
creating a rhetorical effect of calculated venom.

238 *disordered*: Disorderly.
deboshed: A variant form of 'debauched'.
bold: Impudent.

240 *Shows*: Appears.

240–41 *epicurism and lust | Makes it more like a tavern or a
brothel*: The *epicurism* (gluttony) belongs to the *tavern*,
the *lust* to the *brothel*.

242 *a graced palace*: A palace which his grace, the King,
graces.

245 *disquantity your train*: Reduce the number of your
followers.

246 *the remainders that shall still depend*: Those who remain
as your followers.

247 *besort*: Be suitable for.

248 *know . . . you*: Presumably she means 'know you to be
a dangerous old man requiring restraint'.

254 *Woe that*: Woe to the person who.

258 *the sea-monster*: The sea was traditionally a home of
horrors, and perhaps *sea-monster* only means 'the kind
of monster that the sea traditionally produces'. If any
specific sea-monster is meant, that which destroyed
Hippolytus probably fits best into the context: as
described in the 1581 translation of Seneca's *Phaedra*
it is a 'monster' with a 'marble neck'; it is sent as a
punishment for filial ingratitude.

259 *Detested kite*: Vile carrion-bird.

260 *of choice and rarest parts*: Of carefully selected, difficult-
to-find qualities.

262–3 *in the most exact regard support | The worships of their
name*: Are punctilious, even in details, to live up to
their honourable reputation.

265 *engine*: Usually said to be the rack, but the rack does
    not seem like the *small fault*, nor does it wrench the
    frame *From the fixed place*. Some device more like a
    lever or a crow-bar seems to be intended.

266 *the fixed place*: (1) The foundations of the *frame of
    nature*; (2) the natural affection which supports human
    existence.

268 *this gate*: It is not clear which *gate* is intended – the
    ears, the eyes, or the mouth. It is very likely, however,
    that Lear beats his head as the general area of judge-
    ment and folly.

269 *dear*: Precious to me.

275–8 *Into her womb . . . honour her*: Cf. Deuteronomy 28:15,
    18: '. . . if thou wilt not hearken unto the voice of
    the Lord thy God . . . cursed shall be the fruit of thy
    body . . .'

277 *derogate*: Degraded, dishonoured (in strong antithesis
    to *honour* below).

278 *teem*: Bear children.

279 *Create her child of spleen*: Make her a child composed
    entirely of malice.

280 *thwart disnatured*: Perverse and unnatural (that is,
    without filial affection).

282 *cadent*: Dropping.
    fret: Wear away.

283–4 *Turn all her mother's pains and benefits | To laughter
    and contempt*: Treat any cares and pains of mother-
    hood that Gonerill may experience with scornful
    laughter, and treat her joys in motherhood with
    contempt.

289 *disposition*: Mood.

289–90 *that scope | As dotage gives it*: Meaning, presumably,
    violent talk and little action.

291 *fifty of my followers*: Editors have usually sought to
    explain this by realistic means: fifty followers must
    have been removed, without comment, at some earlier
    stage. I think that we should rather praise the bold
    foreshortening that makes the loss of fifty followers
    seem the consequence of an absence during which

only four lines are spoken. Certainly at 319 there are
A hundred knights, and at 321 and 329 the same number
is repeated.

at a clap: At one stroke.

292 *a fortnight*: The length of time he has been staying
with Gonerill.

296 *Should make thee worth them*: Should value you as if
you were worth the tears of a king.

Blasts and fogs: Blighting influences and disease-bearing
fogs.

297 *untented woundings*: Untentable wounds (too deep to
be probed with a 'tent' or roll of lint).

298 *fond*: Foolish.

299 *Beweep this cause*: If you shed tears over this matter.

300 *loose*: The F word may be the common sixteenth-
century spelling of 'lose' (the eyes lose water when
they are plucked out), or it may be the modern 'loose'
(the eyes release their water). It is probable that
Shakespeare, given the overlap of spelling, did not
distinguish clearly between the two words.

301 *To temper clay*: To soften clay (a base use, like the
treading of mortar, II.2.63–4).

301–2 *Yea, is't come to this?* | *Let it be so*: F omits Q's *yea
. . . this?*, and prints instead *Ha? let it be so*. Both versions
are metrically defective, so it is likely that the F correction should be added to the Q version, not simply
substituted for it. But there is one word which the F
corrector may have meant actually to remove from the
text – the word *yea*, against which F has, throughout
its length, a remarkable prejudice. If so, then *Ha* should
probably be regarded as a substitute rather than an
addition; we cannot keep both exclamations, and I
prefer to retain the earlier one.

303 *kind and comfortable*: Like a true daughter, affectionate
and ready to give comfort.

304–5 *with her nails* | *She'll flay thy wolvish visage*: Ironically,
Lear is made to describe Regan attacking Gonerill in
the manner of one wolf attacking another.

307 *Do you mark that*: Gonerill urges Albany to note the

treason implied in Lear's statement – as if he had said, 'I shall take steps to recover the throne and so depose you.'

308–9 *partial* . . . | *To*: Biased because of.

312–13 *Take the Fool with thee*: 'The literal sense is obvious; but the phrase was a regular farewell gibe: Take the epithet "fool" with you as you go' (G. L. Kittredge).

314–18 *caught her* . . . *daughter* . . . *slaughter* . . . *halter* . . . *after*: The rhymes seem to have been perfect in Elizabethan English: . . . 'hauter' . . . 'auter'.

321 *At point*: Armed ready for action.

322 *buzz*: Whisper of rumour.

324 *in mercy*: At his mercy.

326 *still*: Always.

327 *Not fear still to be taken*: Rather than live all the time in fear of being 'taken away' myself.

334 *my particular fear*: What this particular (or 'personal') fear is does not appear.

336 *compact*: Confirm, strengthen.

338 *milky gentleness and course*: Effeminate and gentle course (hendiadys).

340 *a-taxed for*: The various readings of the substantive texts are (1) Q uncorrected: *alapt*; (2) Q corrected: *attaskt for*; (3) F: *at task for*. The uncorrected Q reading is almost certainly a misreading of 'ataxt' ('t' and 'x' were often misread as 'l' and 'p'). The Q correction is a variant spelling of this; and F is a 'regularization' of Q corrected. An editor's reading should be as close as it intelligibly can to the original form, and in this case an almost complete return is possible; *a-taxed* is a variant form of 'taxed': 'complained of'.

341 *harmful mildness*: Gentleness that may harm the state.

342 *eyes may pierce*: Albany means 'into hidden events'; but we are powerfully reminded of the description of Gonerill in II.4.167: *Her eyes are fierce*.

345 *Well, well – th'event*: Albany declines to continue the dispute, and puts the arbitration of their quarrel to the *event* – the outcome.

1.5

This scene follows straight after I.4. We are now outside Gonerill's castle. Lear makes his old-fashioned attempts to counter Gonerill's compact with Regan, while the Fool bodingly prepares us for disaster.

0 *Knight*: F reads *Gentleman* – no doubt one of the Knights of the previous scene.

1 *before*: Ahead of me.

Gloucester: The town, presumably, rather than the Earl. But Shakespeare, no doubt, assumed that the Earl lived in or near the town. Dover Wilson prints 'Cornwall', on the grounds that Lear could not know that Regan, the recipient of the letter, is at Gloucester. But Shakespeare often makes these 'errors' of anticipation, not noticeable in the theatre.

2–3 *Acquaint my daughter no further . . . the letter*: Lear already distrusts Regan, and wishes not to give her any ammunition for an attack on his interpretation of the recent past.

8 *in's*: In his.

were't: The 'it' is his 'brain' or (alternatively) (the same sense) *brains*.

9 *kibes*: Chilblains.

11–12 *Thy wit shall not go slipshod*: There is no need for you to be shod in slippers (because of the chilblains in your wits), for your journey to Regan shows you lack wits, even in your heels. The train of thought is started by the *diligence* promised by Kent.

14 *use thee kindly*: As the next clause shows, he really means 'treat you according to her kind, or her nature', but he allows the possible meaning 'be kind to you' to point to Lear's expectation. Her 'kind' is as a sister to Gonerill rather than a daughter to Lear.

15 *she's as like this as a crab's like an apple*: Regan is as like Gonerill as a sour apple is like an apple (that is, identical in 'kind').

18 *She will taste as like this as a crab does to a crab*: The experience of Regan will be as sour and indigestible as the experience of Gonerill.

19 *on's*: Of his.

22 *of either side's nose*: On either side of his nose.

23 *what a man cannot smell out he may spy into*: The Fool is picking up his *I can tell what I can tell* (16). Man is given organs of perception that, used properly, may protect him from folly.

24 *I did her wrong*: Presumably Cordelia is meant. We recognize this immediately; but it is not clear *why* we do so.

29 *put's*: Put his.

31 *forget my nature*: That is, cease to be a kind father.

37 *To take't again perforce*: 'He is meditating on his resumption of royalty' (Dr Johnson).
   perforce: By violent means.
   Monster ingratitude: Cf. I.4.256–8.

43 *mad*: The first occasion when Lear leads our thoughts in this direction; no doubt he is picking up the *wise* of the preceding line, in its meaning 'sane'. As Coleridge remarks, 'The deepest tragic notes are often struck by a half sense of an impending blow' (*Coleridge on Shakespeare*, ed. Terence Hawkes (1969), p. 205).

48–9 *She that's a maid . . . cut shorter*: This couplet with its indecent pun on *things* has been supposed to be not Shakespeare's; but indecency and authenticity are quite compatible.

48 *departure*: Probably pronounced 'depart-er'.

II.1

The parts of the plot begin to separate out into their constituent elements, evil with evil, good with good. Edmund completes his triumph over *A credulous father and a brother noble*; Cornwall and Regan move in to support him. Edgar, now associated with Lear's knights (93–4), is exiled (like Kent and Cordelia).

0 *Enter . . . doors*: Here, and at II.2.0 and III.1.0, I have substituted a modern equivalent for the stage direction in F (*Enter . . . seuerally*). Entries and exits 'severally' – at opposite stage doors (cf. III.1.55 and III.7.106) – are used by Shakespeare to give visual effect to meet-

ings from far apart, or departures to undertake different
activities.

 1 *Curan*: It is rare for Shakespeare to give a proper name
   to a character as little individualized as Curan is here
   (his only appearance). It is not clear why he does so
   at this point.

 6 *news*: Here takes a plural agreement.

 8 *ear-kissing*: Most editors prefer Q's *eare-bussing*. *bussing*
   is certainly the more vivid word; but it is a vulgar error
   to suppose that Shakespeare's vocabulary is characterized principally by its use of quaint and vivid elements.
   arguments: Topics of conversation.

10–11 *likely wars toward 'twixt the Dukes of Cornwall and
   Albany*: The first of frequent references to wars likely
   to occur (*toward*) between the Dukes.

 14 *The better! best*: So much the better! In fact, nothing
   better could happen.

 15 *perforce*: Of necessity, without my seeking it.

 17 *one thing of a queasy question*: A matter that requires
   delicate handling. He refers, presumably, to the
   disposing of Edgar.
   queasy: Literally, 'liable to vomit'.

 18 *Briefness*: Speed of action.
   Briefness and fortune work: I hope that quick action and
   good luck will help me,

 19 *Descend*: At I.2.174 Edgar retired to Edmund's lodging.
   Presumably it is from this hiding place that he now
   'descends'.

23–6 *the Duke of Cornwall . . . the Duke of Albany*: Edmund
   was entirely ignorant of these matters only thirteen
   lines before. This is a good example of his quick-
   thinking opportunism.

 26 *Upon his party 'gainst the Duke of Albany*: First Edmund
   suggested Edgar's peril from Cornwall; now he
   reverses the case and suggests that Edgar may have
   spoken too boldly on the side of Cornwall against
   Albany and so excited the latter's wrath. The prime
   object is to create a world teeming with dangers.

 27 *Advise yourself*: Consider the matter.

29 *In cunning*: As a clever device.

30 *quit you*: Defend yourself in the fight (with also, perhaps, a sense of *quit* meaning 'depart').

34-5 *I have seen drunkards | Do more than this in sport*: 'Stabbing of arms', and mixing the blood with wine drunk to a mistress, was a practice of the gallants of Shakespeare's age.

37-9 *in the dark . . . auspicious mistress*: Note Edmund's gift for theatrical invention – these details are well designed to affect the credulous Gloucester.

38-9 *Mumbling of wicked charms . . . where is he*: Edmund appeals to Gloucester's tendency to superstition. Gloucester's reply is, however, severely practical. There is some comedy in the cross-purposes of Edmund trying to get Edgar out of the way, and divert attention to himself, and Gloucester bent on the capture of his son.

41 *Fled this way*: As the eighteenth-century editor Capell said, Edmund should point in the wrong direction.

45 *bend*: Aim (like a bow). Cf. II.4.222.

48-9 *how loathly opposite I stood | To*: With what loathing I opposed.

49 *fell motion*: With a fierce thrust.

50 *preparèd sword*: At I.2.167 Edmund told Edgar to go armed. We may assume that Edgar has given substance to the story by entering (19) with his sword drawn (*preparèd*).

51 *unprovided*: Unprepared, unprotected.
   latched: The F reading is less easy than Q's *lanch'd* (or 'lanced'); but the fact that the change was made gives it a claim to credence. To 'latch' is to 'catch' or 'nick', and this may seem more appropriate to the minor wound that Edmund has inflicted on himself than the stronger 'lanced'.

52 *my best alarumed spirits*: My best energies called up by the *alarum* of battle.

54 *gasted*: Terrified.

55 *Let him fly far*: However far he flies.

57 *And found – dispatch*: Presumably the pause is filled in

by some gesture, such as drawing his hand across his
throat.

58 *arch and patron*: Arch-patron (hendiadys).

61 *to the stake*: Metaphorically: 'to the place of final
inescapable reckoning'.

64 *pight*: (Past participle of 'pitch') firmly fixed (like tent-
pegs).

curst speech: Angry words.

65 *discover*: Reveal.

66 *unpossessing bastard*: Bastards were in law deemed incapable of inheriting land.

67–9 *would the reposal | Of any trust, virtue, or worth in
thee | Make thy words faithed*: Would the fact that trust
has been placed in you, or any virtue or worth that
you possess in yourself, make people believe what you
say?

71 *character*: Handwriting (in the letter Edmund showed
in I.2).

71–2 *turn it all | To thy suggestion, plot, and damnèd prac-
tice*: Explain it as being due to your temptations, your
plotting, and your wicked intriguing.

73–6 *thou must make a dullard of the world . . . make thee
seek it*: You would have to make mankind very stupid
to stop them thinking that you had full, ready, and
powerful motives to seek my death, given the advantages that would come to you if I were dead.

76 *strange and fastened*: Fixed firm in his unnaturalness.

77 *deny his letter*: In 70–71.

got: Begot.

Tucket: Personal trumpet call.

79 *ports*: Probably 'sea-ports'; but it may mean the gates
of walled towns.

80–81 *his picture | I will send far and near*: An early version
of the 'wanted' poster outside police-stations.

83 *natural boy*: Gloucester means one who has expressed
'natural' loyalty to his father; but since a 'natural son'
is a bastard, there is an ironic twist to the phrase.

84 *capable*: Of inheriting land; that is, legitimized by
process of law.

89 *my old heart is cracked; it's cracked*: The repetition suggests the sentimental self-pity that is a part of Gloucester's basic temperament. Cf. *lady, lady* (92) and *too bad, too bad* (95).

90, 91 *my father's godson . . . He whom my father named*: Regan immediately capitalizes on the new situation, to identify all wickedness with her father.

95–6 *I know not . . . Yes, madam . . .*: Gloucester's response to Regan's efforts to blame her father is not very satisfactory; he is too sunk in self-pity to catch her drift. It is Edmund, with his clear eye for the main chance, who gives her the reply she wants, thus establishing at first sight the natural rapport between them.

96 *consort*: Accented on the second syllable. This is usually derogatory: 'gang, mob'.

97 *though*: If.
ill affected: Ill disposed.

98 *put him on*: Urged him to undertake.

99 *expense*: Spending.

102 *my house*: Notice the mannish and commanding air of Regan and the merely confirmatory role of Cornwall in this exchange.

105 *A child-like office*: The duties that are appropriate to a true son. Coming from Cornwall the words have an irony appropriate to Edmund.

106 *He did bewray his practice*: Edmund revealed Edgar's plot.

110 *Be feared of doing harm*: Give rise to the fear of his harmful deeds.

110–11 *Make your own purpose | How in my strength you please*: Fulfil your purpose (of capturing Edgar) by whatever means you like, drawing on my resources as it suits you.

113 *ours*: One of my followers. Note the royal plural.

114 *we shall much need*: With the implication: 'in the troubled times ahead of us' – whether in wars with Lear or wars with Albany is not certain.

116 *Truly, however else*: Even if my imperfections prevent me from being as efficient as I am true.

118 *Thus out of season, threading dark-eyed night*: Notice
how imperiously Regan takes over Cornwall's narrative and makes it her own. *out of season* may imply
that it is winter, a bad time for travelling, or may only
be repeating the point that, in their haste to avoid Lear,
they have travelled all night. The idea of threading
the eye of a needle in the dark, implicit in the imagery
used, conveys the sense of effort and difficulty.

119 *Occasions . . . of some price*: There are reasons (or
'personal requirements') of some importance. *price*
rather than 'prize' seems the most suitable modernization; see the note on I.1.70.

122–3 *which I best thought it fit | To answer from our home*:
Which letters I thought it best and most appropriate
to reply to away from home. Regan wishes to delay
receiving Lear till she has consulted with Gonerill.

123–4 *The several messengers | From hence attend dispatch*:
The men carrying the respective letters are waiting
here for their dismissal.

127 *Which craves the instant use*: Which requires to be
dispatched at once. It is not clear whether *Which* refers
to *counsel* or *businesses*. In Elizabethan English the
singular form *craves* would be equally correct with
either.

II.2

The physical conflict between the two servants, Kent
and Oswald the Steward, foreshadows in a semi-comic
and pathetic vein the grander conflict to come.
Gloucester and Cornwall move into sharper definition.

2 *Ay*: It is not clear why Kent says he is of Gloucester's
household, unless it is to give occasion for further
attacks on Oswald.

3 *we . . . our*: Presumably the plural refers to the attendants who accompany Oswald.

5 *if thou lovest me*: A conventional and rather affected
phrase for 'please', which Kent chooses to take literally.

7, 9 *care . . . care*: Oswald says he does not 'care for' ('like')
Kent. Kent says he could make him *care* ('worry').

8 *Lipsbury pinfold*: No place called *Lipsbury* is known; so it is usually supposed to be an equivalent to 'lip-town', the space between the lips. A *pinfold* is a pound for stray animals. The two words may well imply 'the strongly fenced area between the teeth', the whole phrase meaning: 'If I had you between my teeth I would make you care.'

11 *I know thee*: I can see through you. Notice the pejorative second-person singular throughout this dialogue.

13 *eater of broken meats*: After meals the scraps were collected into a basket, and these were the food of the lowest menials. Kent's general picture of Oswald is of a jumped-up menial pretending to be a gentleman – he is both *base* and *proud*.

14 *shallow*: Incapable of thought.

three-suited: Servant-like. Servants were allowed three suits a year. Cf. III.4.129.

hundred-pound: A great sum if the point is simply that Oswald is a menial. But about this time James I was making knights for a hundred pounds; so that the phrase carries the idea of 'beggarly pretender to gentility'.

15 *filthy-worsted-stocking knave*: Real gentlemen wore silk stockings.

lily-livered: Bloodless, cowardly.

15–16 *action-taking*: Going to law (instead of fighting).

16 *super-serviceable*: This seems to be the only appearance of the word, so it is not clear exactly what it means – perhaps 'anxious to be of service in any way, however dishonourable'.

finical: Fussing about details.

17 *one-trunk-inheriting*: Who inherited only as much as would go into one trunk.

17–18 *wouldst be a bawd in way of good service*: Would do any service, however improper or disgusting, if that was required of you.

19 *composition*: Compound.

22 *addition*: Something added to a man's name to denote his rank – here the names that Kent has 'added' to Oswald.

28–9 *make a sop o'the moonshine of you*: Make a mash of
you, soak you in blood, while the moon shines (or
'while you talk "moonshine"' – nonsense).

29–30 *cullionly barbermonger*: Base fop, never out of the
barber's shop.

33 *Vanity the puppet*: Gonerill, seen as a morality-play
figure of Self-Regard, performed in a puppet play.
There is also the sense of Gonerill as a puppet who
should not speak except with her father's voice – the
sense of the unnatural revolt of the puppet against the
puppeteer.

puppet: We should be aware of not only the modern
sense of 'marionette', but also the earlier sense of
'doll' (poppet).

35 *carbonado your shanks*: Slash your legs as if they were
meat for broiling.

35–6 *Come your ways*: Come on.

39 *neat slave*: Elegant rascal.

42 *With you*: I'll fight with you.
goodman boy: Master child, you who have set yourself
up with more authority than your years authorize.
and you please: If you like. For *and* F prints *if*, which is
probably a modernization. See An Account of the Text.

43 *flesh ye*: Introduce you to bloodshed.

48 *difference*: Dispute.

51 *disclaims in thee*: Denies any part in making you.

51–2 *a tailor made thee*: The proverb is that 'The tailor
makes the man' – with the sense that social status is
derived from clothes. Kent pushes this one stage
further: Oswald is made, not simply socially but in
every sense, by his clothes.

55–6 *A tailor . . . A stone-cutter or a painter could not have
made him so ill . . .*: The tailor was one of the more
despised of Elizabethan tradesmen, often thought of
as cringing and effeminate.

62 *thou unnecessary letter*: Zed was thought *unnecessary*
because most of its functions in English are taken over
by 's', and because Latin manages without it. Similarly
Oswald is a superfluous element in society.

63 *unbolted*: Unsifted, unkneaded; requiring to be trodden down (like lumpy mortar) before he can be useful.

64 *jakes*: Lavatory.

65 *wagtail*: G. L. Kittredge suggests that Oswald is too scared to stand still, and therefore reminds Kent of the uneasy tail-jerking of the wagtail. The word was often used in this period to mean 'wanton'.

67 *beastly*: Beast-like (not knowing the *reverence* etc. proper to human society).

68 *privilege*: To break the bounds of normal social decorum.

70–71 *should wear a sword* | *Who wears no honesty*: Carries the symbol of manhood, but lacks an honourable character.

72 *the holy cords*: The bonds of natural affection that bind the individual to society.

73 *t' intrinse t'unloose*: Too inward, secret, hidden (in their mode of tying) to be untied. Thus the bonds of matrimony or of filial obedience (or of royal duty) cannot be 'untied' (returned to their separate condition), but can be 'bitten' apart so that *love cools, friendship falls off*, etc. Oswald's nature is thus turned towards one of the central problems of the play.
smooth: Promote by flattery.

74 *rebel*: In the typical image of man, passion can only emerge when it *rebels* against its overseer, reason.

75 *Being*: F's *Being* and Q's *Bring* seem equally good; and therefore, in the absence of other evidence, we must prefer the F reading.

76 *Renege*: Deny. Cf. IV.6.98–100.
turn their halcyon beaks: The kingfisher (or *halcyon*) was supposed, if hung up, to vary direction with the wind. So flattering servants only possess opinions to point in whatever direction the passions of their masters require.

79 *epileptic visage*: Oswald is presumably trying to smile and at the same time twitching with terror.

80 *Smile*: F follows Q's unusual spelling *Smoile*. Editors have sometimes thought that this reflected Kent's

dialect disguise as Caius; but such an isolated expression of it would be pointless.

81–2 *Goose, if I had you . . . Camelot*: An obscure passage, which must have the general sense: 'If I had you at command I would make you add flight to your cackling laughter, like a goose being driven.'

81 *Goose*: Foolish person.

Sarum Plain: Salisbury Plain.

82 *Camelot*: The legendary capital of Arthur's kingdom; it is not known where it was situated; some Elizabethans believed it was at Winchester.

88 *likes me not*: Does not please me.

94–6 *doth affect . . . from his nature*: Pretends to a blunt rudeness of manner, and twists the habit (*garb*) of plainspeaking away from its (*his*) true nature (truth), turning it towards deception.

98 *And they will take it, so; if not, he's plain*: If people will swallow his rudeness, then that's all right; if they object, then he defends himself by the claim that this is just plain-speaking.

100 *more corrupter*: The double comparative is a common Elizabethan usage.

101 *silly-ducking observants*: Obsequious attendants making themselves foolish with their low bows.

102 *stretch their duties nicely*: Strain themselves to carry out their duties with the greatest finesse.

104, 105 *aspect . . . influence*: Astrological terms. Kent's parody of the *observants*' courtly dialect leads him to describe Cornwall as a planet.

104 *aspect*: Accented on the second syllable.

106 *flickering Phoebus' front*: The fiery forehead of the sun.

107 *my dialect*: That of a plain-spoken man.

110–11 *though I should win your displeasure to entreat me to't*: It is difficult to paraphrase this; perhaps the easiest interpretation is: 'though I should manage to overcome your displeasure to the extent that you would entreat me to be a knave'.

115 *upon his misconstruction*: As a result of his (the King's) misunderstanding of me.

116 *he, compact*: Kent, being in league with the King.
     flattering his displeasure: To gratify his mood of anger.

117 *being down, insulted*: When I was down, he abused me.

118–19 *put upon him such a deal of man | That worthied him*:
     Made himself out to be such a hero that others thought
     him worth something.

120 *For him attempting who was self-subdued*: For attacking
     a man who gave in without a struggle.

121 *fleshment*: Excitement of accomplishing. To 'flesh' was
     to inflict injury in warfare, especially for the first time.
     dread exploit: Ironical.

122–3 *None of these rogues and cowards | But Ajax is their
     fool*: Either (1) 'To hear people of his kind speak you
     would think the great hero Ajax was a fool beside
     them' or (2) 'Rogues and cowards can deceive great
     men like Cornwall (or Ajax)'.

124 *ancient knave . . . reverend braggart*: The same idea is
     repeated: Kent is old and therefore should be revered;
     but he is a knave and a braggart.

129 *grace and person*: Both his mystical body as King and
     his *person* as man.

132 *till noon*: The moon is still shining; the sun begins to
     rise some thirty lines later (161).

135 *being*: Since you are.

136 *colour*: Character.

137 *bring away*: Bring along.

140 *check*: Rebuke.

141 *contemned'st*: Most despised.

152 *Will not be rubbed*: Cannot bear to be hindered. A 'rub'
     in bowls is anything that impedes the bowl.

153 *watched . . . hard*: Made myself stay awake.

158 *approve the common saw*: Prove the truth of the well-
     known saying. The particular *saw* is no doubt suggested
     by the rising of the sun.

159–60 *out of Heaven's benediction comest | To the warm sun*:
     Come from good to bad.

161 *beacon to this under globe*: The sun.

162 *comfortable*: Comforting.

163–4 *Nothing almost sees miracles | But misery*: Miracles (like this letter from Cordelia) are especially likely to occur to those in the lowest and most depressed condition. Maynard Mack thinks there is a reference to Acts 16, where Paul and Silas, placed in the stocks in Philippi, 'prayed and lauded God' and were released by an earthquake (*King Lear in Our Time* (1966), p. 56).

166 *my obscurèd course*: My disguised way of life.

166–8 *and 'shall find time ... their remedies'*: Obscurely worded and perhaps corrupt. Some of the dislocation of sense may be due to Kent's reading out phrases from the letter. The general meaning must be that Cordelia will intervene and try to put things right.

167 *this enormous state*: This abnormal and wicked state of affairs.

168–9 *o'erwatched ... eyes*: Eyes made weary by being kept from sleep.

171 *He sleeps*: I give no exit here. I believe that Kent remains on stage throughout the next scene and is discovered by Lear in II.4 still onstage. We may prefer to imagine that the stocks are set in a recess and are concealed by the drawing of a curtain.

II.3

This one-speech scene serves to give a short breathing-space in the effectively continuous action in the courtyard of Gloucester's castle which occupies II.2 and II.4. It also allows us to be aware of the transformation of Edgar into Poor Tom so that when we hear his name (III.4.37 and 41) and see him (III.4.43) we know with whom we are dealing.

1 *proclaimed*: As an outlaw. See II.1.59.

2 *by the happy hollow of a tree*: By the fortunate accident that there was a hollow tree in which I could hide.

3 *No port is free*: See II.1.79.

6 *am bethought*: Have a mind.

7 *most poorest*: The double superlative, like the double comparative (see II.2.100), is a means of giving emphasis.

8 *in contempt of man*: Despising the pretensions of humanity (to be superior to the beasts).

10 *Blanket my loins*: A useful indication of the stage appearance of the 'naked' Tom – he wore a piece of blanket as a loin-cloth.

elf: Tangle into elf-locks. (Matted hair was thought to be the result of elvish malice.)

11 *with presented nakedness outface*: By persecuting himself, by *presenting* his nakedness to the storm, Edgar 'stares down' the hostile world.

14 *Bedlam beggars*: Beggars who claim they have been inmates of the Bethlehem (*Bedlam*) madhouse, and have licences to go about begging for their keep. 'This fellow . . . that sat half-naked . . . from the girdle upward . . . he swears he hath been in Bedlam and will talk franticly of purpose; you see pins stuck in sundry places of his native flesh, especially in his arms, which pain he gladly puts himself to . . . only to make you believe he is out of his wits; he calls himself by the name of *Poor Tom* and, coming near anybody, cries out, *Poor Tom is a-cold*' (Thomas Dekker, *The Bellman of London*, 1608).

15 *mortified*: Dead to feeling (like *numbed*).

17 *object*: Spectacle.

low: Lowly, humble.

18 *pelting*: Paltry.

19 *bans*: Cursings.

20 *Poor Turlygod! Poor Tom*: Edgar enacts the role he must now fulfil. *Turlygod* is a word no one has explained.

21 *That's something yet; Edgar I nothing am*: As Poor Tom there is some kind of existence for me; as Edgar I cannot exist.

II.4

The climactic scene at the end of the protasis or exposition of the play. Beginning at the level of the affront to Kent, the tension mounts through Lear's dispute with Regan and Cornwall – conducted via Gloucester and so avoiding full-scale confrontation – and reaches its first climax when Gonerill arrives and we have the full orchestration of I.1 repeated, answering the 'I give

you' of the opening with a conclusive 'We take'. This
dispute only dies into another kind of climax as Lear's
speeches expand to prophetic frenzy, as the storm thun-
ders closer, and as Lear rushes to join the cosmic furies,
and the wicked withdraw to safety.

3–4 *purpose . . . Of this remove*: Intention to move from
   one house to another.

6 *Makest thou this shame thy pastime*: Do you sit in the
   stocks for fun?

7 *cruel garters*: (1) The stocks; (2) crewel (worsted) cross-
   garters.

10 *wooden nether-stocks*: Stocks as stockings.

11 *place*: (1) Rank (as King's messenger); (2) the place
   (where you sit) due to you.

13 *son*: Son-in-law.

19 *Yes*: Given the regular symmetry of this exchange one
   might expect 'Yes, yes' here; but one can hardly change
   the text for such a reason, even though the unreliable
   Q is the only authority for 18–19.

23 *upon respect*: Either (1) 'against a man whose role
   required respect' or (2) 'deliberately'.

24 *Resolve me with all modest haste*: Tell me with speed,
   but be temperate.

26 *Coming from us*: Given that you came as a royal
   messenger.

28–9 *from the place that showed | My duty kneeling*: From
   the kneeling posture that showed my duty.

29–30 *a reeking post, | Stewed in his haste*: A sweating
   messenger, soaked in the sweat his haste had produced.

32 *spite of intermission*: In spite of the gasps and pauses
   that his breathless condition required.

33 *presently*: Immediately.
   on whose contents: When they had read them.

34 *meiny*: Household menials.

40 *Displayed so saucily*: Acted in so obviously insolent a
   way.

41 *man than wit*: Courage than discretion.

45 *wild geese*: They fly south in the autumn. The events
   that Kent has described convey the same message as

do wild geese seen flying south – the winter of displeasure and unkindness is to get worse.

47 *blind*: To the needs of their parents.

48 *bear bags*: Keep their money-bags.

51 *turns the key*: Opens the door.

52–3 *dolours for thy daughters*: (1) Griefs because of your daughters; (2) dollars in exchange for your daughters

53 *tell*: (1) Speak of; (2) count.

54, 55 *mother . . . Hysterica passio*: A feeling of suffocation and giddiness thought to begin in the womb ('mother', '*hystera*' in Greek) and to affect the patient by climbing to the heart and then to the throat. One of the demoniacs in Harsnet's *A Declaration of Egregious Popish Impostures* (1603) suffered from the mother.

56 *Thy element's below*: Your appropriate place is below. The 'mother' is not simply a medical condition appropriate to Lear; it is a visceral symbol of the breakdown in hierarchy, when the lower elements climb up to threaten or destroy the superior ones.

62 *And*: If.

62–3 *set i' the stocks for that question*: The question is subversive, for the answer must be that kings who lose their power also lose their followers.

65–6 *an ant . . . no labouring i'the winter*: Aesop's provident ant laboured when labour was profitable (in the summer); so Lear's followers stopped following when the winter of their master's fortune made following unprofitable.

66–9 *All that follow their noses . . . him that's stinking*: Those who go straight still follow what they see, and they can see Lear's downfall. Even the blind man who cannot *see* his downfall can smell the stink of failure.

69 *a great wheel*: A great man.

73 *ha' . . . use*: This emendation assumes that the F reading, *I would hause none but knaues follow it* (where *hause* replaces the Q *haue*), derives from a correction *ha use* written in the margin of Q. It is assumed that this was intended to replace Q's *haue* by *ha* and Q's *follow* by *use*. The F compositor, however, attributed both the corrections to *haue* and left *follow* intact.

74–7 *That sir . . . in the storm*: The servant's progress described here is very close to that which Iago praises in *Othello*, I.1.49–54.

74 *sir*: Man (here specifically a servant).

75 *for form*: Out of habit or convention.

76 *pack*: Depart.

80–81 *The knave turns fool that runs away;* | *The fool no knave, perdy*: If this is textually correct it implies a sudden switch from worldly wisdom to spiritual truth: 'The knave (servant) who deserts his master must eventually be seen as a fool; but this fool will stay, and so, in God's name, is no knave.'

83 *Not i'the stocks, fool*: In the context this is equivalent to saying that Kent is no knave.

85 *fetches*: Tricks.

86 *images of revolt and flying-off*: Representative of disobedience and desertion and the rejection of natural ties.

88 *quality*: Character.

91 *What 'quality'*: Lear is still in the world where individuality is far less important than status and relationship. When king and father command, character is no excuse.

97 *commands, tends, service*: This is F's reading. The text here is difficult if not impossible to sort out. The Q corrector's *commands her seruice* is probably mere tidying up without authority. The original (uncorrected) Q's *come and tends seruice*, because it is nonsense, probably represents an honest attempt to read the manuscript. If F was printed from the uncorrected form of the Q page we could base little on its preservation of the Q reading; on the other hand, if F was printed from the corrected page, its readings would imply a fresh look at the manuscript, and the coincidence with the uncorrected Q reading would prove authenticity. I think we must print either 'commands, tends' or something that looks like 'come and tends' in Elizabethan handwriting. The usual reading of modern editors, 'commands, tends', makes

sense, but not good sense. Lear is making plain forceful demands, not complex or ironic ones like 'commands her service and tends his own'. 'True service' is a possible reading, and one easily misread in Elizabethan handwriting as *tends service*.

101 *still*: Always.

101–2 *neglect all office | Whereto our health is bound*: Fail to fulfil the duties which are required of us when we are in health.

105 *am fallen out with my more headier will*: Am no longer friendly to my more reckless impulse.

107 *Death on my state*: An oath – 'May my kingly power come to an end' – which is already fulfilled.

109 *remotion*: Either (1) 'removal from one house to the other' or (2) 'holding themselves remote from me'.

110 *practice*: Stratagem.

111 *and's wife*: Not 'my daughter'.

112 *presently*: At once.

113 *chamber*: Bedroom.

114 *cry sleep to death*: Kills off sleep by the noise it makes.

116 *rising heart*: A further stage in the *hysterica passio*.

117–20 *as the cockney did . . . down*: *cockney* probably means here 'a pampered and foolish person'. She had little experience of making eel-pies, put the eels in without killing them, and, when they tried to wriggle out of the pastry, rapped them on the heads, crying, 'Down, you roguish creatures.' So Lear's heart tries to 'rise' out of the situation his folly has created and must be *knapped* ('struck').

120–21 *'Twas her brother . . . buttered his hay*: Cheating ostlers were said to butter hay to stop the horses eating it. The cockney's *brother* (that is, one of the same breed of tender-hearted fools) tries to be kind and succeeds in being destructive (like Lear).

126–7 *divorce me from thy mother's tomb, | Sepulchring an adult'ress*: Posthumously divorce your mother, proved unfaithful to me (by your unfilial conduct).

127 It has been suggested that Kent should exit here.

129 *naught*: Wicked.

130 *like a vulture*: Shakespeare may be remembering the torment of Prometheus, whose liver (believed to be the seat of the passions) was endlessly devoured by a vulture.

133–5 *I have hope . . . she to scant her duty*: The sense is clear: 'I trust that she does not know how to scant her duty as well as you know how to undervalue her'; but it is not easy to make the words mean this. The most probable explanation of the fact that the literal sense seems opposite to the required sense is that *scant* adds a second negative idea to that in *less know*; Shakespeare is anxious to stress the negative, but fails to notice that he has one too many, and that 'she to do her duty' would be more accurate.

138 *riots*: Regan and Gonerill use the same vocabulary for the knights. See I.3.7, I.4.199 and 240, and II.1.93.

144 *state*: Physical and mental condition (but with an ironic echo of *state* meaning 'power, royalty').

148 *becomes the house*: Is appropriate to the household (where the father is 'the head of the house').

150 *Age is unnecessary*: In a survival-of-the-fittest world (which Gonerill and Regan are setting up) the aged cannot be justified; no one needs them. If they are to be given *raiment, bed, and food* it must be out of charity.

154 *abated*: Deprived.

158–9 *Strike her young bones . . . with lameness*: Deform the bones of her unborn child.

159 *taking airs*: Infectious vapours.

161–3 *Infect her beauty . . . blister*: You noxious vapours that rise from bogs when the sun shines on them, fall down on her, blister her face and mar her beauty.

166 *tender-hefted*: Endowed with a tender sensibility (literally, 'set into a delicate handle').

170 *sizes*: Allowances.

171–2 *oppose the bolt | Against my coming in*: The climax of these deprivations is, ironically enough, the one which Regan is shortly to put into practice.

173 *The offices of nature, bond of childhood*: The duties that are natural to our state, such as the bond of affection between child and parent.

174 *Effects of courtesy*: Manifestations of a courtly disposition.

174–5 *gratitude.* | *Thy half o'the kingdom* . . .: It is worth noticing that Lear, even at this point, climaxes his arguments, not with the claims of nature or courtesy, but with the economic argument.

178 *approves*: Confirms.

180 *easy-borrowed pride*: *pride* often means 'ostentatious adornment'. Oswald's splendid livery and his steward's chain (cf. Malvolio) are easy to put on and take off. What is more, they depend on the whim of 'her grace'.

186 *Allow*: Approve.

188 *beard*: An emblem of age, and therefore of authority and deserving.

191 *that indiscretion finds*: That want of judgement (like yours) discovers to be so.

192 *sides*: The sides of the chest, strained by the swellings and passions of the heart.

193 *hold*: Hold out, remain intact.

195 *Deserved much less advancement*: The stocks are a low seat, and a disgraceful punishment; but they are higher than he deserves.

196 *being weak, seem so*: Don't act as if you had strength you do not possess. Shakespeare quickly transfers the contest from Cornwall to the daughters. The central conflict must not be obscured by subsidiary issues.

201 *entertainment*: Proper reception.

204 *wage against the enmity o'th'air*: Struggle against the hostile environment of the open air.

205 *the wolf and owl*: Solitary and rapacious animals, hunting by night.

206 *Necessity's sharp pinch*: The phrase is governed by *choose*, in apposition to *To be . . . owl*. *Necessity* is both 'poverty' and 'fate'.

207 *hot-blooded*: Passionate (supposed to be a French characteristic) and therefore likely to be violent.

209 *knee*: Kneel before.
     squire-like: Like a body-servant.

211 *sumpter*: Pack-horse, drudge.

212 *groom*: Servant.

219 *embossed*: Swollen (to a knob or 'boss').

220 *corrupted*: By the *disease . . . Which I must needs call mine.*

221 *come when it will*: Notice the confidence that shame is bound to be visited upon her, sooner or later.

222 *the thunder-bearer shoot*: Jupiter aim his thunder-bolts (at you).

223 *high-judging*: Who judges from on high.

229 *mingle reason with your passion*: View your passionate outbursts with the cold eye of reason.

230 *Must be content to think you old, and so —*: Have no choice but to see you as senile, with the result that . . . Regan's contempt for his failure to accept his own senility chokes her utterance: the whole thing is so obvious that there is no point in speaking further.

234 *sith that*: Since. On *that*, see the note on I.1.248.
    charge: Expense.

240 *slack ye*: Be negligent to you (as Oswald was commanded in I.3.10).

241 *control them*: Call them to account.

244 *place or notice*: Lodging or official recognition.

246 *Made you my guardians, my depositaries*: Put you in charge of my estate, made you my trustees.

251 *well-favoured*: Fair of face.

257 *To follow*: To be your followers.

259 *reason not the need*: Don't try to apply rational calculation to *need* (as in 256).

259–60 *Our basest beggars | Are in the poorest thing superfluous*: Even the most deprived of men have among their few possessions something that is beyond (*superfluous* to) their basic 'needs'.

261–2 *Allow not nature more than nature needs — | Man's life is cheap as beast's*: The usual punctuation of this involves a comma after *needs*, with the sense: 'If you do not allow nature more than is necessary, then man's life will have to be reckoned as cheap as a beast's.' This seems to me too rational and hypothetical an

argument for Lear at this point. He is (I take it) angrily
mimicking the computational arguments of his daughters: 'In your terms even the beggar's rags are superfluous. Don't bother to believe that human nature has
needs greater than those of animal nature, for it is as
easy (or *cheap*) to buy a human life as an animal life.'

263–5 *If only to go warm . . . keeps thee warm*: Let us define
'the gorgeous' in dress as 'able to keep you warm'; yet
nature does not need even that kind of gorgeousness
in spite of the little warmth your gorgeous dresses do
provide.

265 *for*: As for.

268 *wretched in both*: This is the first time that Lear has
described the wretchedness as against the dignity of
age.

270 *fool me not so much*: Don't let me be such a fool.
Realizing the wretched passivity of age, Lear prays to
be given the 'nobility' of manly anger, even of revenge.

276–7 *they shall be | The terrors of the earth*: Shakespeare
does not hesitate to show Lear's alternative to
weeping, his *noble anger*, as absurd boasting. Lear's
nobility depends not on his power to terrorize the
earth, but on his ability to assimilate into his passions
those terrors of the earth which begin to make their
sounds heard almost immediately.

280–81 *break into . . . flaws | Or ere I'll weep. O Fool, I shall
go mad*: The alternative to melting into tears (the
woman's way) is to explode into fragments (*flaws*).
And immediately Lear indicates the nature of this
explosion, the fragmentation of sanity that is to ensue.

283 *and's*: And his.

284 *bestowed*: Accommodated.

285 *from rest*: From his bed.

287 *For his particular*: As far as he himself is concerned.

293 *He leads himself*: He is under no guidance but that of
his own will.

296 *ruffle*: Rage, brawl.

298–9 *The injuries that they themselves procure | Must be their
schoolmasters*: They have to learn their lesson in being

punished by the consequences of their own wilful
actions.

300 *a desperate train*: The *riotous knights* once again.

301–2 *apt | To have his ear abused*: This is an example of a stan-
dard shift to which Regan and Gonerill resort: that their
unkindness to their father is provoked by others, such as
riotous knights, who mislead him ('abuse his ear'), and
must therefore bear the responsibility for his suffering.

III.1

A bridge-passage between two scenes of higher
dramatic tension. The narrative account of Lear's
behaviour describes some of the meanings that we
should attach to the *action* of III.2. Shakespeare gives
here, at the very moment when evil has established its
undisputed ascendancy, a glimpse of the counter-
movement gathering momentum at Dover.

0 *still*: Perhaps 'as before' (at II.4.279), but more probably 'continuously'.

2 *One minded like the weather*: The first statement of the
equation between the inner world and the stormy
weather which is so important in the next few scenes.

4 *Contending*: Both (1) 'physically struggling against' and
(2) 'competing in violence and anger'.
the fretful elements: The angry weather.

5–6 *Bids the wind . . . 'bove the main*: Lear commands the
earth to return to the state before creation separated
water and earth.

6 *main*: Mainland.

8 *eyeless rage*: Blind, indiscriminate wrath.

9 *make nothing of*: Treat as worthless.

10 *his little world of man*: Lear as a microcosm or model
of the external world.
out-storm: The Q reading, *outscorne*, is possible and
therefore tempting (there is no F text at this point).
But Elizabethan printers and transcribers frequently
confused 'c' and 't', as well as 'm' and 'n'. *out-storm*
picks up and develops the important and central idea
of the microcosm in a way which would be typically
Shakespearian.

11   *to-and-fro conflicting*: Blowing now one way, now another.

12   *the cub-drawn bear would couch*: The bear, drained of her milk by her cubs and therefore ravenous, would lie in shelter.

14   *unbonneted*: Not wearing a hat (a stronger idea then than now: totally abandoning self-respect as well as self-protection).

15   *bids what will take all*: Offers the world to any power which cares to have it. *take all* is usually associated with the gambler's cry when he stakes everything on the last throw.

16   *out-jest*: Overcome by the force of his jokes.

17   *heart-struck injuries*: Injuries that are like blows on the heart.

18   *upon the warrant of my note*: Justified by my knowledge (of you).

19   *Commend . . . to you*: Recommend to your care.
     dear: Important.

22   *their great stars*: Their fortune of being great.

23   *who seem no less*: Who seem indeed to be real servants.

24   *France*: The King of France.

24–5 *speculations | Intelligent of our state*: Observers collecting political intelligence.

26–9 *Either in snuffs . . . but furnishings*: Three things that the King of France may have learned, and that may be encouraging him to invade, are: (1) the division between Albany and Cornwall; (2) the harsh treatment of King Lear, as if he were a horse pulled back on a tight rein (a pun on 'reign'), given no freedom of movement; (3) *something deeper*, which explains both (1) and (2), making these mere *furnishings* or accidentals. It seems pointless to speculate on the nature of this *something deeper*; it is part of the deep shadow that belongs to the picture.

26   *snuffs and packings*: Huffiness and secret plots to secure revenge.

29–30 *furnishings – | But true it is*: The dash expresses a refusal by Kent to speculate further; he returns to what is known as a fact – the French invasion.

30 *power*: Army.

31 *scattered*: Presumably refers to the dispersal of the royal power shown in the first scene of the play.

32 *Wise in our negligence*: Taking advantage of our neglect (of national security).

feet: Footholds.

33-4 *are at point | To show their open banner*: Are prepared to unfurl their flag, and declare themselves.

34 *Now to you*: Now I am going to suggest what you can do.

35 *my credit*: Your belief in me.

35-6 *so far | To*: So far as to.

37 *making just report*: For making an exact report.

38 *unnatural and bemadding sorrow*: Sorrow caused (unnaturally) by his own flesh and blood, so as to drive him mad.

39 *plain*: Complain.

42 *office*: Duty, function.

45 *out-wall*: Outside appearance. Kent is still dressed as Caius the servant.

46 *What it contains*: The *ring* mentioned in the next line.

48 *fellow*: Sometimes glossed 'companion'; but more likely to mean 'lower-class person, servant'.

52 *to effect*: In their consequences.

53-4 *in which your pain | That way*: In which matter I beg you to take pains by searching in that direction.

III.2

Lear and the Fool stumble across a stage now representing 'the heath' where man is fully exposed to the hostile physical world. Shakespeare uses the extension of this hostility in the storm to talk about the storm of passions in Lear's mind. Kent remains an emblem of loyal endurance; but Lear is more and more detached from any sense of an individual self to which one may be usefully loyal.

1 *your cheeks*: The image is derived from the personifications of the winds shown puffing their cheeks at the corners of old maps.

2   *cataracts and hurricanoes*: Water from the heavens and
    from the seas. Here, as in *Troilus and Cressida*, V.2.168
    – the only other occurrence of the word in Shakespeare
    – 'hurricane' is used to mean 'waterspout'. Lear is
    asking for a second deluge, or for a return to the state
    before the creation of man.

3   *cocks*: Weathercocks (on the top of the *steeples*).

4   *thought-executing*: Acting as fast as thought.

5   *Vaunt-curriers of oak-cleaving thunderbolts*: The *fires* of
    the lightning are the advance guard of the thunder's
    'bolts' or missiles, which are so powerful that they split
    the oak-tree. *Vaunt-curriers* are those who run in the
    'van' of the main body. I have avoided the usual
    modernization 'Vaunt-couriers' (F has *Vaunt-curriors*,
    Q, *vaunt-currers*) because it brings distracting associ-
    ations into the line.

7   *Strike flat the thick rotundity o'the world*: Hit so hard
    that the roundness of the world will be smashed flat.
    The suggestion of round-bellied fertility being frus-
    trated may also be present; this would lead directly to
    the imagery of the following lines.

8   *Crack Nature's moulds*: Break the patterns by which all
    things are created in their kinds.
    all germens spill: Destroy all the seeds out of which all
    matter is formed.

10 *court holy-water*: The flattery a man must sprinkle to
    belong to the court.

16 *I tax not you . . . with*: I do not accuse you of.

18 *subscription*: Obedience, allegiance.

21–2 *yet I call you servile ministers, | That will*: I call you
    servile agents, in that you are willing to.

23 *high-engendered battles*: Battalions coming from the
    heavens.

25–6 *a good head-piece*: (1) A good head covering; (2) good
    sense.

27–9 *The cod-piece that will . . . shall louse*: The man who
    finds a home for his penis before he has a roof over his
    head is destined for lice-infested beggary.

27 *cod-piece*: A case for the male genitalia ('cods') attached

to the breeches, often, as Alexander Dyce says, 'osten-
tatiously indelicate' in this period. Here (by metonymy
of the covering for the thing covered) the penis.

30 *So beggars marry many*: Obscure; does *many* refer to
the lice or the women?

31–3 *The man that makes . . . cry woe*: Another inversion
of order; based on the proverb: 'Set not at thy heart
what should be at thy heel.' If you lay your delight
in what you should spurn, you will be liable to suffer
for it, just as, if you valued your toe as highly as you
should value your heart, its ailments would loom as
large.

35–6 *For there was never yet fair woman but she made mouths
in a glass*: To 'make mouths' carries, as well as the
obvious meaning, the sense of 'treat with contempt'.
Apparently a foolish non sequitur, the sentence may
be a return to the theme of the daughters: 'Women
are by nature likely to despise what they see.'

40 *grace and a cod-piece*: The spiritual and the physical,
the King (his grace) and the fool. The idea of a *wise
man* is introduced to make the choice of roles uncer-
tain. The professional fool often wore a particularly
prominent cod-piece; but Lear, like the cod-piece above
(27), had children before he had wisdom.

44 *Gallow*: Frighten (more properly 'gally').
wanderers of the dark: Nocturnal animals.

48–9 *carry* | *Th'affliction nor the fear*: Endure the physical
affliction or the terror it inspires.

49–60 *Let the great gods . . . than sinning*: Lear's speech should
be contrasted with the preceding one by Kent. Kent
speaks of the physical effect of the storm. Lear, careless of this, concentrates on its moral meaning.

50 *pudder*: Hubbub (a variant form of 'pother').

51 *Find out their enemies now*: The *enemies* (criminals),
terrified by the storm, will confess their crimes.

53 *bloody hand*: Murderer. Cf. III.4.89.

54 *simular of virtue*: False claimant to chastity.

55 *Caitiff*: Base wretch.

56 *under covert and convenient seeming*: Behind a surface

appearance that was effective to conceal the truth and
fitting for the nefarious purposes planned.

57 *practised on*: Plotted against.

58 *Rive*: Break out.

continents: Hiding-places, bounds that hold you in.

58-9 *cry* | *These dreadful summoners grace*: Cry for mercy
to the elements that are sounding a summons to God's
court (as the *summoners* call offenders before the eccle-
siastical courts).

59-60 *I am a man* | *More sinned against than sinning*: *I* should
be emphasized, in contrast to the *Close pent-up guilts*
of other people.

60 *bare-headed*: See the note on III.1.14.

63, 64 *hard*: Unpitying.

67 *scanted*: Limited.

69 *my fellow*: Kent.

70-71 *The art of our necessities is strange* | *And can make vile
things precious*: Necessity has a strange art (like that of
the alchemist who turns base metal into gold) which
makes things that we despised when we were prosperous seem precious when we are in need.

71 *vile*: Here and at III.4.138, III.7.82, IV.2.38 and 47, and
IV.6.278, Q and F read *vild* (or *vilde*), common alternative forms of the word in Elizabethan English.

72-3 *I have one part in my heart* | *That's sorry yet for thee*:
This may seem to imply a radical limitation on Lear's
sympathy for a *fool and knave*. Perhaps we should read
'. . . sorry yet – for thee' ('I have a part of me still
capable of feeling sorrow, and that part is concerned
with you').

74-7 *He that has . . . every day*: This is a stanza derived from
the popular song that Feste sings at the end of *Twelfth
Night*. Lear's mention of his *wits* (67) reminds the Fool
of the song, with its obviously appropriate refrainline,
and he uses it to enshrine the lesson that our wits must
be adapted to our fortunes.

79 *a brave night to cool a courtesan*: It is not clear why the
comment on the weather takes this form. Perhaps a
pun is intended on 'night'/'knight'. If so, this would

explain the sudden switch to medieval parody in the lines following.

81–94 *When priests . . . used with feet*: The *prophecy* begins as a parody of a passage attributed in the Elizabethan period to Chaucer:

> When faith faileth in priestès saws,
> And lordès hests are holden for laws,
> And robbery is holden purchase,
> And lechery is holden solace,
> Then shall the land of Albion
> Be brought to great confusion.

Shakespeare turns this into a satiric statement of things that really do happen in his own day. The next 'stanza' involves a list of things not satirical and real, but utopian and ideal. In F this is followed by four lines of generalization (85–6, 93–4), but as the passage is made up of two separate couplets saying different things, and as the first couplet completes the pseudo-Chaucerian matter of the first stanza, it seems best to follow the practice of those editors who have placed the couplets one at the end of each stanza.

81 *more in word than matter*: Better at talking about virtue than practising it.

83 *nobles are their tailors' tutors*: Fashion-mad noblemen tell their tailors how to cut their elaborate clothes (as in Shakespeare's time).

84 *No heretics burned but wenches' suitors*: When love is more important than religion. *burned* may be a reference to the flames of love or to the physical effects of the pox.

86 *confusion*: Four syllables: con-fu-si-on.

90 *Nor . . . not*: In Elizabethan English two negatives do not necessarily make a positive.
    cutpurses come not to throngs: The cutpurse, like his modern equivalent, the pickpocket, pushed in among large crowds, where he could cut and steal purses – commonly worn hanging from the belt – with greater ease.

91 *When usurers tell their gold i'the field*: Usurers were a part of city life, opposed to the traditional agricultural sources of wealth. Perhaps *gold i'the field* refers to grain, so that the phrase means 'when usurers turn farmers', or perhaps 'are willing to lend to farmers'.

91 *tell*: Count.

92 *do churches build*: Use their wealth for religious purposes.

94 *going shall be used with feet*: Feet will be used for walking on ('an intentionally absurd truism', says G. L. Kittredge).

95–6 *Merlin . . . I live before his time*: According to Geoffrey of Monmouth, Lear lived during the eighth century BC, and Arthur during the sixth century AD.

III.3

In this prose scene, Gloucester's fate marches forward to the same betrayal as has already overtaken Lear. His pity for Lear keeps before us what is happening on the heath, but interrupts the lyrical passions of approaching madness with reminders of ordinary life.

1–2 *unnatural*: Because it is their father that Gonerill and Regan have mistreated.

3 *pity*: Be merciful to (a use of the verb not elsewhere recorded, but cognate with 'have pity on' in the same sense).

7 *Go to*: No more of that.

8 *a worse matter*: Perhaps this refers to the French invasion, which is what the letter in fact describes (III.5.9–10). But in 9–10 the invasion seems a separate matter. Perhaps the *worse matter* is yet another piece of the 'shadow' in which Shakespeare chooses to place the conflict of Albany and Cornwall; Cf. *something deeper* (III.1.28, and the note on III.1.26–9).

10 *closet*: Cabinet for private papers.

11 *home*: All the way, thoroughly.

12 *footed*: Landed, got a foothold. The same unusual word is used at III.7.45 of the French invasion (cf. III.1.32).

13 *look*: Seek.

18 *toward*: About to happen.

19 *This courtesy forbid thee*: Helping Lear, which he was
forbidden to do.

21 *a fair deserving*: Deserving of a fair reward.

III.4

A direct continuation of III.2. Kent's concern for the
physical well-being of the King is frustrated finally by
the appearance of naked Tom, an apparition that
releases Lear's last hold on his own identity and
submerges his sanity in his sense of all the oppressed
and dispossessed of the world. Fool, King and Bedlam
begin to forge a new dialect, a rapt recitation of inner
visions, compared to which the common-sense solic-
itudes of Kent and Gloucester seem external and superficial.

3 *nature*: Human nature.

11–12 *When the mind's free | The body's delicate*: When the
mind is free of worry, it can afford to attend to the
body's petty complaints of discomfort.

15 *as this mouth should tear this hand*: As if one part should
harm another part of the same body (all of whose
functions are for the united good of the whole). Lear
sees himself and his daughters as part of such a body.

20 *frank heart*: Generous love.

25 *things would hurt me more*: The internal *tempest* of his
thoughts of filial ingratitude.

26 *houseless poverty*: *Poor naked wretches* who have no
covering from the storm.

27 *I'll pray*: The 'prayer' that Lear says before he goes to
sleep is a highly unorthodox one, not for his own
safety during the night, but for that of *wretches*; and
not to the gods, but to the objects of their power.

31 *Your looped and windowed raggedness*: Your ragged
clothes, full of 'windows' (which were normally
unglazed in Shakespeare's time) and loop-holes.

32 *seasons*: Times, weather conditions.

33 *Take physic, pomp*: Let the pompous man of authority
learn how to be (morally) healthy.

35 *shake the superflux*: Shake off superfluous possessions.

37 *Fathom and half*: Edgar takes up the cry of the sailor

singing out the depth of water his ship is passing through. The hovel is presumably half-submerged by the rainstorm.

37 *Poor Tom*: See the note on II.3.14.

44 *Away*: Keep away from me.

The foul fiend follows me: The mad were often supposed to be possessed or followed by devils.

45 *Through the sharp hawthorn blow the cold winds*: This has the air of a quotation from a song. Bishop Percy (1729–1811) has, in his *Reliques of Ancient English Poetry* (1765), a ballad ('The Friar of Orders Grey') with the line 'See through the hawthorn blows the cold wind, and drizzly rain doth fall'; but this ballad appears to be Percy's invention, patched together from scraps of Shakespeare. The Q reading, *cold wind*, is supported by the same song-fragment below (95).

46 *Humh*: Edgar shivers with cold.

Go to thy bed and warm thee: The beggar Christopher Sly says something very similar in *The Taming of the Shrew*, Induction 1.7–8 – so it may well be another catchphrase, possibly in reply to Jeronimo's famous 'What outcries pluck me from my naked bed' (*The Spanish Tragedy*, II.5.1).

47 *Didst thou give all to thy daughters*: The first words that can be used to prove that Lear has finally lost his hold on external reality, is 'mad'. The appearance of 'Poor Tom' is undoubtedly intended to be the catalyst that releases the inner forces that have been beating in Lear's mind. Immediately after the *Poor naked wretches* speech he finds a figure with whom he can wholly identify himself and whose role (of madman) he can take over.

52, 53 *knives . . . halters . . . ratsbane*: These are the traditional gifts (the poison is usually less specific) given by the Devil to the man who is in a state of despair, in the hope that he may kill himself and bring his soul into a state of perpetual damnation.

53 *porridge*: Soup.

55 *course*: Hunt.

thy five wits: These were defined as 'common wit, imagination, fantasy, estimation, memory'; or perhaps this
is another way of saying 'your five senses' (taste, smell,
sight, hearing, touch).

56 *O do, de, do, de, do, de*: This set of sounds is probably
meant to represent Tom's teeth chattering with cold.

57 *star-blasting*: Being struck down by disease (disease
was often supposed to be the result of the 'influence'
of the stars).

taking: Being 'taken' with an infection.

58–9 *There could I have him now*: Tom searches for lice and
devils at the same time.

64–5 *plagues that in the pendulous air | Hang fated*: Like *star-
blasting* (57), this alludes to the idea that disease is
poured down by planetary influence as a punishment
on the wicked. Stored up in the stars, it hangs (*pendulous*) like fate over the future of wrong-doers.

65 *light*: Alight.

67, 68 *subdued . . . unkind*: The accent in both cases falls on
the first syllable.

67 *subdued nature*: Brought down the human state.

70 *little mercy on their flesh*: Referring to Edgar's nakedness, and to the thorns and sprigs (or splinters) stuck
in his arms. When Edwin Booth was playing Lear he
'drew a thorn or wooden spike from Edgar's arm and
thrust it into his own': A. C. Sprague, *Shakespeare and
the Actors* (1944), p. 291.

71 *Judicious*: Appropriate, fitting.

72 *pelican daughters*: The pelican's young (according to the
medieval bestiaries) smite their father and kill him. The
mother pelican first hits back, and then revives the dead
children by shedding her own blood over them – thus
becoming the symbol of Christ-like loving self-sacrifice.
Lear sees Gonerill and Regan as assaulting him and also
demanding that he sacrifice himself for them.

73 *Pillicock*: Suggested by *pelican*. It seems both to have
meant a darling, a beloved, and to have been a playful
word for penis (picking up the idea from *flesh begot* in
71).

74 *Alow, alow, loo, loo*: Some sort of cry of sporting encouragement seems to be intended.

75 *This cold night will turn us all to fools*: Note that as Edgar takes over the role of the broken, rhapsodic, song-singing madman, the Fool is reduced to the role of the balanced observer.

77–9 *Take heed . . . proud array*: A crazy parody of the ten commandments.

78–9 *commit not with man's sworn spouse*: Do not commit adultery with one who is sworn wife to another.

79 *proud array*: Fine clothes. The idea of clothes leads Tom naturally to his next remark about the cold.

82 *servingman*: It is not clear whether this refers to a servant in the ordinary sense (with a *mistress* whose first role is to command the household) or to a 'servant' (that is, lover) with a 'mistress' (that is, a beloved).

83 *wore gloves in my cap*: Gallants wore their mistress's gloves in their cap.

88 *the Turk*: The Grand Turk, the Sultan, famous for his seraglio.

89 *light of ear*: 'Credulous of evil' (Dr Johnson).

89–90 *hog in sloth . . . lion in prey*: The seven deadly sins were often represented in art and literature by animals, illustrating the predominant passion or the particular 'beast in man' that was intended.

90 *stealth*: Both 'stealing' and 'stealthiness'.
dog in madness: The dog represents madness because the transmission of rabies to man makes the mad dog particularly notable.
prey: The act of preying, pillage, violence.

93 *plackets*: Slits in the front of petticoats.

95 *Still . . . cold wind*: The same song-fragment as in 45.

96 *Says suum, mun, nonny*: Some kind of refrain seems to be intended, and the Q version, *hay no on ny*, is an approximation to the traditional 'hey, nonny, nonny'. The F reading, given here, is likely to be nearer to the original, because more difficult. Perhaps it represents an imitation of the *cold wind* whistling through the hawthorn.

97 *Dolphin, my boy, boy, sesey! Let him trot by*: Perhaps
these are more song-fragments – but, if so, the songs
have perished. *Dolphin* may be a horse, *sesey* may be
the French '*cesseʒ*' – but all this is merest conjecture.

98 *answer*: Encounter.

99 *body . . . skies*: The microcosm/macrocosm analogy
once again.

99–100 *Is man no more than this? Consider him well*: Shakespeare
may have been remembering Hebrews 2:6: 'What is
man, that thou shouldst be mindful of him? Or the
son of man, that thou wouldst consider him?' (Geneva
Bible, 1587), or Florio's Montaigne: '. . . miserable
man; whom if you consider well, what is he?' ('An
Apology of Raymond Sebond', 'Tudor Translations'
(1893), Vol. II, p. 172).

100–101 *Thou owest . . . no*: You are not indebted to . . . for.

101 *beast*: Specifically 'cattle'.

102 *cat*: Civet cat (the source of some perfumes).
sophisticated: Adulterated by the addition of clothes
etc. away from the pure (naked) state of man (*the thing
itself*).

103 *Unaccommodated*: Unfurnished (with clothes etc.),
unsupported by a well-fitting environment.

104 *forked*: Having two legs.

105 *lendings*: The clothes 'lent' to man by the *beast*, the
worm, the *sheep*, etc. Lear aims, by tearing off his
clothes, to identify himself with *the thing itself*, with
Poor Tom.
unbutton: As a king he commands his *valet de chambre*
to undress him; as a demented moralist he tears off his
clothes with his own hands.
He tears off his clothes: Capell added *Kent and the Fool
strive to hinder him*.

106 *naughty*: Bad. The word was quite without the childish
connotations it has since acquired.

107 *swim*: Suggested both by the rain and by Lear's strip-
ping off his clothes.
a wild field: A waste heath, a wilderness.

107–8 *an old lecher's heart*: This undoubtedly refers to

Gloucester with his torch, the lechery which begot Edmund, and the evidence of *heart* shown by his succouring of the King. To secure a naturalistic explanation, we must suppose that the Fool spies Gloucester after *swim in*, though it is not clear how an actor could convey this.

110 *Flibberdigibbet*: The name of one of the devils who danced with a supposed demoniac in Harsnet's *Declaration*. See. IV.1.60.

111 *curfew . . . till the first cock*: Said to be from 9 p.m. till midnight; but may have the more general sense of 'from dusk till dawn' – when evil spirits were most free.

111–12 *the web and the pin*: Cataract of the eye.

112 *squenies*: Causes to squint.

113 *white*: Almost ripe.

115–18 *S'Withold . . . aroint thee*: F's *Swithold* presumably refers to Saint Withold, elsewhere in Elizabethan literature a defender against harms. Here he is a defender against the *nightmare* – the demon that descends on people when they are asleep. The saint paces the wold (*'old*) three times (the magic number) and when he meets the nightmare and her nine (three times three) offspring he commands her to *alight* (get off the sleeper's chest) and *plight her troth* (swear – that she will do no harm). And so he (Edgar) can bid all witches *aroint* (begone!).

115 *'old*: Wold (rolling upland).

124 *todpole*: An alternative form of 'tadpole'.
     the wall-newt and the water: The lizard and the water-newt.

124–5 *in the fury of his heart, when the foul fiend rages*: When the fit of madness is on him.

126 *sallets*: Salads, tasty morsels.
     the ditch-dog: The dead dog thrown into a ditch.

127 *the green mantle of the standing pool*: The scum of the stagnant pond.

128 *whipped from tithing to tithing*: Elizabethan law required vagabonds to be whipped publicly and sent into another parish (*tithing*), where presumably the same thing happened again.

stock-punished: Set in the stocks.

129–30 *three suits . . . six shirts*: The allowance of a serv-ingman, such as Edgar alleges he has been (82).

132–3 *But mice . . . seven long year*: This is a version of a couplet from the popular medieval romance, *Bevis of Hampton*. In the old-fashioned language of *Bevis*, *deer* means 'animals'.

134 *Beware my follower! Peace, Smulkin*: Edgar warns them of the dangers of his familiar spirit or devil, called *Smulkin* after one of the devils in Harsnet's *Declaration*. The name must have been suggested by *mice*, since in Harsnet Smulkin went out of the possessed man's right ear 'in the form of a mouse'.

136–7 *The prince of darkness is a gentleman; Modo he's called and Mahu*: To Gloucester's complaint about the company, Edgar replies that the devils he has about him are noblemen. In Harsnet, Modo and Mahu are grand commanders of legions of devils.

138–9 *Our flesh and blood . . . doth hate what gets it*: Our chil-dren hate their parents.

138 *vile*: See the note on III.2.71.

139 *gets*: Begets.

140 *Poor Tom's a-cold*: Edgar fends off the relevance of Gloucester's complaint about his son by retreating into the role of the Bedlam beggar.

147 *philosopher*: Expert in 'natural philosophy' or science. Perhaps it is Edgar's 'philosophical approach' (that is, acceptance of his hardships) that gives Lear the idea that he is a philosopher.

148 *the cause of thunder*: One of the 'secrets of nature' which a 'philosopher' or professional wise man would be expected to explain. It is apposite both to the immediate weather and to the larger questions of God's justice.

150 *learnèd Theban*: Greek sage.

151 *What is your study*: In which branch of learning do you specialize? Edgar picks up *study* in the other sense: 'zealous endeavour'.

152 *prevent*: Forestall.

154 *Importune*: Accented on the second syllable.

160 *outlawed from my blood*: (1) Legally made an outlaw (as in II.1.59–62 and 109–10); (2) disowned as my son and heir (II.1.82–4).

164 *I do beseech your grace* –: Some action is clearly intended. The New Cambridge edition suggests: 'Gloucester takes his arm, trying to separate him from his "philosopher"; Lear refuses.'
cry you mercy: I beg your pardon (I didn't notice you).

169 *With him*: Both words are heavily emphasized. Lear is impatient of the efforts to divert him from the conference with his 'philosopher'.

170 *still*: Continuously.

171 *soothe him*: Humour him.

172 *Take him you on*: Kent should take ahead the 'philosopher' Edgar so that Lear can be persuaded to follow to the farmhouse.

175 *No words . . . Hush*: Presumably an indication (to the audience) that they are approaching the castle.

176 *Child Roland to the dark tower came*: Perhaps another line from a romance. *Child* is '*Infante*' ('Prince'); Roland or Orlando is the most famous of Charlemagne's paladins. The *dark tower* is certainly Gloucester's castle in the immediate reference, sinister enough in the *King Lear* story, whatever it may have been in the lost Roland story referred to here.

177–8 *'Fie, foh, and fum,* | *I smell the blood of a British man'*: Here the Roland fragment seems to modulate into 'Jack, the Giant-killer'. It may be no accident that Edgar, returning to his home, remembers the story of another son's triumphant return. The *tower* may have suggested the beanstalk.

III.5

The final fruits of Edmund's 'nature' are shown in the planned destruction of his natural father, his adoption into the love of Cornwall, and his acquistion of the 'legitimate' title of Earl of Gloucester.

2 *censured*: Judged.

2, 3 *nature . . . loyalty*: Family affection . . . loyalty to the state.

3 *something fears me*: Somewhat concerns me.

6–7 *a provoking merit set a-work by a reprovable badness in himself*: This is puzzling, because it is not clear whether the reference is to Edgar or Gloucester. Most probably the meaning is: 'The fact that death was only Gloucester's due reward (*merit*) must also have provoked Edgar to act; but a man must be bad before he will allow himself to be provoked to parricide for such a reason.'

9 *to be*: That I am.

just: Loyal to the state.

9–10 *approves him an intelligent party to the advantages of France*: Proves that he is a spy, seeking to give advantage to the French side.

17–18 *that he may be ready for our apprehension*: So that we may arrest him without any trouble.

19 *comforting*: Giving aid to.

20 *stuff his suspicion more fully*: Augment Cornwall's suspicion of Gloucester as a spy.

persever: Equivalent to the modern 'persevere', but with the accent on the second syllable.

22 *my blood*: My natural loyalty to my father.

III.6

The scene takes us inside the farmhouse towards which Gloucester was conducting his companions at the end of III.4. The antiphonally placed voices of the three madmen – lunatic King, court fool, feigned Bedlam – weave the obsessive themes of betrayal, demoniac possession, and injustice into the most complex lyric structure in modern drama.

2 *piece out*: Augment.

6 *Fraterretto*: One of the demonic names in Harsnet.

7 *Pray, innocent*: Often thought to be addressed to the Fool (the *innocent*).

10 *yeoman*: A man who owns property but is not a gentleman, that is, does not have a coat-of-arms.

15–16 *To have a thousand . . . upon 'em*: While Edgar and the Fool follow their separate trains of thought, Lear's mind is fixed on Gonerill and Regan; here he imagines them suffering the torments of Hell.

17 *bites*: The foul fiend in the form of a louse or flea; cf. III.4.152.

18 *the tameness of a wolf*: The implication is that the wolf can never be tamed.

18–19 *a horse's health*: 'A horse is above all other animals subject to diseases' (Dr Johnson).

20 *arraign them*: Lear abandons the idea of the torments of Hell, and turns to the image of a trial for Gonerill and Regan.

21 *justicer*: Judge.

23 *he*: Possibly Lear, but probably 'the Fiend', with whom Edgar's speeches are continuously concerned.

23–4 *Want'st thou eyes at trial, madam*: The *madam at trial* must be Gonerill or Regan; but it is not clear what *Want'st thou eyes* means. It must connect with the glaring of the fiend in the previous sentence. Perhaps it means 'Can't you see who's looking at you?'

25–6 *Come o'er the burn . . . hath a leak*: Edgar sings a snatch of popular song, which the Fool completes, providing a reason (doubtless obscene) why Bessy should avoid having to do with her lover. See p. 160.

29–30 *in the voice of a nightingale*: No doubt suggested by the Fool's singing.

30 *Hoppedance*: Derived from Harsnet's 'Hoberdidance'.

31 *white herring*: Unsmoked herring.
    Croak: The Elizabethans spoke of 'croaking guts' where we speak of 'rumbling tummies'. The noise is supposed to indicate hunger, which explains the next sentence. In Harsnet some 'croaking' was said to be the voice of a demon.
    black angel: Black being the devil's colour, a *black angel* would be a demon.

33 *amazed*: In a maze, dumbfounded (stronger than the modern sense).

34 *cushings*: An earlier form of 'cushions'.

35 *their evidence*: The witnesses against them.

36 *robed*: This no doubt refers to Tom's *Blanket* (II.3.10).
    thy place: On the judges' bench.

37 *yokefellow*: Fellow.

yokefellow of equity: The Courts of Justice and of
Equity were the two main branches of the English
legal system. In this trial, exceptionally, the two are
combined (as at the trial of Mary, Queen of Scots).

38 *Bench by his side*: Join him on the judges' bench.

commission: A body to whom power (in this case, judicial power) is delegated from the crown, specifically
'the commission of the peace', the body of justices of
the peace.

41-4 *Sleepest or wakest . . . no harm*: Dr Johnson remarked:
'This seems to be a stanza of some pastoral song. A
shepherd is desired to pipe, and the request is enforced
by a promise that though his sheep be in the corn, i.e.
committing trespass by his negligence, yet a single tune
upon his pipe shall secure them from the pound.' The
nursery rhyme of 'Little Boy Blue' is an obvious analogy.

43 *for one blast*: As a result of even a single blast.

minikin: Either (1) shrill or (2) pretty, neat, fine.

45 *Pur, the cat is grey*: The cat may be another demon or
familiar, as often in witchcraft. *Pur* may be the noise
it makes, or its name ('Purre' is the name of a devil
in Harsnet).

51 *I took you for a joint-stool*: A proverbial insulting
'excuse' for not noticing someone. A *joint-stool* is a
stool made by jointing together pieces of wood.

52 *another*: Regan.

warped looks: Twisted, distorted features.

53 *What store her heart is made on*: What kind of material
her heart is made of. Cf. 75-6.

54 *Arms, arms, sword, fire*: It is not clear what *fire* is doing
in this list, which is concerned with means of stopping Regan's escape. If 'fire' could mean 'fire your
muskets', this would be acceptable; but there is no
evidence that the word could be so used in 1605.

Corruption in the place: Even the court of law is corrupt;
the judge has connived at the prisoner's escape.

56 *Bless thy five wits*: Edgar lapses into his jargon (cf.
III.4.55), unable, as his next utterance shows, to sustain
his part in the charade.

61–2 *The little dogs and all . . . they bark at me*: I am now
so despicable that even the little lap-dogs (perhaps
bitches, by their names) know they can bark at me.

65 *or . . . or*: Either . . . or.

66 *Tooth that poisons*: The only sense in which a dog's
tooth *poisons* is through rabies.

68 *brach or lym*: Bitch-hound or bloodhound.

69 *bobtail tike*: Cur with its tail 'bobbed' (cut short).
trundle-tail: Dog with a long drooping tail trundling
(trailing) behind it.

72 *leapt the hatch*: Jumped over the closed lower half of
a divided door.

73 *Do, de, de, de*: At III.4.56 a similar collection of syllables was supposed to represent Tom's teeth chattering.
Sese: Most editors change to 'Sessa', but one unex-
plained sound seems as good as another. Cf. III.4.97.

73–4 *Come, march . . . market-towns*: Tom addresses himself,
to take his attention away from the painful scene before
him. He resolves to set out for the places of resort
most likely to yield good begging.

74 *thy horn is dry*: A formula used by the Bedlamites in
begging for drink. It appears that they wore an ox-
horn round their necks into which they poured the
drink that was given them. In the present context it
must also mean 'I have no more words for this situation'; in this scene Edgar says no more in his Tom
persona.

75 *anatomize*: Dissect.

75–6 *what breeds about her heart*: As if some hard deposit
was forming on it. Lear's mind may have moved in
this direction because of Edgar's *dry* (74) and his reference to *horn*, which is formed by the process to which
Lear alludes in reference to Regan's heart.

76–7 *Is there any cause in nature that makes these hard hearts*:
hard hearts were well-known theological phenomena,
caused by falling from grace. Despairing of super-
natural causes, Lear asks for a natural, anatomical,
reason.

77 *entertain*: Take into my service.

78–9 *fashion of your garments . . . Persian*: Tom's blanket now reminds Lear of the traditionally pompous garments of the Persians.

81–2 *draw the curtains. So, so*: Lear imagines himself on a luxurious bed, with his servant drawing the bed-curtains.

82 *We'll go to supper i'the morning*: Lear presumably remembers he has not had his supper. 'Never mind,' he says to himself, 'we can eat it at breakfast time.'

83 *I'll go to bed at noon*: These are the last words that the Fool speaks in the play and they have been thought (rather sentimentally) to refer to his going to his grave in the prime of life. But they are more likely to draw on the proverbial sense of 'going to bed at noon': that is, 'playing the fool'.

89 *drive*: The *litter* is presumably horse-drawn.

94–5 *to some provision | Give thee . . . conduct*: Take you where you can get supplies.

96 *balmed thy broken sinews*: Healed your shattered nerves. Shakespeare gives to Lear the physical condition that followed torture on the rack; but the rack he has been on is a mental one.

98 *Stand in hard cure*: Will be hard to cure.

100–101 *When we our betters see bearing our woes, | We scarcely think our miseries our foes*: It is so disturbing to see our superiors oppressed by the same miseries as beset us that we almost cease to notice our own pains; we begin to think of these pains as not ours at all, but only levelled against the superior people.

102–3 *Who alone suffers, suffers most i'the mind, | Leaving free things and happy shows behind*: The principal suffering of the man who suffers on his own is the sense of having left behind him the whole world of carefree lives and joyful sights.

104–5 *But then the mind much sufferance doth o'erskip | When grief hath mates, and bearing fellowship*: We avoid much suffering when we know other people in the same plight who have to bear the same woes (a proverbial idea).

106 *portable*: Bearable.

108 *He childed as I fathered*: He with children who seek his life, as I have a father who seeks my life.

109 *Mark the high noises*: Watch what's going on in the world of important people.

   thyself bewray: Reveal yourself (as Edgar).

110–11 *When false opinion, whose wrong thoughts defile thee,* | *In thy just proof repeals and reconciles thee*: When the false story about you, which has made you seem morally corrupt, is proved wrong and you are shown to be just, so that you can be recalled to your true station and reconciled (with your father).

112 *What will hap more*: Whatever else happens.

113 *Lurk*: Keep in hiding.

III.7

The violent assaults on the mind and dignity of Lear are now paralleled by a physical assault on the eyes of Gloucester. No counter-movement is strong enough to stop this barbarism; but the intervention of the servants marks the beginning of an upswing of the pendulum. A first defeat for wickedness appears in the death of Cornwall.

1 *Post speedily*: Hasten.

   my lord: Of Albany.

2 *this letter*: The letter about Cordelia's landing that Gloucester told Edmund about (III.3.9) and that Edmund conveyed to Cornwall (III.5.9).

7 *sister*: Sister-in-law (Gonerill, on her way to Albany).

9–10 *Advise the Duke where you are going to a most festinate preparation*: Advise the Duke of Albany, to whom you are going, to make speedy preparations (for war).

10–11 *Our posts shall be swift and intelligent*: Our couriers will move rapidly and convey full information.

12 *my lord of Gloucester*: Edmund has already been promoted though his father is still alive. Cf. 14.

16 *Hot questrists after him*: Eagerly searching for him. 'Questrist' seems to be Shakespeare's invention (from 'quest').

17 *the lord's*: Gloucester's.

24 *pass upon his life*: Pass a death sentence on him.

25–6 *our power | Shall do a cursty to our wrath*: We will use
our power (as co-sovereigns) in a way that gives precedence to our wrath.

26 *curtsy*: I have modernized to the form that gives the
better rhythm, and (marginally) the better sense, but
we should notice that 'courtesy' and 'curtsy' were not
distinguished by the Elizabethans.

27 *control*: Curb, restrain.

28 *Ingrateful fox*: He has shown ingratitude by failing in
loyalty to his *arch and patron* Cornwall; he has been
foxy in his sly and secretive dealing with Lear and his
friends.

29 *corky*: Dry, withered.

33 *none*: No traitor.

37 *Naughty*: Wicked.

39 *quicken and accuse thee*: Come to life (as people) and
speak against your actions.

40 *hospitable favours*: This is usually said to mean 'the
features (*favours*) of your host'; but perhaps 'the indul-
gences of my hospitality' is simpler.

41 *ruffle thus*: Treat with this outrage.

42 *late*: Lately.

43 *Be simple-answered*: Give us a straight answer.

45 *footed*: Landed.

46 *To whose hands you have sent the lunatic King*: This
completes the question begun in 44. *lunatic King* is a
good example of Shakespearian foreshortening: Regan
has had no opportunity to learn about Lear's lunacy.

51 *at peril*: Under the threat of punishment.

53 *I am tied to the stake, and I must stand the course*: Like
a bear in bear-baiting, I am tied to the stake, the dogs
are attacking me, and I must endure it till the bout is
ended.

57 *anointed flesh*: The holy oil with which he was anointed
at his coronation sanctified his person, and made physical assault on him a sacrilege.
rash boarish fangs: *rash*, the Q reading for F's *sticke*, is
not only more picturesque but also more accurate, since

it is the hunting term for the slashing sideways movement of the boar's tusks. The three 'sh' sounds in the
line imply a slow deliberate delivery.

59–60 *would have buoyed up | And quenched the stellèd fires*:
Would have risen up, like a buoy on the swell, high
enough to extinguish the stars (with the implication of
formlessness overcoming the pattern of order).

60 *stellèd fires*: The context shows that these must be the
stars. 'Stelled' is not known elsewhere as an adjective.
Shakespeare uses it as a participle, meaning 'delin-
eated'; but it is easier to suppose that here he is making
up a new word, meaning 'starry', from the Latin *stella*.

61 *holp*: Old form of the past tense of 'help'.

62 *dern*: Dread, dark.

64 *All cruels else subscribe*: This is a famous crux, for
which any interpretation must be tentative. One
problem is whether the clause belongs with what
precedes or what follows. Supposing the former, I
suggest 'Assent to any other cruel thing you like (but
open the door to these poor creatures)'; the usual interpretation is: 'All other cruel creatures yield to pity (so
you should do so too, and turn the key).'

65 *wingèd Vengeance*: Perhaps this means only 'swift
vengeance'; but it is more likely to imply vengeance
as an angel of divine wrath.

75–6 *If you did wear a beard upon your chin | I'd shake it*: If
you were a man I would attack you.

77 *My villain*: My serf (daring to argue with me! – the
same point as in 79).

78 *the chance of anger*: The risk of what may happen when
angry men fight.

82 *Lest it see more, prevent it*: So that your remaining eye
shall not see any more mischief done to Cornwall, I
will anticipate the mischief, on that very eye.
vile: See the note on III.2.71.

85 *enkindle all the sparks of nature*: Let your family loyalty
blaze into anger.

86 *quit*: Repay.

88 *overture*: Revelation (accented on the second syllable).

90–91 *Edgar was abused.* | *Kind gods, forgive me that*:
       Gloucester's insight into moral and factual truth comes
       with great suddenness: 'So Edgar was slandered –
       forgive me for my part in that.' Note the absence of
       recrimination and the assumption that normal good-
       ness still exists.

93 *How look you*: How do you look on yourself, how are
    you?

97 *Untimely*: Cornwall's one feeling seems to be regret
    that the wound will interfere with his schedule for
    leading the army against Cordelia.

100 *meet the old course of death*: Die in the normal way.

101 *Women will all turn monsters*: A repetition of the point
    made about men in 98–9: 'In that case women too will
    lose their moral sense, and behave monstrously.'

103 *roguish madness*: This is the reading of Q uncorrected;
    Q corrected omits *roguish*. The epithet seems, however,
    too Shakespearian to be accidental and we must suppose
    that the corrector made a slip.

104 *Allows itself to anything*: Lends itself to any task that
    may be imposed on him.

IV.I

       A scene showing the struggle to recover meaning and
       value in the world. Edgar's determination to endure
       and Gloucester's determination to die counterpoint one
       another in a tone moving between the grotesque and
       the affectionate.

1–2 *better thus, and known to be contemned,* | *Than still
    contemned and flattered*: It is better to be a beggar and
    know what people think about you (contempt) than to
    be despised (as at a court) though flattered. The punc-
    tuation in F and that in Q both allow the following
    phrase, *To be worst*, to be included in the sentence; but
    it seems better to attach it to the following lines, and
    F's punctuation can be read in this way.

3 *most dejected thing of fortune*: Thing most dejected (or
    cast down) by fortune.

4 *Stands still in esperance*: Remains always in possession
    of hope.

4 *fear*: Of something worse about to happen.

6 *The worst returns to laughter*: Any change, when you are at the worst, is bound to be change for the better.

7 *Thou unsubstantial air that I embrace*: With my nakedness I embrace the air, and I approve of it, even though it is lacking in substance, in wealth, in gifts, in comforts.

9 *Owes nothing to thy blasts*: Because the wind's help led only to the worst, Edgar is free of obligation, and therefore can embrace his 'creditor' without fear.

10 *parti-eyed*: The uncorrected Q reading, *poorlie, leed*, was no doubt responsible for the F reading, *poorely led*; but since this gives a modicum of sense it has been generally accepted. The Q correction, *parti, eyd*, on the other hand, must be the result of a second attempt to read the manuscript, and is the nearest to Shakespeare we can come. It is usually supposed to be unintelligible as it stands; but in F a comma is often a substitute for a hyphen, and may be so here. If we make this substitution we then have *parti-eyed*, a phrase like 'parti-coloured' or 'parti-coated' (*Love's Labour's Lost*, V.2.761), 'party-bow' (the rainbow), 'party-flowers', or 'parti-membered' (having different members). *parti-eyed* would mean 'having his eyes looking like a fool's coat in the red of blood and the white of eggs'. This provides a grotesque image, but there is no shortage of these in *King Lear*. Gloucester's eyes are the striking point about him, and Edgar would be expected to mention them. It may be better that he should refer to them as grotesque than dilute his response (and ours) by noticing only the social quality of his guide.

11–12 *But that thy strange mutations make us hate thee | Life would not yield to age*: If it were not for these strange switches in fortune from good to bad, and the hatred of life that this generates, we would not be willing to accept old age and death (or perhaps 'we would not age at all').

18 *I have no way*: I have lost my path through life.

19 *I stumbled when I saw*: When I had my eyes I missed

my moral footing, and tripped over false judgements.

20–21 *Our means secure us, and our mere defects | Prove our commodities*: Our possessions (such as eyes) make us secure or over-confident, and total (*mere*) deprivation may prove an advantage.

22 *The food of thy abusèd father's wrath*: I used you to feed my anger on, when I was deceived (*abusèd*).

23 *in my touch*: By touching you.

25 *Who is't can say 'I am at the worst'*: The scene up to this point may be taken as an illustration of the folly of Edgar's initial confidence in *To be worst*.

27–8 *The worst is not, | So long as we can say 'This is the worst'*: The kind of consolation in which you say to yourself (as Edgar did in 1–6) 'I am now at the lowest point' is a sure indication of a buoyancy of hope that separates you from the real *worst*.

33 *think a man a worm*: Perhaps a reminiscence of Job 25:6: 'man that is but corruption, and the son of man, which is a worm?'.

36–7 *As flies to wanton boys are we to the gods; | They kill us for their sport*: As playful and irresponsible boys make games out of the lives of flies, not really caring whether they live or die, so the gods (on this evidence) seem to be having fun with mankind's misery and death.

37 *How should this be*: How can the mental even more than the physical condition of Gloucester have changed so radically?

38 *Bad is the trade that must play fool to sorrow*: It is a bad business to have to spend your time uttering folly to a man (like my father) distressed by sorrow.

39 *Angering itself and others*: Creating general anger, because of its inappropriateness.

43 *I'the way toward Dover*: Along the Dover road.

46 *'Tis the time's plague*: It is the kind of horror appropriate to our times.

47 *or rather do thy pleasure*: Gloucester withdraws the command, remembering that it is quite inappropriate to his condition; 'Do what you wish' is the most he is entitled to say.

49 *'parel*: Apparel.

50 *Come on't what will*: Whatever may happen (to me) as
a result.

51 *I cannot daub it further*: That's the best I can do (in
pretending to be Poor Tom).

55 *stile and gate, horse-way and footpath*: Each kind of path
has its appropriate obstacle – the stile for the footpath,
the gate for the horse-way (bridle-path).

56 *Tom hath been scared*: The landscape is for Tom a series
of places to be scared in, where the foul fiend has
appeared.

58–60 *Obidicut; Hobbididence . . . Mahu . . . Modo . . .
Flibberdigibber*: Harsnet's forms are 'Hoberdicut',
'Hoberdidance', 'Maho', 'Modu', 'Fliberdigibbet', and,
allowing for the probability that the Q reporters would
have difficulty in remembering these outlandish names
correctly, perhaps we should prefer Harsnet's spellings.
Q's *Stiberdigebit* is a clear compositor's misreading of
a manuscript form like Harsnet's (F is defective at this
point). Cf. the Q form at III.4.110: *fliberdegibek*.
Above (III.6.30) Shakespeare represents Harsnet's
'Hoberdidance' as *Hoppedance*.

60–62 *Flibberdigibbet, of mopping and mowing, who since
possesses chambermaids and waiting-women*: 'Fliberdigibbet' is a dancing devil in Harsnet, and a 'flib-
bertigibbet' is a flighty chattering woman (hence,
presumably, Harsnet's devil's name). The vices he
represents here are in an appropriate key: *mopping
and mowing* – grimacing and twisting the face, like
chambermaids in their mistress's looking-glass. There
are three 'possessed' chambermaids in Harsnet.

61 *since*: Since they left Tom.

64 *Have humbled to all strokes*: Have brought to the acceptance of every kind of misery.

64–5 *That I am wretched | Makes thee the happier*: Since (as
in III.6.104–5) misery loves company.

65 *Heavens deal so*: So that one man's misery should be
comforted by another's.
still: Always.

66   *the superfluous and lust-dieted man*: The man who has
     too much (cf. *superflux*, III.4.35) and who sates himself
     on his pleasures.

67   *slaves your ordinance*: Does what he likes with (makes
     a slave out of) the divine rule (that one man should
     help another).

67–8 *will not see | Because he does not feel*: *see* means 'under-
     stand' and *feel* 'have fellow-feeling with'; but Glou-
     cester is also thinking of his own condition, brought
     to 'see' how things are when he can only know them
     by touch. Cf. 23–4.

69   *So distribution should undo excess*: The gods' powers
     would deprive the superfluous man of his excess and
     shake the superflux to those in need.

72   *bending*: Bending over, overhanging.

73   *fearfully*: Frighteningly.
     confinèd: Shut in (by the land on both sides of the
     English Channel).

IV.2

The upswing towards good is advanced by an extraordinary and unprepared volte-face. Albany has now
become a man of clear moral commitment (though
less clear in his commitment to action), opposed to the
faction of his wife Gonerill and her intended para-
mour, Edmund.

1–2 *Welcome . . . way*: She welcomes him to her castle,
     where they have now arrived. She is surprised that her
     house-keeping husband has not come out of the castle
     to greet them.

8   *sot*: Fool.

9   *turned the wrong side out*: That is, reversed the moral
     judgements – called Gloucester's loyal service *treachery*
     and Edmund's treachery *loyal service*.

11   *What like*: What he should like.

12   *cowish*: Cowardly, effeminate.

13   *undertake*: Take responsibility for any enterprise.

13–14 *He'll not feel wrongs | Which tie him to an answer*: He
     will ignore insults which require him to 'answer' them
     by challenging the wrong-doer to fight. It is for this

reason he is ignoring the French invasion.

14–15 *Our wishes on the way* | *May prove effects*: What we
talked of and wished for as we came here together may
well come to pass. Presumably the idea of Albany's
cowardice gives Gonerill the further idea of getting
rid of him, so making effective their wish for union.

15 *my brother*: My brother-in-law (Cornwall).

16 *Hasten his musters*: Speed up his enlistment of soldiers.
powers: Troops.

17 *I must change arms . . .*: (1) I must change into military accountrements; (2) my husband and I must
exchange the work we do with our arms: he must take
the distaff, and I will get the sword.

20 *in your own behalf*: Thinking of yourself (and not of
your loyalty to the cause).

21 *mistress*: With a double-entendre.

21–8 *mistress's command . . . bed*: The passage is full of
sexual innuendoes stronger than anything said explicitly, as in *stretch thy spirits*, *Conceive*, *ranks of death*,
services, *usurps my bed*.

24 *Conceive*: Think what this implies.

25 *Yours in the ranks of death*: Edmund slightly over-acts
the role of swashbuckling lover that has been foisted
on him, though Gonerill does not seem to notice
anything amiss.
death: Often used as a metaphor for 'orgasm'.

27 *a woman's services*: The service that a woman naturally
gives to a real *man*.

28 *A fool usurps my bed*: I am possessed by a fool (Albany)
who does not know how to command. The uncorrected
Q reading, *My foote usurps my body*, is the source of
F's *My Foole usurpes my body*; Q corrected reads *A
foole usurps my bed*; which implies a second look at the
manuscript, whereas the F reading need imply no more
than an obvious correction of the copy-text (Q uncorrected). *bed* seems better in meaning also, since it is
the connubial possession of her he objects to rather
than sexual possession. Cf. IV.6.265–6, where in her
letter of *mistress's command* she speaks of *his bed my*

gaol; from the loathed warmth whereof deliver me.

29 *I have been worth the whistling*: This is based on the
proverb: 'It is a poor dog that is not worth the
whistling.' The meaning is: 'So you have decided at
last to come looking for me, since even "a poor dog
is worth whistling for".'

30–31 *not worth the dust . . . your face*: Albany picks up *worth
the whistling* and twists it round so that the sarcasm
rebounds: 'Even the wind that cares nothing for you
whistles as it throws dust at you and that's too good
for you; that's how much whistling you are worth.'

31 *I fear your disposition*: That Gonerill was worthless and
neutral (like the *dust*) would not cause *fear*; but her
disposition, the tendency of her character, is not neutral,
but frighteningly destructive.

32 *contemns its origin*: Disdains the source from which it
springs (Lear in this case).
its: Q uncorrected reads *it*, which could sometimes be
used for 'its', but usually appears in Shakespeare in
contexts of childish talk. The fact that the Q corrector
changed 'it' to *ith* implies either that he did not find
the reading plausible or that it did not correspond to
what he thought he saw in his copy. *ith* (that is, 'in
the') does not make sense; but it would be easy to
mistake 's' for 'h' in the manuscript.

33 *Cannot be bordered certain in itself*: Cannot be contained,
or trusted to act in one way rather than another (and
therefore must be *feared*).

34–5 *herself will sliver and disbranch | From her material sap*:
will tear herself from the stock on which she grew, as
one tears a branch from a tree. *material* means 'which
gave her her (moral and physical) substance'.

36 *to deadly use*: A use proper to dead wood – to be burned.
Cf. Hebrews 6:8: 'But that ground which beareth
thorns and briars is rejected and is nigh unto cursing;
whose end is to be burned.' It may be that this is
referred to below in *text*.

37 *No more; the text is foolish*: Stop preaching at me on a
subject that makes no sense.

38, 47 *vile*: See the note on III.2.71.

39 *Filths savour but themselves*: Filthy minds can only smell (and relish) their own odour.

42 *head-lugged bear*: Bear pulled along by the ring in its nose (and therefore in no good temper).

44 *brother*: Brother-in-law (Cornwall).

45 *A man, a prince, by him so benefited*: A cumulative list of three reasons why Cornwall should not have acted thus: (1) he was a human being; (2) what is more, he was a prince, one with moral standards higher than those of mere humanity; (3) most of all, he was greatly in Lear's debt.

46 *their visible spirits*: Not their invisible spirits (who are, presumably, all around us all the time) but manifest interventions, like those which will precede the Last Judgement.

49–50 *prey on itself | Like monsters of the deep*: The life of the sea creatures, where the big fishes eat up the little ones, was a common image of final moral disorder or chaos.

50 *Milk-livered man*: Gonerill can only see Albany's feverish moral vision as a result of lack of courage to seize the real situation, lack of blood in his liver, a substitution of female *Milk* for male blood. In this she resembles Lady Macbeth before the murder of Duncan.

51 *bear'st . . . a head for wrongs*: Your head is only an object for other people to rain their wrongful blows on.

52–3 *an eye discerning | Thine honour from thy suffering*: A capacity to see how far endurance is proper and how far suffering ought to be resented and revenged. Cf. 13–14.

54–5 *Fools do those villains . . . their mischief*: It is foolish to object to punishment which *precedes* crimes. Lear has not yet collaborated with the French, but he will; Gloucester's case must also be in the mind of Gonerill and of the audience, though Albany has not yet heard of his punishment.

56 *noiseless land*: Noise is made equivalent to warlike

preparation or resistance: Albany should beat his drum
and march against the enemy.

57 *thy state begins to threat*: The Q corrector's change
from *slayer* to *state* seems quite acceptable. A new
grammatical subject in 57 could only weaken the
antithesis between *France* and *thou*. But the other
change – *begin threats* to *begins thereat* – cannot be
accepted as it stands, since it makes no sense. What
would be ideal would be a relevant word easily
mistaken for 'thereat', but none has been found; *to
threat* makes good sense but it is not very like 'thereat'.

58 *a moral fool*: Foolish enough to sit and argue to moral
pros and cons (instead of taking up arms).

59 *See thyself*: Contemplate your own condition (not
mine).

60–61 *Proper deformity shows not in the fiend | So horrid as in
woman*: Devilish grimaces are uglier in a woman than
they would be on the devil's face, for they are appropriate (*Proper*) to him.

62 *changèd and self-covered thing*: One who has *changèd*
her appearance so that it no longer corresponds to her
reality, who has *covered* or concealed the fiend within
her behind the female graces of her external self.

63 *Be-monster not thy feature*: Don't show in your external
appearance the monster that lives within you.
     Were't my fitness: If it were appropriate for me.

65–6 *dislocate and tear | Thy flesh and bones*: Dislocate the
bones and tear the flesh.

66 *Howe'er thou art a fiend*: However great a fiend you are,
in reality.

68 *Marry, your manhood! Mew*: Good heavens, you and
your talk of your 'manhood' (in shielding my *woman's
shape*)! I'll show you what I think of it.
     Mew: Derisive cat-call.

73 *that he bred*: That he kept or supported in his household.
     thrilled with remorse: Pierced through with feelings of
compassion.

76 *amongst them*: Presumably 'amongst the other servants'.

78 *Hath plucked him after*: Has made him follow his servant into death.

79 *justicers*: (Heavenly) judges.

   nether crimes: Crimes committed down here on earth.

83, 86–7 *One way I like this well. . . . Another way | The news is not so tart*: These both refer to the same thought: Cornwall's death brings one step nearer the possibility of undivided rule over Britain.

85 *the building in my fancy*: The dream of marrying Edmund that my amorous inclinations (*fancy*) have built up.

86 *hateful*: Because she will be left as Albany's wife, and will have to watch her sister enjoying Edmund.

90 *back*: On his way back.

IV.3

A series of short scenes (in or near Dover) marks, as often at this point in a Shakespearian tragedy, the alternate postures of the competing armies. But the battle in *King Lear* is less important than the moral attitudes of those involved. In IV.3 Kent and a Gentleman narrate the facts of the coming reunion between Lear and Cordelia, and (more important) the values that attach to Lear's shame and to Cordelia's radiant and healing beauty.

3 *imperfect*: Incomplete.

9 *letters*: If the mission which the Gentleman undertakes to Cordelia in III.1 is the same one referred to here, the verbal message has been transformed into *letters*. This is understandable, as the inconsistency would allow Shakespeare to make better dramatic effects at both points.

12 *trilled*: The *Oxford English Dictionary* says that 'trill' implies 'a more continuous motion than is expressed by trickle'.

14 *her passion who . . .*: Her emotion which . . .

16–17 *patience and sorrow strove | Who should express her goodliest*: Her passions and her power of control appeared like competitors in her face and her temper, each seeming to make her more lovely than the other.

19 *Were like a better way*: This is difficult to construe, and
so to punctuate: *like* may refer back to *Sunshine and rain*
(the smiles and tears were like simultaneous sunshine
and rain), or it may mean 'were like one another' (each
resembled the other and in this relationship revealed *a
better way*), or perhaps 'were like a vision of the way to
Heaven'. In any case the meaning aimed at must be that
she expressed a new mode of connection, not found in
nature and better than what is found there.

20 *seem*: Historic present. Since the eighteenth century
this has been regularized to the past 'seemed'; but
Shakespeare's usage elsewhere justifies the original
reading.

23 *a rarity most beloved*: As much sought-after and precious
as *pearls* and *diamonds* – or the beauty of Cordelia in
her patience.

24 *become*: Adorn.
verbal: In words (beyond what was conveyed by her
looks).

25–6 *heaved the name of father . . . as if it pressed her heart*:
The use of *heave* and *heart* should remind us of *I
cannot heave | My heart into my mouth* in I.1.91–2.
Cordelia is throughout the play characterized by a lack
of fluent rhetoric.

29 *Let pity not be believed*: Let me believe (on this evidence)
that pity does not exist.

31 *clamour moistened*: Sprinkled with this *holy water* the
outcry of her grief.

34 *one self mate and make*: One and the same husband
and wife. ('Make' like 'mate' can apply to either
spouse.)

37 *the King*: Of France.

42 *A sovereign shame so elbows him*: A dominating sense
of shame so crowds and jostles him.

44 *foreign casualties*: The chances of existence in a foreign
land.

51 *Some dear cause*: An important reason. The real reason
is Shakespeare's desire to keep the revelation of Kent's
identity till the last scene.

IV.4

Cordelia enacts the part the preceding scene described.
The fertile English landscape is used to evoke both the
ungoverned wildness of the King (in preparation for
IV.6) and the natural powers of restoration that
Cordelia can call up.

0 *with drum and colours*: With drums beating and flags
waving (indicative of battle order).

1 *he*: The one you have just been describing to me.

2 *mad as the vexed sea*: Tossed and turned by his passions,
as unpredictable as the movement of a stormy sea.

3–5 *rank fumiter . . . Darnel*: These flowers seem, so far as
they are identifiable, to be of bitter, pungent or
poisonous kinds and therefore an appropriate 'crown
of thorns' for the mad King; but they also reflect the
state of natural growth to which he has allied himself.

3 *furrow-weeds*: Weeds that spring up in the furrows of
ploughed land.

4 *hardokes*: F; Q: *hor-docks*; not accurately identifiable;
sometimes equated with burdocks, hoar-docks,
harlocks (= charlocks), and other possibilities.

5–6 *idle weeds that grow | In our sustaining corn*: Lear is
associated with the rank and random uselessness of
the weeds, set in contrast to the planned and useful
grain which sustains life. The *century* of soldiers, the
organized life of Cordelia's army, is, on the other
hand, like the *sustaining corn*.

6 *century*: Is it an accident that Cordelia sends forth a
hundred men to restore the King who lost his 'hundred
knights'?

7 *the high-grown field*: It is now, for symbolic purposes,
high summer at Dover. The height of Lear's escape
into 'natural' chaos is supported by a natural riot of
vegetation.

8 *What can man's wisdom*: What can human science do.

10 *outward worth*: Wealth. We should recognize the same
Cordelia as in I.1, despising the outward shows that
others prize.

12 *foster-nurse*: She who cherishes and supports.

13 *provoke*: Induce.

14 *simples*: Herbs.

   operative: Effective.

15–17 *blest secrets ... unpublished virtues of the earth*, | *Spring with my tears*: The hidden or unknown recuperative powers of herbs are to spring out of the earth as the herbs themselves do after a spring shower.

17 *aidant and remediate*: Rare words, with the sense of 'aiding and remedying', used here to fit into the remote and incantatory atmosphere of Cordelia's prayer.

19 *ungoverned rage*: Violent and unchecked temper.

20 *means*: That is, his reason.

24 *It is thy business that I go about*: Cordelia forswears personal political ambition and proclaims Lear's restoration as her only war-aim. But the echo of Christ's answer when found by his parents in the temple, 'I must be about my Father's business' (Luke 2:49), is presumably not accidental.

26 *importuned*: Importunate, beseeching. The Q reading, important, has the same meaning.

27–8 *No blown ambition ... But love*: 1 Corinthians 13:4–5 seems to have been in Shakespeare's mind: 'Charity ... is not puffed up, is not ambitious, seeketh not her own' (Rheims version). In the Bishops' Bible it reads: 'Love ... swelleth not, dealeth not dishonestly, seeketh not her own ...'

IV.5

The self-seeking wickedness of Gonerill and Regan has found out its own punishment in the desire that both feel for the person of Edmund. General destructive hate here is in strong contrast to the love and protectiveness that was the keynote of the preceding scene.

0 *Oswald*: Oswald has delivered to Regan the letter that Gonerill promised to send at IV.2.87; and he has mentioned, it appears, that he is carrying another letter, from Gonerill to Edmund.

2 *with much ado*: Making a great fuss about it. This reflects Gonerill's view of Albany's moral scruples.

4 *Lord Edmund spake not with your lord at home*: Regan asks Oswald to confirm what he has already told her.

8 *Faith*: Regan's uncharacteristic oath is presumably designed to make palatable what may seem to Oswald to be a mere evasion.

9 *ignorance*: Lack of (political) understanding.

13 *nighted*: (1) Benighted; (2) on which (since he is blind) night has fallen.

13–14 *moreover to descry* | *The strength o'th'enemy*: The quick shift from moral pretension – which she does not properly understand – to practical political realities is typical of Regan.

20–21 *Belike –* | *Some things – I know not what . . .*: Regan's incoherence betokens her attempt to think how she can overcome her sister's advantage with Edmund and Oswald's uncooperativeness.

22 *I had rather –*: Presumably Oswald wished to state (once again) his loyalty to his mistress, in something like 'I had rather die than disobey my lady'.

25 *œillades*: This French word (defined in Cotgrave's French dictionary of 1611 as 'an amorous look, affectionate wink . . . passionate cast of the eye, a sheep's eye') was almost naturalized in the Elizabethan age (in the pronunciation indicated by the F spelling, *Eliads*), but has now reverted to foreignness.

26 *of her bosom*: In her confidence.

29 *I do advise you take this note*: I recommend that you take note of what I am about to say.

30 *talked*: Here almost a technical term for the coming to agreement which preceded marriage.

31 *more convenient is he for my hand*: It is more fitting that he should marry me. In normal parlance the lady's hand is *given* in marriage. Here, as elsewhere, Regan and Gonerill take the masculine role; their hands are not there to be given, but to seize on what they desire.

32 *You may gather more*: I have left things unsaid, which you can well guess at.

33 *give him this*: Some commentators assume that she gives a love-token rather than a letter. Certainly only one

letter is clearly mentioned when Oswald dies – that
from Gonerill; but it may be implied that he was
carrying more than one (see the note on IV.6.248);
one given by Regan at this point is not ruled out.

40 *What party I do follow*: Like a good politician Oswald
seizes on the opportunity to conclude by expressing
the solidarity of Gonerill and Regan.

IV.6

The expected reconciliation of Lear and Cordelia is
postponed to allow the stories of the blind Gloucester
and the mad Lear to cross and reach a common climax.
This stupendous scene covers three different actions:
(1) Gloucester in despair is brought to accept his lot
by the strange exercise of falling over an imaginary
Dover Cliff. This grotesque and emblematic episode
prepares us for (2) the entry of Lear crowned with
flowers, now the master of a torrential vein of mad
moral eloquence. The broken reverence of Gloucester,
never far from despair, and the free-wheeling phan-
tasmagoric energy of Lear point up two opposite ways
of reacting to oppression and impotence. But both are
now in the care of loving children. The 'capture' and
cure of Lear belong to the next scene; in the third part
of this scene we see Gloucester saved from the courtly
wickedness of Oswald by the cudgel of Edgar (now
A most poor man). The denouement of the Gloucester
plot is prepared for by the time-honoured device of
an intercepted letter.

0 *in peasant's clothes*: This is added to show that the Old
Man has kept the promise given at IV.1.49; Oswald
below (231) calls Edgar a *peasant*.

1 *that same hill*: The hill we talked about (Dover Cliff
as described in IV.1.72–3).

7–8 *thou speak'st | In better phrase*: Edgar now speaks in
verse.

11–24 *How fearful . . . headlong*: Marshall McLuhan calls the
Dover Cliff speech a 'Unique piece of three-dimensional verbal art . . . What Shakespeare does here is
to place five flat panels of two dimensions one behind

the other. By giving these flat panels a diagonal twist they succeed each other, as it were, in a perspective from the "stand-still" point' (*The Gutenberg Galaxy* (1962), pp. 16, 17). The set-piece description built up, layer by layer, by accumulation of small details is designed both to convey to the blind Gloucester the standards of measurement he should apply to the precipice and to convey to the audience the powerful and coherent nature of poetic illusion, by which Gloucester's 'cure' is to be effected.

13 *choughs*: Members of the crow family (pronounced 'chuffs').

15 *sampire*: Samphire (or 'Saint Pierre'; a maritime rock-herb, used in pickling, and gathered on cliffs for this purpose).

18 *yon*: Here and at 118 and 152, F changed Q's *yon* to *yond*. This is a recurrent F mannerism, spread across several plays, and seems to reflect its modernizing tendencies (see An Account of the Text) rather than its concern for accuracy.

   yon tall anchoring bark: That sailing vessel there at anchor.

19 *Diminished to her cock*: Looking as small as her cock-boat or dinghy.

   her cock, a buoy: Her cock-boat looks as small as a buoy.

21 *th'unnumbered idle pebble*: The innumerable loosely shifting pebbles. *pebble* is the old collective plural.

23–4 *Lest my brain turn, and the deficient sight | Topple down*: Lest I lose my mental (and physical) balance, so that the eyes which have failed me fall down with the rest of me.

27 *Would I not leap upright*: If I were as close to the edge as you are I would not dare even to jerk myself into an upright position (or 'dare to jump up vertically, so as to land on the same spot').

28 *another purse*: In addition to the one given at IV.1.63.

30 *Prosper it with thee*: Make it multiply when in your possession.

32 *With all my heart*: I endorse heartily what you have

said; I am going to fare well where I am going (to my death).

36 *Shake patiently my great affliction off*: End my painful life, but not in passionate despair.

38 *opposeless*: That permit no opposition.

39 *My snuff and loathèd part of nature*: The mere blackened wick of my senility, with its offensive smell – all that is left of the candle of my natural life.

41 *Gone*: I have gone (as he was instructed in 30).

42–4 *I know not . . . to the theft*: I think that imagination may cause death when life gives itself up willingly.

44 *where he thought*: At the foot of the cliff.

47 *pass indeed*: Pass away, die, in reality.

49 *gossamer*: The Q and F spellings – *gosmore*, *Goʒemore* – indicate the expected two-syllable pronunciation.

52 *Hast heavy substance*: Are made of flesh, are not a ghost.

53 *at each*: One on top of the other.

57 *chalky bourn*: Chalk boundary (of England: Dover Cliff).

58 *The shrill-gorged lark*: Even the lark with its shrill, penetrating voice.

63 *beguile*: Trick.
   beguile the tyrant's rage: Gloucester is thinking not of his own particular case, but of the traditional defence of suicide as it appeared among the Romans, and especially the Roman Stoics under the tyranny of such emperors as Nero or Domitian.

65 *Feel you your legs*: Have you any feeling in your legs?

71 *welked and waved like the enridgèd sea*: Twisted and ridged like the waves of the sea. F's *enraged* is an obvious vulgarization.

72 *happy father*: Fortunate old man. Here, as in 255 and 286, the true relationship is expressed by Edgar in a context which muffles its specific meaning.

73 *the clearest gods*: The spotless and most pure gods.

73–4 *make them honours | Of men's impossibilities*: Do things that are impossible for men to do, and so make themselves to be honoured by men.

75 *remember*: Perhaps he remembers the fiend-like behaviour

of the Bedlamite; perhaps he remembers the morality of endurance proper to a religious man.

76–7 *till it do cry out itself | 'Enough, enough', and die*: Till affliction itself tire of afflicting me and give up (as I have been tempted to do).

80 *free*: Unburdened by guilt or self-reproach. Typically, the moral poise that Edgar achieves here is immediately subverted by the entry of Lear.

81–2 *The safer sense will ne'er accommodate | His master thus*: This is usually said to refer to Lear's mad clothes ('Nobody sane would go around like that'). I take Edgar to be saying: 'Sights like this cannot be accommodated inside a sane view of the world', *His master* referring not to Lear, but to the possessor of such a *safer sense* ('saner view').

83–92 *they cannot touch ... Give the word*: Lear's madness expresses itself in a string of commands and observations, entirely disjointed in content, but linked by modulations of imagery. Thus *touch* – (1) arrest; (2) test gold – leads to *coining*, which leads to *press-money*; the idea of recruiting soldiers with *press-money* leads to images of archery, of challenges, of *brown bills* (halberdiers) and passwords – a tissue of ideas interrupted only by the *mouse* and the *toasted cheese*.

83 *they cannot touch me for coining*: Coining lay within the royal prerogative.

85 *side-piercing*: Heart-rending (but with a reminiscence of Christ on the Cross (John 19:34)).

86 *Nature's above art in that respect*: Perhaps 'It is better to be the king who creates the coinage than the image of the king that the coin bears', for only the latter can be counterfeited.

87 *press-money*: The sum paid to a recruit when he was 'impressed', seized for the army.

87–8 *a crow-keeper*: A farmer's boy, not a military expert.

88 *Draw ... a clothier's yard*: Extend the bow for the full length of an arrow (a cloth-yard long).

90 *do't*: Catch the mouse.

There's my gauntlet; I'll prove it on a giant: Lear throws down his 'gauntlet' and challenges anyone (be he a giant) to dispute his verdict.

91–2 *O, well flown, bird! I' the clout*: The *bird* may be a falcon, or may refer to the arrow which hits the *clout* (the target).

92 *Hewgh*: The noise made by the arrow.

Give the word: For the first time in the scene, Lear shows an awareness of other people beside him; and his immediate impulse is to challenge them, demand the password that distinguishes friend from foe.

93 *Sweet marjoram*: An appropriate password, since the herb was used for diseases of the brain.

96 *Gonerill with a white beard*: It seems as if something in Gloucester's action or tone of voice suggests flattery. I have suggested that Gloucester, when he recognizes the King's voice, falls to his knees like a loyal servant. Lear's mind immediately harks back to Gonerill as archetype of flatterers – and *this* Gonerill has a white beard.

96–7 *They flattered me like a dog*: As always, Shakespeare sees the dog species as characterized by false fawning on its master.

97–8 *told me I had the white hairs in my beard ere the black ones were there*: Since this refers to flattery, the *white hairs* must be those of wisdom rather than age. The *I* must be emphasized, for he is reminded of all this by the sight of Gloucester's beard.

98–9 *To say 'ay' and 'no' to everything that I said*: Agreeing (or pretending to agree) with everything I said.

99–100 *'Ay' and 'no' too was no good divinity*: Several passages in the New Testament might seem to supply the *divinity* that the flatterers erred against. Matthew 5:37 – 'But let your communication be yea, yea; nay, nay. For whatsoever is more than these cometh of evil' – is possible as a source; the actual injunction is against the oaths that may be added to 'yea, yea' or 'nay, nay', but it is preceded by 'Neither shalt thou swear by thy head, because thou canst not make one hair white or black', which might seem to have suggested

96–8 here. In 2 Corinthians 1:17–20 Paul defends himself against a charge of lightness by asserting that 'our preaching to you was not yea and nay' (was not ambiguous).

102–3 *there I found 'em, there I smelt 'em out*: In these matters I was able to see through their lies and discover them for the flatterers they were.

106 *trick*: Individual peculiarity.

107 *Is't not the King*: Nevill Coghill (*Shakespeare's Professional Skills* (1964), pp. 25–6) says 'the act of homage that brings Gloucester to his knees, a loyal subject, leaves him there a seeming culprit, for that is how Lear interprets the ambiguity in kneeling; and now Gloucester's guilt is to be thrust home'.

109 *thy cause*: Your case; the charge against you.

110 *Adultery*: The key distinction here and throughout the speech is between 'natural' or illegal sexuality, which gradually moves from *Adultery*, *lecher*, *copulation*, to the more violent representation of *luxury*, *pell-mell*, *riotous appetite*, and (on the other hand) the legal proprieties embodied in the *King*, the *lawful sheets*, the *women all above*. The process of the speech mimics the collapse of these legal safeguards into the horror of animal sexuality.

115 *kinder*: With the usual sense – 'more naturally child-like'.

117 *luxury*: Lechery.

pell-mell: As if in headlong, indiscriminate, and confused battle.

for I lack soldiers: Indiscriminate lechery is promoted by the King, for surplus population swells his army.

118 *yon*: See the note on 18.

119 *Whose face between her forks presages snow*: Her *forks* are her legs. Her face *presages* or indicates that the other face *between her forks* is frigid or chaste.

120 *minces virtue*: Affects virtue by a show of squeamishness.

120–21 *does shake the head | To hear of pleasure's name*: Shakes her head in disapproval at the very name of pleasure.

122 *fitchew*: Polecat or weasel. 'Polecat' was a cant term for a prostitute.

soilèd: Full-fed with fresh grass (and therefore bursting with sexual enthusiasm).

124 *Down from the waist they are centaurs*: He means that, like centaurs, they are bestial like horses (*soilèd horses*, as above) below the waist. Centaurs were from early times used as images of man's lustful animal impulses.

126 *girdle*: Waist.

inherit: Possess, hold power over.

128-9 *hell ... darkness ... the sulphurous pit – burning, scalding, stench, consumption*: The obvious sexual references point to a climax of hysterical disgust at female sexuality. At the same time the fairly free verse form of the preceding lines breaks down into prose.

129 *consumption*: Destruction (especially by fire).

130-31 *Give me an ounce of civet; good apothecary, sweeten my imagination*: The imagination that has just conjured up *stench* and *consumption* needs a perfume to sweeten its atmosphere. For the purpose Lear will buy civet from Gloucester, now imagined to be an apothecary.

135 *piece of nature*: Probably *piece* has the sense of 'masterpiece'; but the following phrase suggests a contrast between this *ruined piece* (portion) and the *great world* or macrocosm also in the process of being ruined.

137 *I remember thine eyes*: In Lear's unsweetened imagination the horror of Gloucester's eyeless sockets provides an image of the world he recognizes, though he may not be able to recognize unmutilated forms.

138 *squiny*: Squint through half-shut eyes.

blind Cupid: Cupid's traditional blindness and romantic associations give a horrid appropriateness to the use of his name for Edmund's progenitor.

139 *challenge*: Lear seems to revert to the obsession of 90.

142 *take this*: Accept this scene as real. (The speech is an oblique Shakespearian defence of the non-realism of what is before us.)

145 *the case of eyes*: The sockets where the eyes used to be.

146 *are you there with me*: Is that the point you are making?

147–8 *in a heavy case*: In a sad way (with a pun on *case* meaning 'socket').

150 *I see it feelingly*: (1) I recognize it with keen feelings; (2) having no eyes, I can only 'see' it by the feel of it.

151 *What, art mad*: Lear takes Gloucester's *see it feelingly* in the sense of 'know it only imperfectly because I know it only by feel'; and says, 'You must be mad to require eyes to know the way of the world; all the senses convey the same message, the same image of the world as a place of merely superficial social distinctions, with no moral basis.'

152 *yon*: See the note on 18.

153 *simple*: Of humble condition.

153–5 *Hark in thine ear – change places and, handy-dandy . . .*: A whisper to the justice of the peace bribes him to reverse his decision. Then he is as like the thief as one hand is like another. Lear puts his hands behind his back and pretends to shift an object from one to the other. This is the guessing-game of *handy-dandy*: which hand holds the object? Here the object is social status, and it is mere luck to guess which thief is called to the dock and which to the bench.

William R. Elton, in *King Lear and the Gods* (1966), p. 86, n. 24, quotes Thomas Powell's *The Attorney's Academy* (1623), p. 217: '. . . and play at handy-dandy, which is the guardian, or which is the fool'.

158 *creature*: Man in his lowest state and therefore nearest to the animal. 'Creature' was often used of the animal in contradistinction to the human state. An ironic awareness of this may be intended.

159–60 *a dog's obeyed in office*: Obedience is given not to intrinsic worth but to the accident of status.

161 *beadle*: Parish constable (charged with the duty of whipping offenders).
bloody: From the lashing.

164 *The usurer hangs the cozener*: The big cheat is given the

sanction of society and condemns the little cheat. In this period usurers or capitalists were acquiring respectability and were being appointed to offices such as that of magistrate, against the protests of preachers and poets.

165 *Thorough*: An alternative form of 'through'.

great vices do appear: The Q reading, *smal vices do appeare*, makes perfect, if fairly trite, sense. But F corrected it to *great Vices do appeare*, for no reason that is discernible, unless the corrector found it in his 'copy'. We must either accept *great* or explain it away. The F reading can be defended in terms of sense as well as of text: it is not the smallness of their vices that distinguishes the poor, but the exposure to which they are subject. It must be allowed, however, that the antithesis is somewhat muffled by *great*. If the corrector's 'great', written in the margin, was inserted by the compositor of F in the wrong place, we might suppose that 'do great appear' was the original reading; the rhythmical emphasis in the line would then, however, seem to be in the wrong place.

166 *Robes and furred gowns*: The robes of the judges, and perhaps also of the usurers, as in *Measure for Measure*, III.2.7.

Plate: Arm in plate mail.

167 *And the strong lance of justice hurtless breaks*: Notice the sense of effort conveyed by the sound of this line.

hurtless: Without hurting.

168 *a pygmy's straw*: A weak weapon, opposite to a strong lance (cf. *Othello*, V.2.268–9: 'Man but a rush against Othello's breast, | And he retires'). The frogs in the pseudo-Homeric *Battle of the Frogs and Mice* carried rushes for spears. The parallel mock-battle of the cranes and pygmies was also well known in Shakespeare's age, but had not been described in so much detail.

169 *able*: Fortify, give power and capacity to.

170 *Take that of me*: What we think the exact sense of *that* is depends on whether we suppose that Lear is more

obsessed with kingship or with corruption at this point.
If he is concerned with his kingship, what he gives
Gloucester to *able* him will be some document of the
royal prerogative. If corruption is uppermost in his
mind (as I suppose) what he gives is 'money', and what
seals th'accusers' lips is (as in 153–5) a bribe. In either
case his flowers would seem the only things he can
give.

171–3 *Get thee glass eyes . . . thou dost not*: Lear returns, at
the end of his speech, to the subject with which he
started it – Gloucester's failure to 'see' without eyes.
You should be, he says, like a *politician*, one of those
vile persons concerned to control affairs through
'policy' or trickery, who have the art of seeming to
see what they cannot actually see (discovering, for
example, imaginary plots so as to justify repression).
You should be like them and conceal your blindness
behind glass eyes.

171 *glass eyes*: Spectacles.

173–4 *Now, now, now, now! | Pull off my boots. Harder, harder
– so*: Exhausted by his speech, Lear sinks down and
gives the command that might accompany such a
feeling in ordinary life – on returning from hunting
or a journey, for example. The *so* implies satisfaction
when the job is done.

175 *matter and impertinency*: Relevant substance and irrel-
evancy.

181 *wawl*: Cry out.

184 *This's a good block*: It seems possible to detect a series
of actions here. In accordance with good Anglican
practice he takes off his 'hat' (his crown of flowers, I
suppose) when he begins to 'preach' (181). His sermon
has not, however, got beyond a line and a half when
his attention is diverted to the hat he notices he is
holding in his hand. *This's a good block*, he says: 'This
is a well-made hat.'

185 *delicate stratagem*: Cunning trick.

185–6 *to shoe | A troop of horse with felt*: The idea of the *felt*
no doubt comes from the hat-block mentioned before.

The horsemen so shod could steal up on Albany and
Cornwall (seen as responsible for their wives' crimes)
and kill them.

186 *put't in proof*: Put it to the test.

192 *The natural fool of fortune*: Born to be the plaything
of fortune (just recently leading a charge against the
sons-in-law, and now a prisoner).

194 *cut to the brains*: Notice how the expression combines
both physical and mental wounding.

195 *seconds*: Supporters.

196 *a man of salt*: A man of tears.

197–8 *To use . . . I will die*: The text is difficult to determine
at this point. Q reads as here, except that after *dust*
there is a new line and a new speech prefix: *Lear. I will
. . .* This suggests that something is missing, and the
second Quarto (1619) supplies it: *Gent. Good Sir.* This
is tempting, but there is no evidence that Q2's corrections of Q1 are the result of anything more than the
compositor's ingenuity. F omits everything between
water-pots and *I will die*, no doubt because the compositor's eye moved from 'I [Ay] and laying' to the 'I' in
the same line.

198–9 *I will die bravely,* | *Like a smug bridegroom*: *bravely*
means not only 'with courage' but also 'in my fine
attire' (flowers and all). It is this latter sense that leads
to the image of the *smug* (neat, spruce) bridegroom.

202 *there's life in't*: There's still a chance; at least I can make
you run for your captive. Hearing them say that they
obey him, he realizes that the captivity is not as absolute
as he had supposed.
     and: If.

203 *Sa, sa, sa, sa*: A cry of encouragement to the hounds
in hunting.

206–7 *the general curse* | *Which twain have brought her to*: On
the most factual level the *twain* are Gonerill and Regan,
and the *general curse* brought about in nature is the
current state of Britain, with brother against brother
etc. (I.2.106–11). Behind this is the larger idea of the
fallen condition of mankind caused by Adam and Eve

(*twain*). On this level Cordelia is a Christ-like redeeming figure.

208 *gentle*: Honourable.

speed you: God speed you, God prosper you.

210 *sure and vulgar*: It's certain and everybody knows about it.

210–11 *Everyone . . . Which can distinguish sound*: Everyone who has ears to hear.

213 *on speedy foot*: On foot, and advancing rapidly.

213–14 *The main descry | Stands on the hourly thought*: A sighting of the main force of their army is expected from hour to hour.

218 *my worser spirit*: Usually taken to be 'my evil angel'; but it may mean no more than 'my ill thoughts'.

219 *Well pray you*: That's a good thing to be praying for.

221 *tame to*: Submissive, resigned to.

222 *by the art of known and feeling sorrows*: As the result of the workings of sorrows that I have both felt in myself and known in others.

223 *pregnant to*: Disposed to feel.

224 *biding*: Place to stay.

226 *To boot, and boot*: Probably means 'in addition, and may you make *boot* (profit) out of it'.

proclaimed priꝫe: Outlaw proclaimed as having a price on his head.

Most happy: How lucky I am! The self-centred insensitivity of Oswald makes an effective contrast, set against the mutual support of the other characters in the scene.

229 *Briefly thyself remember*: Say your last prayer, and make it short.

230 *friendly*: Friendly to him, since he desires death more than anything else.

231 *bold peasant*: Oswald's words here, as well as the general affection of his language, give Edgar the idea of the vocabulary and the identity he can assume to answer him.

232 *published*: Proclaimed.

233–4 *th'infection of his fortune take | Like hold on thee*: His outlawry attach itself to you as well (for helping him).

235–40 *'Chill . . . 'choud . . . I'ce*: Edgar falls into the stage
rustic (South-western) of the time, in which 'I' is represented by 'Che' or 'Ich', so that 'I will' becomes *'Chill*;
'I should' becomes *'choud*; and 'I shall' becomes *I'ce*.

235 *vurther 'cagion*: Further occasion (in the sense of 'better
cause'). *'cagion* is stage rustic for 'occasion'; the F
spelling 'casion' has some advantage for the mere
reader, but the Q form may well preserve the noise
made on Shakespeare's stage.

237 *go your gate*: Go your way.

238 *And 'choud ha' bin ʒwaggered out of my life*: If fancy
talk had been capable of killing me.

240 *che vor' ye*: I warrant you.

241 *costard*: (Literally, 'apple') head.
ballow: Cudgel. The uncorrected form in Q is *battero*,
which the corrector, obviously relying on native sense
rather than authority, changed to *bat*. F reads *Ballow*,
from which word the uncorrected Q form must derive.
ballow is not common, but J. Wright in his *English
Dialect Dictionary* (6 vols., 1898–1905) seems to have
found some examples.

244 *'Chill pick your teeth*: This suggests that Edgar has now
a sword or dagger in his possession. If so he must have
acquired it from Oswald – who has still a rapier with
which he makes *foins*. Perhaps in a first bout (at 242)
Edgar has his ballow, Oswald his sword and dagger;
Edgar beats down Oswald's dagger and seizes it.

245 *foins*: Rapier thrusts (in the new Continental style).

248, 256 *letters*: Two letters may be meant: (1) the one from
Gonerill read out below; (2) one from Regan, perhaps
given at IV.5.33 (see the note). However, only one
letter is mentioned below; and 'letters' can be used in
the plural with only singular meaning.

258 *deathsman*: Executioner.

259 *Leave*: Grant us your leave.

261 *Their papers*: To rip their papers.

263 *want*: Lack.

264 *fruitfully offered*: Organized (by Gonerill) so that there
will be results.

There is nothing done: The victory will be meaningless.

267 *for your labour*: (1) As a recompense for your labour;
(2) as a place for your (amorous) labours.

268 *servant*: This is usually glossed as 'lover', but it may
be nothing more than conventional politeness. The
strange addition of Q, *and for you her owne for Venter*,
has not been explained, and seems best left out of the
text.

270 *indistinguished space of woman's will*: How far beyond
apprehension is the range of woman's lust!

272–3 *Here in the sands | Thee I'll rake up*: It is not clear how
this shallow burial of Oswald was accomplished on
Shakespeare's stage. Presumably Edgar had to drag
the body out of sight, either now (277) or at the end
of the scene.

273 *unsanctified*: A curious way of saying 'wicked',
suggested presumably by the thought that the sands in
which he is proposing to bury Oswald – unsanctified
ground – are appropriate to the character of the man
buried.

274 *in the mature time*: When the time is ripe.

275 *ungracious paper*: Wicked letter.

276 *the death-practised Duke*: Albany, whose death is being
practised or plotted.

278 *how stiff is my vile sense*: How unresponsive and unpliant
my feelings are, *vile* (basely physical) in this very inca-
pacity to give way before *huge sorrows*.
vile: See the note on III.2.71.

279 *ingenious*: Fully conscious.

282–3 *woes by wrong imaginations lose | The knowledge of
themselves*: Woes would cease to know their own pain
by entering into the illusions of the insane.

IV.7

The reunion of Cordelia and Kent prepares the way
for the reunion of Cordelia and Lear. The sense of
awaking out of a nightmare of cruelty into a world of
natural kindness makes this scene an island of paradisal
calm in a maelstrom of horror.

3 *every measure fail me*: No matter how much I try to

do, I will not be able to do enough to recompense you.
Cordelia and Kent pick up the arithmetical ideas about
desert which prevailed in I.1.

5 *All my reports go with the modest truth*: Let not what
you say of me be excessive but merely report the truth.

6 *Nor more, nor clipped, but so*: Neither exaggerated, nor
cut short, but just as they happened. The word *clipped*
picks up the coinage idea implicit in *paid* above (4).
suited: Clothed. Kent still wears the servant's livery
he wore as Caius.

7 *weeds*: Clothes.

9 *Yet to be known shortens my made intent*: To reveal
myself now would anticipate the plan I have made. It
is not clear what Kent's *intent* could be – perhaps a
last-minute climactic revelation. But it must be
confessed that this suits Shakespeare's interests more
obviously than Kent's. It is a regular characteristic of
Shakespeare's dramatic art that he delays the pene-
tration of disguise till the final denouement.

10 *My boon I make it*: The favour I beg is.

16 *Th'untuned and jarring senses O wind up*: The slack-
ened strings of his mind no longer yield sense or
harmony (true relationships) but jar against one
another. He needs the pegs screwed up and the
harmony restored.

17 *child-changèd*: (1) Changed (to madness) by the cruel-
ties of his children; (2) (less probably) changed into
second childishness.

21, 23 *DOCTOR . . . GENTLEMAN*: These are the speech-
prefixes given by Q. As F omits the Doctor from this
scene, it allots both speeches to the Gentleman. All
previous editors transpose the speeches, giving the
first to the Gentleman and the second to the Doctor.
See the next note.

22 *Enter Gentleman*: F has an entry for the Gentleman at
the beginning of the scene (substituting for the
Doctor); Q has no entry for him, but gives 23–4 as
his first speech. The addition of his entry here restores
Q's opening of the scene and its distribution of

speeches at 21 and 23; and it explains why, at 91 below,
the Gentleman knows nothing of Kent's identity.

Enter . . . Lear in a chair: This is the F reading; Q has
no entry for Lear. In spite of some awkwardness there
can be little doubt that F is correct. It restores Lear to
his 'throne'; it makes his falling to his knees a plausible action, which 'discovery' in a bed (as indicated
in many editions) does not. The entry at this point
might seem too early; since Cordelia is asked to *Be by*
in the next line it might be taken that her father is not
present. I suggest, however, that, when Lear is carried
on, Cordelia falls to her knees, at that point of the
stage where she is standing. The Gentleman says *Be
by* and prepares to wake him; Cordelia's *Very well* is
not, however, followed by any immediate movement.
The Doctor repeats the request in a less indirect form:
Please you draw near, and only now does Cordelia
move forward and kneel again by Lear's chair.

24 *temperance*: Calm behaviour.

Music sounds offstage: Shakespeare and his contemporaries often use music as part of a process of mental
healing, or to represent dramatically the magic power
or healing force of nature. Cf. *Pericles*, III.2.87–94,
The Tempest, I.2.392–4 and *Henry VIII*, III.1.2–14.

30 *white flakes*: Snow-white hair.

31 *challenge*: Demand.

33 *deep dread-bolted thunder*: Thunder with the thunder-
bolt that causes deep dread.

35 *cross lightning*: Zigzag (fork) lightning.

perdu: A '*sentinelle perdue*' was an especially daring
soldier who was placed (as a spy or a scout) so close
to the enemy that he was considered virtually lost.

36 *this thin helm*: The thin hair of old age.

38 *fain*: Glad.

39 *rogues forlorn*: Abandoned vagrants.

40 *short and musty straw*: Long dry straw would make the
best bed; short, broken-up straw, damp or mouldy,
would not protect from the cold and wet.

42 *concluded all*: Come to an end altogether.

Speak to him: Cordelia's sense of shame and guilt, together with her temperament, so notably reticent in I.1, prompts her to retreat behind the Doctor.

45–8 *out o'the grave . . . molten lead*: Lear supposes that he is experiencing the life after death (as in some sense he is). He takes it that Cordelia is in heaven and that he is in hell. The *wheel of fire* was a common apocryphal appurtenance of the Christian hell (as was *molten lead*). But these images may have more force today as expressions of the psychological torments of guilt.

47 *that*: So that.

53 *abused*: 'In a strange mist of uncertainty' (Dr Johnson).

54 *thus*: Thus bewildered and lost.

60 *fond*: Silly.

64 *this man*: Kent.

65 *mainly*: Very much.

71 *Be your tears wet*: Are your tears real, or am I still snared in illusion?

76 *your own kingdom*: The kingdom which is (still) yours.

80 *even o'er the time*: Fill up the gap in time (by reliving the experience he has passed through).

82 *Till further settling*: Till he is better settled in his mind.

83 *You must bear with me*: Presumably he leans on her as he leaves, so that the verb has both a physical and a mental reference.

85 *Holds it true*: Does it continue to be accepted as true.

92 *look about*: Be wary.

92–3 *The powers of the kingdom*: The British forces (as against Cordelia's French ones).

94 *arbitrament*: Deciding of the dispute.

96–7 *My point and period will be throughly wrought, | Or well or ill*: The sentence of my life and my purpose will be brought to a fully worked-out conclusion or full stop, and it will be clear whether it has been for good or for ill.

96 *throughly*: This, the Q reading – F omits the passage – is a common Elizabethan alternative for 'thoroughly'.

V.I

> The snare of jealous lust draws more tightly around Regan, Gonerill, and Edmund. Meantime the preparations for the battle go ahead; but a further reckoning, beyond the battle, is prepared for.

1   *his last purpose*: To fight with Regan and Edmund against Cordelia.

4   *constant pleasure*: Settled resolution.

5   *Our sister's man is certainly miscarried*: When Regan parted with Oswald (in IV.5) he was on his way to Edmund. She assumes that something has happened to him.

6   *doubted*: Feared.

9   *In honoured love*: In an honourable way. Edmund has become a (verbal) devotee to the idea of honour.

10–11   *found my brother's way | To the forfended place*: Played her husband's role in that part of her body *forfended* ('forbidden') to you (by the commandment against adultery).

12–13   *conjunct | And bosomed with her, as far as we call hers*: Coupled and intimate with her, to the fullest extent.

15   *I never shall endure her*: That is, if the two of you become too intimate.

16   *familiar*: Unduly intimate.

22   *the rigour of our state*: The harshness of our administration.

25–7   *It touches us . . . oppose*: I am moved (to be *valiant* and fight) because this is a French invasion of Britain; but in so far as France's purpose is to embolden the King (and others with just cause of complaint) I am not touched. Albany's language is excessively harsh; the fact that Q is our only text at this point makes corruption a real possibility.

28   *you speak nobly*: See the note on 9.
    Why is this reasoned: What is the point of this academic talk about reasons for fighting? The important thing is to fight.

30   *domestic and particular broils*: Family and individual quarrels.

32 *th'ancient of war*: The most experienced warriors.

33 *presently*: Immediately.

37 *the riddle*: Gonerill detects behind Regan's words the
fear of leaving her with Edmund while she goes with
Albany to the council of war.

40 *this letter*: The letter from Gonerill to Edmund which
Edgar took from Oswald's dead body.

44 *avouchèd*: Guaranteed.

46 *machination*: The plots and counter-plots that belong
to the *business of the world*.

47 *I was forbid it*: By Shakespeare, who does not wish any
anticipation here of the denouement in V.3.

52 *Here*: Edmund hands Albany a paper.

53 *diligent discovery*: Careful reconnaissance.

54 *greet the time*: Go forward to welcome the occasion.

56 *jealous*: Suspicious, watchful.

61–2 *And hardly shall I carry out my side, | Her husband being
alive*: The emphasis falls on *Her*. He is now talking
about 'enjoying' Gonerill. He cannot *take* Regan
because of Gonerill's opposition; it is difficult to fulfil
his side of the bargain with Gonerill (that is, satisfy
her lust) because her husband is alive.

62 *Now then*: Let me see, let me think it out.

63 *countenance for the battle*: Authority, support, while the
battle is in progress.

65 *taking off*: Killing.

68 *Shall*: They shall.

69 *Stands*: Depends.

V.2

Gloucester, still guided by Edgar, waits while Lear and
Cordelia lose the battle.

1 *father*: As at IV.6.72, a general word of respect rather
than a revelation of the particular relationship.

2 *host*: Shelterer.

4 *Alarum and retreat within*: The climactic battle of *King
Lear* is treated very cursorily. Shakespeare is interested
in motives and in results, but the actual process of the
battle is unimportant to him. The real battle between
good and evil must be fought out elsewhere.

9–10 *Men must endure | Their going hence even as their coming hither*: Just as childbirth involves pain and trouble, so death is not just a matter of sitting and rotting, but a painful process that has to be struggled through till it be granted from above.

11 *Ripeness is all*: Man's duty is not to wait to *rot*, but to await the time of *Ripeness*, which is the time appointed for death. That is all that matters.

V.3

In the chaos following the battle a still moment of resignation is achieved by the captive Lear and Cordelia. Albany strives to organize justice, and Edgar appears like a deus ex machina to defeat Edmund. The lust of the sisters destroys both of them. But the turn towards justice, which seems to be confirmed by the deaths of the wicked, is suddenly halted and even reversed by the entry of Lear with Cordelia dead from prison. His own death follows as a corollary on this; Albany and Edgar are left to bear *The weight of this sad time*.

1 *Good guard*: Keep a strict guard on them.

2–3 *their greater pleasures . . . That*: The more explicit decisions of those who.

16 *take upon's*: Assume the burden of.

17 *God's*: I assume that only one God is meant, even though this requires a monotheistic faith from the pagan Lear.

wear out: Survive beyond.

22–3 *He that parts us shall bring a brand from heaven | And fire us hence like foxes*: Foxes are driven out of their holes by fire and smoke (and then killed). But the fire that parts Lear and Cordelia will have to be more than human. Perhaps Lear is thinking of the final conflagration, at the Last Judgement.

24 *The good-years shall devour them*: It is not clear what kind of bogey-men are meant by *The good-years*. But the tone of the statement seems to be that of a father's homely reassurance to a frightened child.

fell: Skin.

30–31 *make thy way | To noble fortunes*: Become a nobleman.

31–2 *men | Are as the time is*: Moral principles change according to circumstances.

33 *Does not become a sword*: Is not appropriate for a soldier.

36 *write happy*: Call yourself a fortunate man.

37 *carry it*: Arrange it.

41 *your valiant strain*: The valour that you have derived from your ancestors. Note the implicit denial, in this, of Edmund's bastardy speech, I.2.1–22.

46 *equally*: With justice.

49 *title*: (1) Kingship; (2) legal right to the possession of the land.

51 *impressed lances*: Conscript pikemen (but the reverberations of the strongly physical side of the image should also be noted: common humanity might turn back on us, and press their points into the very eyeballs which should control them in a commanding vision of how things must be).

57–8 *And the best quarrels in the heat are cursed | By those that feel their sharpness*: Even good arguments are hateful at this moment of passionate involvement, when we are all suffering the pains and losses of battle. Edmund stalls for time to get Lear and Cordelia killed, pretending that they would not, at the moment, get a fair hearing at their trial.

62 *we*: Regan has assumed the plural of royalty.

66 *immediacy*: The condition of being 'immediate' to my sovereignty, next in line.

69 *your addition*: The title you have given him.

70 *compeers*: Equals.

75–9 *General . . . master*: Regan creates Edmund *General* of the city (herself) which she surrenders. He has conquered her *walls* (her 'resistance') and now has the right to dispose of her soldiers etc. She gives in unconditionally.

79 *enjoy him*: By linguistic convention, men 'enjoy' women, not vice versa. The application to Regan marks her masculine and commanding nature.

80 *The let-alone lies not in your good will*: The power to

hinder it does not lie within the scope of your consent.

83 *hear reason*: Albany does not seem to be arguing for talk rather than action, since almost immediately he calls for the trumpet to sound. His speech contains the details of the complex situation, the 'reasons' which will be needed to *prove title*.

84–5 *and, in thy attaint,* | *This gilded serpent*: And I also arrest Gonerill who has provided the *attaint* or accusation against you. The F word, *arrest*, is clearly a mistaken repetition of the word in the line above. Note the style of this whole speech: Albany slips into the quasi-legal formality and paradox of the deus ex machina.

85 *sister*: Sister-in-law.

87 *sub-contracted*: Only *sub*-contracted because she is already contracted to Albany.

89 *If you will marry, make your loves to me*: If Gonerill and Edmund are contracted to one another, then Albany is the only man free to enter into a new relationship.

90 *An interlude*: What an old-fashioned little farce! 'Interludes' were short, often humorous, plays of the pre-Shakespearian period.

94 *make it*: Perhaps equivalent to 'make it good', fulfil it.

95 *in nothing*: In no point.

97 *medicine*: Poison.

98–9 *What in the world he is* | *That*: Whatever the rank of the person who.

99 *villain-like*: Like a slave.

103 *thy single virtue*: Your unaided valour.

108–15 *A trumpet sounds . . .*: Considerable textual confusion surrounds this heraldic occasion. The text (112) speaks of three trumpet calls. F in fact has four, one before the reading of the challenge and three after; Albany commands the first and the Herald the other three. Q has three trumpet calls, the first commanded by a *Captain*, the second and the third by *Bastard* (that is, Edmund). Editors often try to compromise between the two versions, but since they are alternative organ-

izations of the same thing it seems best to stick to one
– F's in this case.

115 *a trumpet*: A trumpeter.

120 *canker-bit*: Worm-eaten.

122 *cope*: Match.

127–8 *Behold; it is the privilege of mine honours,* | *My oath,
and my profession*: See my sword; the right to draw it
is the privilege conferred on me by my honour, by my
oath of knighthood, and my religious vows ('profes-
sions').

129 *Maugre*: In spite of.

130 *thy . . . fire-new fortune*: Your new-minted rank as military leader and earl.

134 *extremest upward*: Topmost part.

136 *toad-spotted traitor*: Spotted (stained) with treason as
the toad is spotted (allegedly with venom).

141 *thy tongue some 'say of breeding breathes*: The way you
speak gives some *assay* or proof of the quality of your
upbringing. But perhaps F's *say* only means 'speech'.

142 *nicely*: By being meticulous.

145 *the hell-hated lie*: The lie (that I am a traitor) which I
hate as I hate hell.

146–8 *Which, for they yet . . . rest for ever*: The mere return
of accusations to your head and heart glances off your
armour; but my sword will push them straight into
your heart, and there they will remain. *Which* probably refers back both to *treasons* and to *heart* ('into
which').

146 *for*: Because.

148, 149 *Edmund falls . . . to Edgar, about to kill Edmund*: I have
inserted these stage directions to explain Albany's
words, which are not clearly directed in the text. Some
have supposed that it is Gonerill who says *Save him,
save him!*, which solves the problem in another way.

149 *practice*: Plotting.

152 *cozened and beguiled*: Tricked and deceived.

153 *this paper*: The letter from Gonerill to Edmund which
passed through the hands of Oswald and Edgar. It is
not clear if the 'stopping' is to be physical or mental.

153 *Hold, sir*: It is not clear to whom this is addressed. Perhaps it is to Edgar, with his sword once again at Edmund's throat.

156 *the laws are mine, not thine*: Presumably because she is the daughter of the sovereign (the source of legality), and Albany only the consort.

157 *Who can arraign me*: As sovereign she cannot be brought to trial.

159 *desperate*: In the state of despair, theologically defined as 'having lost any sense of Divine Grace', and therefore liable to commit suicide. This is why she has to be 'governed' or restrained.

163 *noble*: Of good breeding. The same idea is picked up in Edgar's *no less in blood* ('of no worse breeding') in 165. Edmund has relapsed from the revolutionary posture of his I.2 soliloquy into traditional conceptions of nobility and breeding.

166 *If more*: If legitimacy confers more nobility than illegitimacy does.

168 *our pleasant vices*: The vicious acts which give us pleasure.

170–71 *The dark and vicious place where thee he got | Cost him his eyes*: The darkness of sin resulted in the physical darkness of his blind state.

171–2 *'Tis true. | The wheel is come full circle*: Edmund picks up Edgar's point about the poetic justice of Destiny (*'Tis true*), and applies it to himself. He made Edgar his enemy, he embraced force and deceit as methods; and now the disguised Edgar has conquered him by force. We should remember how he alleged Edgar's sword had wounded him in II.1. Now he is killed by the method he used to start his career.

181–97 *The bloody proclamation ... Burst smilingly*: The narrative of important and moving events offstage, told by a messenger, traditionally makes its effect by a more rhetorical, more statuesque mode than is usual in dramatic poetry. The example here (properly called a *period* – a classical paragraph – in 202) involves continuously suspended syntax carrying the narration forward without a single full-stop.

181   *The bloody proclamation*: The proclamation (see II.3.1)
      that he should be put to death if found.

183–4 *we the pain of death would hourly die | Rather than die
      at once*: We prefer to suffer the pain of death every hour
      of our life rather than die quickly and get it over with.

194, 196–7 *his flawed heart . . . smilingly*: His cracked (*flawed*)
      heart burst under the contrary pressures of joy and
      grief; but this was not a death in despair; at the moment
      of death he knew joy.

201   *dissolve*: Weep myself into liquid.

202   *a period*: A complete sentence, with its own consum-
      mation and final point of punctuation.

203–5 *but another . . . And top extremity*: The first *period* was
      an 'amplification' (in the language of rhetoric) of one
      sorrow (Gloucester's); to amplify another sorrow
      (Kent's) in the same way would take one beyond the
      period (limit) of what one can stand. Kent's *period* is
      in fact shorter than Gloucester's.

206   *big*: Ready to burst forth.

207   *worst estate*: Poorest condition (when he was Poor
      Tom).

209   *so endured*: Lived as Poor Tom.

211   *threw him on my father*: Threw himself on the body of
      the dead Gloucester.

214   *puissant*: Overpowering.
      the strings of life: The heart-strings (but I think the
      vocal cords are also in Shakespeare's mind: the violence
      of his outcry cracked both vocal cords and heart-
      strings).

216   *tranced*: In a trance, unconscious.

218   *his enemy king*: King Lear, who had (I.1.178) declared
      himself his enemy.

221   *smokes*: Steams.

222   *from the heart of –*: The failure to complete the state-
      ment allows the *coup de théâtre* of suggesting for a
      moment that it is Cordelia who is killed.

227   *marry*: Join together.

231–2 *the compliment | Which very manners urges*: The formal

courtesies which good manners alone would cause us
to observe.

233 *aye good night*: Farewell for ever. We are not told, and
need not know, whether Kent has a premonition of
Lear's death or assumes that his own death is immi-
nent, as may be suggested by *the strings of life* | *Began
to crack* (214–15). In either case, his dramatic task is
done.

235 *brought out*: Out, in the theatrical sense being used here,
means 'out, on to the stage'; in these terms 'in' means
'inside the stage-façade, behind the stage'. F's *brought
out* implies a theatrical origin for the 'copy' behind it,
just as Q's *brought in* implies a literary 'copy' not used
for stage purposes. The dead daughters are all brought
back on to the stage to reassemble there the cast of
I.1.

236 *object*: Spectacle of pity or horror.

243 *brief*: Quick.

249 *EDGAR Haste thee for thy life*: I follow F here (Q,
followed by many editors, gives the speech to *Duke* –
that is, Albany – and makes Edgar exit, bringing him
onstage again with Lear). Edgar must be placed on
the stage beside Edmund; he takes the sword from him
and gives it, with his instructions, to the Officer.

252–3 *blame upon her own despair,* | *That she fordid herself*: If
we compare the language applied in 289–90 to the
deaths of Gonerill and Regan (*fordone themselves,* |
And desperately are dead) we can see the ironic repetition of the first act here: there is an attempt to make
Cordelia seem to behave in the same way as her sisters,
but it does not succeed.

254 *The gods defend her*: A. C. Bradley and others have
seen an ironic relationship between this and the stage
direction immediately following: *Enter Lear with
Cordelia in his arms*.

255 *O, you are men of stones*: I think that the primary idea
here is of statues, silent, frozen-still (in horror), and
impermeable by grief. The overall image governing
the following lines may be that of a funerary chapel

or pantheon with statues and a vault: but as this is *heaven's vault* an intentional confusion between the living and the dead is created.

256 *Had I your tongues and eyes*: It is not clear how they could use their *eyes* to make *heaven's vault crack*, except that tongues used for outcry and eyes used for weeping come irresistibly together. Perhaps the only point made is that Lear's eyes are failing him (as in 280). *tongues* and *eyes* represent within the human microcosm the sources of thunder and lightning in the macrocosm – the vault of heaven. Thus the tempest is recalled.

260 *stone*: Mirror (perhaps short for 'specular stone', a species of mica, selenite, or talc).

261 *the promised end*: The end of the world (as foretold in Mark 13). Kent may also mean 'the end that Lear promised himself when he divided the kingdom'.

262 *image*: Representation. Similarly, Macduff calls the death of Duncan 'The Great Doom's image' (*Macbeth*, II.3.75).
Fall and cease: Let the heavens fall and life on earth cease.

269 *stay a little*: We should notice the ironic relation of this second (permanent) exile to the first.

272 *I killed the slave*: So much for the *noble fortunes* promised at 31.

274 *falchion*: An old-fashioned word for sword, appropriate to the memory of Lear's youth, as is the 'long sword' that Justice Shallow (in *The Merry Wives of Windsor*, II.1.209) remembers from *his* youth.

275 *him*: This is F's reading; Q has *them*. In meaning they seem to be indifferent – which gives F, the better text, the preference.

276 *these same crosses spoil me*: These troubles of my old age have spoiled me (as a swordsman).

278–9 *If Fortune brag of two she loved and hated | One of them we behold*: The two people are clearly Lear and Kent, both fortunate and unfortunate in extreme degrees. Each beholds *One* – they are looking at one another.

280 *This is a dull sight*: Often thought to be a complaint
      about his fading eyesight rather than a comment on
      what he sees before him.

285 *I'll see that straight*: I'll attend to that immediately. Lear
      copes with the tedium of people who try to distract
      him from Cordelia by promising to attend to them
      later.

286 *your first of difference and decay*: From the beginning
      of your change and decline of fortune.

288 *Nor no man else*: This completes his preceding sentence
      (*I am the very man . . . Nor no man else*), but also begins
      his reply to Lear's *welcome* ('I am not welcome, nor is
      anyone else – *All's . . . deadly*').
      deadly: Death-like.

289 *fordone themselves*: Destroyed themselves.

290 *desperately are dead*: Have died in a state of despair.
      This suggests an assumption that they both committed
      suicide (even though we know that Regan was
      poisoned by Gonerill), thus bringing the moral pattern
      to a neat conclusion.

291 *He knows not what he sees*: The point seems to be that
      Lear's *sight*, rather than his utterance, has become
      imperfect. This ties in with *present us to him* in the next
      line and with the references above to failing sight (256
      and 280) – which do not fit with F's *He knowes not
      what he saies*.

292 *bootless*: Useless, profitless.

295 *this great decay*: Lear himself, and the situation which
      surrounds him.

296 *us, we*: Albany, as sovereign ruler of Britain, assumes
      the royal plural.

299 *With boot, and . . . addition*: With something extra
      (presumably new titles of honour).

302 *O, see, see*: What exactly draws their attention is not
      clear, but it must be some new posture of Lear as he
      cradles Cordelia in his arms, or picks her up again, or
      kneels at her side.

303 *my poor fool*: Presumably Cordelia is meant (since she
      is the centre of his attention, and was hanged), 'poor

fool' being a common Shakespearian form of parental
endearment. It is impossible to know if the reminiscence of the Fool's title is accidental or intentional. It
has been suggested that the same boy actor played
both parts; but the Fool is likely to have been played
by Robert Armin.

no life: I take it that Lear is making a general point
('Let all life cease') rather than the particular one:
'There is no life left in Cordelia.'

307 *this button*: Presumably the button at his own throat, which
seems to be causing his feeling of suffocation. But it
could equally well be a button on Cordelia's garment.

308 *Do you see this? Look on her! Look, her lips*: Clearly
Lear imagines he sees Cordelia coming to life again.
Whether this means that 'Lear dies of joy' (as A. C.
Bradley suggested) or that he is in a mere delirium is
more doubtful, and not very important for the play as
a whole. It would be difficult for any actor to project
a precise interpretation.

312 *the rack of this tough world*: The torture-machine that
stretches a man between hope and despair. The *tough*
suggests that it is the body that is referred to, as the
rack of the spirit.

321–4 *The weight . . . live so long*: Q gives the final speech to
Albany (*Duke*). Tragedies commonly end with a
generalizing speech from the most senior survivor,
and this may have been in the Q pirates' minds. F
corrects to *Edgar*, and certainly the *we that are young*
sounds better in the mouth of Edgar. We may also
notice that Albany in 317 addresses both Kent and
Edgar, and that (apart from this speech) Edgar has no
reply.

321 *weight*: Sadness. The use of the word may imply that
Edgar is already carrying Lear (or Cordelia) from the
stage.

322 *Speak what we feel, not what we ought to say*: Regal
formality has broken down into individual feelings.
There may be in this an element of apology for taking
the last speech from Albany.

The National: three theatres and so much more…
www.nationaltheatre.org.uk

In its three theatres on London's South Bank, the National presents an eclectic mix of new plays and classics, with seven or eight shows in repertory at any one time.

And there's more. Step inside and enjoy free exhibitions, backstage tours, talks and readings, a great theatre bookshop and plenty of places to eat and drink.

Sign-up as an e-member at www.nationaltheatre.org.uk/join and we'll keep you up-to-date with everything that's going on.

NT NATIONAL THEATRE
SOUTH BANK
LONDON SE1 9PX

PENGUIN SHAKESPEARE

OTHELLO
WILLIAM SHAKESPEARE

WWW.PENGUINSHAKESPEARE.COM

A popular soldier and newly married man, Othello seems to be in an enviable position. And yet, when his supposed friend sows doubts in his mind about his wife's fidelity, he is gradually consumed by suspicion. In this powerful tragedy, innocence is corrupted and trust is eroded as every relationship is drawn into a tangled web of jealousies.

This book includes a general introduction to Shakespeare's life and the Elizabethan theatre, a separate introduction to *Othello*, a chronology of his works, suggestions for further reading, an essay discussing performance options on both stage and screen, and a commentary.

Edited by Kenneth Muir

With an introduction by Tom McAlindon

General Editor: Stanley Wells

Penguin Shakespeare

MACBETH
WILLIAM SHAKESPEARE

WWW.PENGUINSHAKESPEARE.COM

Promised a golden future as ruler of Scotland by three sinister witches, Macbeth murders the king to ensure his ambitions come true. But he soon learns the meaning of terror – killing once, he must kill again and again, and the dead return to haunt him. A story of war, witchcraft and bloodshed, *Macbeth* also depicts the relationship between husbands and wives, and the risks they are prepared to take to achieve their desires.

This book includes a general introduction to Shakespeare's life and the Elizabethan theatre, a separate introduction to *Macbeth*, a chronology of his works, suggestions for further reading, an essay discussing performance options on both stage and screen, and a commentary.

Edited by George Hunter

With an introduction by Carol Rutter

General Editor: Stanley Wells

PENGUIN SHAKESPEARE

HAMLET
WILLIAM SHAKESPEARE

WWW.PENGUINSHAKESPEARE.COM

A young Prince meets with his father's ghost, who alleges that his own brother, now married to his widow, murdered him. The Prince devises a scheme to test the truth of the ghost's accusation, feigning wild madness while plotting a brutal revenge. But his apparent insanity soon begins to wreak havoc on innocent and guilty alike.

This book includes a general introduction to Shakespeare's life and the Elizabethan theatre, a separate introduction to *Hamlet*, a chronology of his works, suggestions for further reading, an essay discussing performance options on both stage and screen by Paul Prescott, and a commentary.

Edited by T. J. B. Spencer

With an introduction by Alan Sinfield

General Editor: Stanley Wells

Read more in Penguin

PENGUIN SHAKESPEARE